𝕸OZLANDIA

Morrissey Fans in the Borderlands

by Melissa Mora Hidalgo

A Headpress Book

TABLE OF CONTENTS

for my Baby Dear

and now my heart is full

ACKNOWLEDGMENTS

FIRST AND FOREMOST, THANK YOU, MORRISSEY, AND thank you, Morrissey and Smiths fans everywhere. This book exists because of you.

It also exists because a lot of people gave their time, love, energy, and resources during all phases of this project. Thank you to David Kerekes at Headpress for believing in this project and publishing this book. And dood, thank you, Jen Otter Bickerdike, for being the best.

In many ways, this book is borne out of my early exposure to music, especially the kind my mom and dad listened to. In Los Angeles in the late 1970s and 1980s, it was KRTH-101 'oldies' rock and soul from the 1950s and 1960s for my mama. She loves cumbias, disco, and Eric Burdon & The Animals. My dad loves jazz, blues, and the 'classic rock' of seventies bands like Steely Dan, The Who, and Jethro Tull. He took me to my first concert ever: Olivia Newton-John in 1982. I was eight and in the depths of my first girl-crush. My mom was supposed to take me, but she was about to give birth to my little sister, so my dad did his fatherly duty and took his tomboy daughter to see Sandra Dee herself. He was a good sport. He did not like Olivia or her music, but he liked all kinds of jazz, and lucky for both of us, a smooth jazz artist called Tom Scott was Olivia's supporting act that night. Thank goodness for Tom Scott.

Growing up, I heard a lot of music my parents both liked, which meant it was played at home and in the car and turned up loud. Everything from Mark Anthony's Nuyo-Rican salsa, eighties-era Madonna and Michael Jackson songs, and of course, 'brown-eyed soul' by Santana, Tierra, and Los Lobos, the local heroes from East LA. I also had a cool Tío, may he rest in peace, who collected albums, deejayed parties, and made me the best mixtapes of the coolest music. At the tender young ages of eight, nine, ten years old, I heard bands and musicians like Prince, Missing Persons, Thompson Twins, Human League, the B-52s, Falco, and ABC for the first time. From my grandparents on both sides, I learned to appreciate, and eventually love, what I only knew as 'Mexican music,' whether cumbias, conjunto, or corridos. Singers like Vicente Fernández, Javier Solis, Juan Gabriel, Linda Ronstadt, and Paquita la del Barrio remind me of my paternal and materal grandparents from both sides of the border. With love, I thank my mom, dad, Tío and Tía, and all of my grandparents for these formative musical moments that influenced my love of music, especially, and inevitably, Morrissey's.

I am forever grateful to my sisters, Melinda Hidalgo Carrillo and Monica Hidalgo, and Alexis de la Rocha. They are my co-writers in a sense. We have endless shared experiences of countless Morrissey concerts, tribute band shows, MorrisseyOke nights, and other fan events, particularly since the mid-2000s. We all knew what it was like to grow up Chicana/Latina in the late 1980s and early 1990s in suburban Whittier/La Habra, on the border of Los Angeles and Orange counties, and we all took to Morrissey and Smiths music, and so many other 'alternative' British bands, during these formative years. Little did we know then that Alexis would be hosting the most popular Morrissey singalong night in all of Moz Angeles, or that Monica, Melinda and I would form Sheilas Take A Bow, our all-female Ode to Morrissey and The Smiths. Their Moz memories, stories, and insights as fans and musicians are all over this book. I thank them from the bottom of my butchsister heart for their love, energy, and commitment to this world of Morrissey.

También, I thank the menfolk in my life. My compadre, Nathan Carrillo, and my Brotha B, Brandon Mitsunaga, took many pictures, videos, and notes at various shows and events; they lent their eyes, ears, thoughts, time, and labor to this project in their own sweet ways. I thank them for sharing their music history smarts with me. Thanks to Nate for teaching me about local punk and music scenes and for telling me about the Gun Club and Kid Congo. Special thanks to Brotha B for going with me to lots of tribute band shows, for taking me to see Morrissey at the Gibson Amphitheatre in 2009, and for pretty much coming up with the title of this book.

Over the years, I have hung out with good people who have provided stimulating conversations about their connections to Morrissey and the Smiths. Some are big fans, others just love the songs. All of them have shared space with me at various Moz events throughout LA. They have many stories and insights about Moz and Smiths fandom on both sides of the US-Mexican border. Thank you to Neph Vásquez, JoAnna Mixpe Ley, Laura Luna, and Luie García for walking with me and talking with me about Morrissey, Mexicans, and Los Angeles. All of you left your marks on this work in important ways.

I thank my big extended family, especially my aunties, uncles, cousins, and friends like Pat Walker and Isela Reza, who supported me in key ways while I worked on this book. I am grateful for the company, beer, wine, scotch, food, conversation, space to work, and thoughts to mull over, even if some of them had never heard of Morrissey before.

My heartfelt gratitude and much love go to the fierce artists in my life who inspire me to follow my creative spirit and keep on writing. Adelina Anthony and Sharon Bridgforth, my Pa, thank you. Thank you, too, to Karla Legaspy and Marisa Becerra, dear friends and Xicana visionaries who dare to bring our stories to the stage and screen.

I have traversed many Morrissey and Smiths fan communities from the Midlands of England to the Borderlands of California and Texas. 'Moz Angeles' is my home base, so I thank the fans in LA first, especially those I have met at Moz events like MorrisseyOke at Eastside Luv; Smiths and Morrissey night at Part Time Punks; Morrissey concert after parties at the Grand Star; tribute nights at Sage, Mal's Bar, Spike's, and the New Wave Bar; the Smiths and Morrissey Convention at The Avalon; Rosie Bojangles's Sing Your Life Sundaze dance parties at Footsies; and countless other Morrissey Smiths themed events that put Moz Angeles on the map. Special thanks to Clover Dean, Clever Swine, Hapie-ssey, Liz H., Mozz Liz, MozKrew East LA, Juliet 'Romeo Girl' Wong, Anita Balandra, and Chato for your passionate fandom and personal touches on this project.

I was fortunate to be able to attend the 2015 Moz Army Meet in Manchester, England. I met so many of the fans I knew only as 'Breakfast Champions' on Twitter. It was a wonderful and unforgettable time. Thank you to all the lovely fans and online friends I met at the Star and Garter that night, especially Donna Bishop, Denis Carroll, Maria Stewart, and the Donevan sisters. Thank you to all of the Moz Army, and very special thanks to its founder, Julie Hamill, for her time and contributions to our world of Morrissey. Big thanks to Dickie Felton of Liverpool, another great Moz fan and man about town, for his time, generosity, and books about Morrissey fans. I also thank Craig Gill, drummer of Inspiral Carpets and organizer of the great Manchester Music Tours. Thank you, too, to the Salford Lads Club.

I thank the many other fans I met on my travels in 2014 and 2015 around New York, the UK, Spain, and France, and who all shared their Smiths Morrissey love stories with me. In particular, I thank Marina García-Vásquez, co-founder of Mex in the City, an arts and culture collective based in New York City, and host of 'Mex Moz,' an occasional Morrissey Smiths dance party and fan celebration in NYC.

I have one foot in this lovely, lively world of Morrissey and Smiths fandom that spans space and time; I have another foot in the world of formal scholarly pursuits and academe. This project benefits from, and emerges in, the spaces of my life where these two worlds converge and diverge. I value the support of faculty colleagues, scholars, and allies in the fields of liteature, politics, media studies, sociology, cultural studies, musicology, and Chicana/o-Latina/o studies. In particular, I thank Drs. Nigel Boyle, Alexandra Juhasz, Adrian Pantoja, Micaela Díaz-Sánchez, Frank Galarte, Alexandro J. Gradilla, and Erualdo González for their insightful contributions and collegial support at formative stages of this project. My biggest thanks go to Drs. Eoin Devereux, Martin J. Power, Aileen Dillane at the University of Limerick. Their 2011 book, *Morrissey: Fandom, Representations and Identities,* is the first collection of academic articles on Morrissey and a significant contribution to the growing archive of Mozology. Their work inspires mine, and I am proud to call them colleagues, collaborators, and comrades.

This project also benefits from my own academic training in literature and cultural studies. My work is informed by cultural, feminist, literary, queer, and US ethnic and Chicana/o studies, as well as by studies of fandom and pop culture that seek to take seriously fans and their critical value. This project has greatly benefitted from the work of scholars and writers such as George Lipsitz, Jack Halberstam, Gaye Theresa Johnson, Henry Jenkins, Karen Tongson, Joshua Gamson, Deborah Paredez, Yvonne Yarbro-Bejarano, Alice Bag, and Cherríe Moraga.

My endless gratitude goes to the artists, musicians, playwrights, and other cultural producers throughout Mozlandia whose work is at the center of this project. So much great work out there by artists such as Shizu Saldamando and Jake Prendez did not make it in these pages, but they are infinitely part of this Moz universe. To those whose work did make it in here in the end, I thank them in order of appearance: to Rio Yañez and Vic Garry, my heartfelt thanks for contributing their strikingly beautiful art work for the cover images; thank you, Alexis de la Rocha, DJ Jess Funk, and Willie Uribe, for making MorrisseyOke possible; thank you to all the tribute bands I have interviewed and watched perform over the years, including Maladjusted, These Handsome Devils, Strangeways, Sweet and Tender Hooligans, and Mariachi Manchester. Special thanks to Edgar Zermeno, Eddie Stephens, Julian Ricardo, Ralph Paredes, Alexandro D. Hernández-Gutiérrez, Gloria Estrada, and José Maldonado for your time and contributions.

I thank my beloved band mates of Sheilas Take A Bow, the first all-gurrrl tribute to Morrissey and the Smiths. To Melinda 'Mindy Keys' Hidalgo Carrillo, Monica 'Moni Rourke' Hidalgo, Toni 'the Poni' Santoyo, Liz 'Lizzy Marr' Gómez, and Melody 'Mellowdee' Skaggs Moran, a founding member, thank you all from the bottom of my singing heart.

Thank you to all the 'Breakfast Champions' who make *Breakfast with the Smiths* the great fan meet-and-tweet every week. To our host, José 'the Mexican Morrissey' Maldonado, and to Breakfast Champions like Roberto Ferdenzi ('The Italian Rapscallion'), Andrea Willoughby Jones, Mason Nguyen, Ed Navarro, the Battis sisters, and so many others, thank you for your tweets and correspondence that formed some of the basis for chapter four. Big thank-yous to Michael Patrick Spillers, Josefina López, Jaime Mayorquin, and everyone who made Teatro Moz possible. Thank you, too, to the South El Monte Arts Collective, Caribbean Fragoza, and to Vicki Vértiz for her poem in chapter five. A very big GRACIAS to Gustavo Arellano for writing the Foreword to this book, and gracias, también, to Lalo Alcaraz for contributing a timeless comic.

I have to thank Morrissey, again, because without him, there would be no fans and no book. And I must thank his musicians, co-writers, and producers who bring Morrissey's music to life. Special thanks to Morrissey's first solo touring band—Boz Boorer, Alain Whyte, Gary Day, Spencer Cobrin—for fond memories of some of the best live Morrissey concert experiences of my young life. And because Morrissey's concerts in Southern California and Texas from 2007–2016 comprise a large part of this book's sound and vision, I want to thank his most current touring band—Boz Boorer, Jesse Tobias, Matt Walker, (Solomon Walker), Mando López, and Gustavo Manzur. Gracias, friends.

To all the fans I have met throughout the world of Morrissey, thank you.

And to the one person who has lived with this project day in and day out, who has witnessed the tears of joy and pain that come with writing a first book, who has been by my side, kept me company, travelled with me all over the place, listened to my endless chatter, and attended more Morrissey and Smiths events than she ever bargained for: thank you to my beautiful partner, Stacy I. Macías. She was a Smiths fan before I was a Morrissey fan. Her sharp insights, her thoughtful analyses, her tough critiques, and her generous contributions make this book hers as much as it is mine.

And so, my dearest love, this book is for you.

In memory of Selena, Amy Winehouse,
David Bowie, Prince, and Juan Gabriel

WE NEVER KNEW OUR PLACE

On Steven Patrick and the *Pendejos* Who Stare— Mexicans Really Don't Care

by Gustavo Arellano

MY JOURNALISTIC ACCOMPLISHMENTS: TAKING ON THE Catholic Church's nasty pedophile-priest scandal. Battling white supremacists, neo-Nazis, and Turkish nationalists. Unmasking civic corruption in Orange County, a notorious cesspool of conservatism. Writing a nationally syndicated column called "¡Ask a Mexican!" where I answer people's questions about Mexicans in humorous, informative, invective-filled way.

None of that matters. I'm the guy who wrote the piece about why Mexicans love Morrissey.

About every couple of months for the past decade, a new news outlet— whether radio, television, film, Internet, Snapchat, *something*—discovers that the mercurial Mancunian has a fanatical Mexican following, that tough-looking hombres cry themselves to sleep while listening to Steven Patrick's coda of coos on There Is A Light That Never Goes Out, that cover bands, conventions and shows are almost exclusively attended by these

1

descendants of Moctezuma. And as any lazy reporter inevitably does, they Google certain terms to find other stories on the subjects, to find if their insight is original, quickly realize it ain't—and then they discover my 2002 article for the *OC Weekly* (the alternative weekly I edit) titled "Their Charming Man: Dispatches from the Latino-Morrissey Love-In," and decide to give me a call to do a story anyway.

(They obviously didn't bother with the section of my essay where I announced even then that Latinos-love-Morrissey articles were clichéd, passé, and more than a bit racist. Of course they ignored my warning— Mexicans love Morrissey! What a novel concept! This can go viral!)

Inevitably, those lazy journos fail. Their cardinal sin: treating the love fest as nothing more than a freak show, and thinking of themselves as a mix of Freud, Cortés and Lester Bangs, leading to vacuous, precious prose. I've read and watched them all—real-life Mr. Shanklys, the lot of them.

So as the guy who wrote the piece about why Mexicans love Morrissey, I'm glad that Dr. Melissa Hidalgo is as disgusted and tired with those stories as I am. That's why I can proudly declare that this book you're about to read, *Mozlandia,* is the book that will once and for all stop all the pretenders. Because Hidalgo gets it: rather than pontificate from afar, or parachute into the fandom jungle for a night, she *lives* her subject. Traveling the freeways of L.A., haunting the bars and coffee klatches and radio shows to live and breathe with her tribe, Hidalgo is a New Wave Ernie Pyle, the legendary American World War II correspondent who traveled with Uncle Sam's troops to hear their tales the way they told them. For chrissakes, Hidalgo went to a barbershop to try and get her hair cut in the same place where Morrissey gets his locks sheared, only to get rejected because Londoners have apparently never heard of a lass with a male cut. This is no mere writer trying to make a name for themselves—this is the real deal. Or as our charming man would say, Hidalgo is our quarry.

Confessional time: though I'm the guy who wrote the piece about why Mexicans love Morrissey, I really don't care much about him.

I didn't grow up consciously listening to him so Moz never seeped into my soul. (Years later, though, his songs come back to me as memories. The chugging wails of How Soon Is Now? I now remember as music played during breaks at Dodgers Stadium. The arrogant march of "Glamorous Glue," with its futuristic, fatalistic line "We look to Los Angeles/For the language we use/London is dead, London is dead," is a line I heard in high school, uttered by one of the so-called rebel kids whose sartorial style I can now say was more Morrissey-inspired than taken from James Dean. The "Meat is Murder" cover, adorning the chest of more than one college girl who I never had the nerve to court). I think the man's music is brilliant, but I'll still reach for the Beatles (the band that's ruled my aural life), the Kinks, and other groups before him. I discovered Oscar Wilde before hearing "Cemetry Gates," and I only own the Smiths records—and really, all I listen to is "Rusholme Ruffians," the song that Morrissey wrote for me and *only* me.

Once I became aware of his acolytes, however, I respected the hell out of them and their idol. They represent a wonderful monkey wrench (or, as we'd say in Spanish, a *chinga tu madre*—go fuck your mother; yes, we Mexicans turn slurs into useful nouns) to American and British thought leaders. Since the days of Drake sinking the Spanish Armada, they've insisted that us Spanish speakers should only wear funny hats and listen to music that either sounds like an Aztec Oktoberfest or sing the glories of violence. They cannot imagine that we Mexicans can like music in English, let alone understand the lyrics. They stare as we express solidity with John Lennon, rock out to Led Zeppelin, sway to the Cure.

But it's that devotion to Morrissey that turns the bemusement of those *pendejos* (literally; "pubic hairs"; figuratively, "assholes") into wrath. Their expectations of us as violent imbeciles quickly transforms into disappointment. How dare we—a macho, angry, bullet-happy race—embrace this fey, dour, pasty-skinned sodomite? Of all the artists in the United Kingdom, *this* one inspires the most fervent fans? And if we're capable of this, what's next?

Again, this reveals the stupidity of these chroniclers. The most significant contribution I made to the Mexicans-love-Morrissey canon is the following passage from my original story:

> But check it out: for all the machismo and virulent existentialism that Mexican music espouses, there is another side—a morbid fascination with getting your heart and dreams broken by others, usually in death. In fact, Morrissey's most famous confession of unrequited love, There Is A Light That Never Goes Out, ("And if a double decker bus/Crashes into us/To die by your side/Would be a heavenly way to die") emulates almost sentiment for sentiment Cuco Sanchez's torch song "Cama de Piedra" ("The day that they kill me/May it be with five bullets/And be close to you").

I'm not accusing Morrissey of plagiarism, but rather pointing out how rational it is for Mexicans to have an affinity for his music, and how clueless reporters are that they can't immediately get it like me. I got it, because I understand both sides of the Mexican-Morrissey border. And that's what's so brilliant about Hidalgo's work. Unlike me, she's a die-hard that can also remove her love to dispassionately realize what she can offer and serve not as a mere translator but outright advocate: to tell the world that the world should emulate Moz Angeles.

So read this book with glee. Marvel at Hidalgo's magnificent work, at the true believers who will continue whether clueless writers patronize or ignore them. There *is* a light that never goes out, and that's the torch of Mexicans dancing their life away while the mighty fret about them— these are the riches of the poor.

Gustavo Arellano is editor of OC Weekly, *an alternative newspaper in Orange County, California.*

Not Another 'Why do Mexicans/Latinos Love Morrissey?' Book (As If A Bunch of Them Exist)

I WROTE THIS BOOK BECAUSE I, ALONG WITH MANY other Latina/o fans, got tired of the same ol' questions of 'why' we love Moz. The question of Latino (and more specifically, Mexican and Chicano) Morrissey fandom, and what have now become stock, if not cliched, explanations, are useful starting points, and indeed they highlight important contexts for understanding this seemingly unlikely affinity. In this book, though, I am less interested in asking that question again and producing the same evidence to show that, yes, a lot of Mexicans, Latinos/as and Chicanos/as *do* (as do many other groups of people) love Morrissey. We know these fans and communities exist, and it's not really so strange after all. Rather, I am interested in asking the 'what' and 'how' questions, new questions that provide us with nuance, complexity, insight, and new ways to see, hear, and understand these fan communities in 'Moz Angeles' and around the borderlands.

What do Morrissey fans do to express their fandom? How do these fan expressions take shape? What local, national, global histories and politics inform this fandom? What cultural icons, and creative forms do these fans' expressions take? How do fans take up, appropriate, and relate to Morrissey as a pop culture icon? What can we learn from Morrissey fan cultures that we may not be able to learn from other, more 'appropriate' Chicana/o-Latina/a (sub)cultural expressions? What is unique about Morrissey fan expressions from Chicana/o, Latina/o,

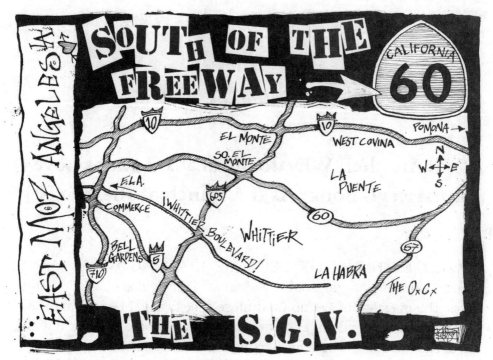

"South of the 60."
Illustration by Michael Robinson, based on a sketch by the author.

Mexican, and other groups who live in the US-Mexico borderlands? And why consider fandom at all? Anything but 'why do Mexicans/why do Latinos love Morrissey?' again.

The first wave of 'why do Latinos love Morrissey' questions and the curiosity around Mexican and Chicano/a fandom in particular began to attract the attention of curious writers and movie makers around the time of the turn of the millennium—1999, 2000, 2001, 2002, years significantly marked by Morrissey's first forays into and encounters with his US Latino/a and Latin American fans. In those years, Morrissey left the UK, fed up with unfavorable treatment by the media in his native country (the 'pernickety chickenshits,' as he calls them) and a lost court case that saw his former band mates sue him for back royalties.

At the turn of the millennium, Morrissey was living in Los Angeles, up in the hills of West Hollywood above Sunset Boulevard. During that time, he made his first solo venture into Latin America on his ¡Oye, Esteban! ('Hey, Steven!') tour, which made stops in Mexico, Chile, Argentina and Brazil. He was the opening act for the Mexican rock group, Jaguares, for shows in Anaheim, Berkeley, and San Diego, California. As Morrissey writes in his *Autobiography*, 'There are no Caucasian faces... The new Morrissey audience is not white—not here, at least.'[1] For Morrissey to call his latest group of fans 'his new Latino hearts' meant that the singer not only acknowledged that brown people were buying tickets and showing up in droves to his concerts, but that he wholly and enthusiastically embraced this 'new' audience (not so new, as it turns out). Moz's love for his 'new Latino hearts' represented a turn away from those in the UK who were perhaps over him, as well as a pointed rejection of 'those self-appointed fusspots,' the London music editors, with whom he shared a mutual dislike.

In 2016, we are in the middle of second wave of media-produced Latino-fan themed questions, this time with more of an emphasis on why the 'Mexicans and Morrissey' connection. The Mexican-Morrissey love affair question has been shored up mainly by the splash made by Mexrrissey in April 2015. The Mexico City-based 'supergoup,' as the *Los Angeles Times* describes them, is comprised of musicians from several of Mexico's top rock/pop bands, led by Camilo Lara of Mexican Institute of Sound. Other members include Ceci Bastida (Tijuana No!), Chetes (Zurdok), Jay De La Cueva (Moderatto/Titán), Adan Jodorowsky (Adanowsky), Liber Teran (Los de Abajo), and Alejandro Flores (described as 'Café Tacuba's favourite violin player' on Mexrrissey's website).[2] Collectively, Mexrrissey have reimagined some of Morrissey's best known songs into Mexican-sounding tunes, meaning a fusion of mariachi, cumbia, samba, and other 'Latin beats,' accompanied by Spanish/English lyrical mashups.

Mexrrissey is less a cover or tribute band and more of a celebratory musical formation that honors and emerges out of a set of affinities between Mexicans and Morrissey that have been nearly three generations in the making. Their contributions to the 'Mexico-Morrissey' affair are there for the world to see and hear. They put on an exciting, endearing live show, and their collective love and respect for Morrissey and his music comes through in their musical renderings of hits like Every Day Is Like Sunday (Cada Día Es Domingo), Suedehead (Estuvo Bien), and Last Of The Famous International Playboys—changed to Playgirls and sung by Ceci Bastida, the only woman in the group.[3] The band received the highest endorsement by Morrissey himself when a screenshot of Mexrrissey's album, playlist, and the link to purchase it appeared on Morrissey's official website, true-to-you.net.

The title of Mexrrissey's album *¡No Manchester!* is a play on a Mexican slang term, 'no manches,' a phrase that communicates disbelief, as in 'no way!' or 'don't mess with me!' The exclamation itself plays on the spirit of disbelief that gives rise to the 'what? Mexicans and Morrissey? no way!' sentiments that influence a lot of the press attention on their project. When Mexrrissey took the world by storm last year, the band received generous media coverage in France, Spain, Australia, the US, and the UK, following tour dates and promotional appearances. Along with Mexrissey came the usual set of questions about the Mexico-Morrissey connection. Yours truly was tapped for no less than five interviews with the likes of *BBC World*, *WNYC*, *NPR*, and *ABC 7* about the 'Morrissey and Mexican fans' question. And now that Mexrrissey's album is out (I write this during the week of its release), as the band plans another tour in the Fall and Winter of 2016–2017—and while founder Camilo Lara's Mexican Institute of Sound prepares to support Morrissey at his headline Día de Muertos concert in Santa Barbara, California, in November 2016—many more interviews with Mexrrissey, write-ups, reviews, and other coverage around the band's Mexican take on Morrissey songs have appeared and will likely continue. Nearly all of these write-ups include that question or a variation of it: why is Morrissey so big in Mexico?

Heck, even Larry King wanted to know. In a landmark television interview with Morrissey in August 2015, the US news personality inquired about the singer's popularity in Mexico. King: 'Why Mexico?'; Morrissey: 'I don't know. It's a beautiful thing.' Morrissey continued, attributing his Mexican fans' ardor to their 'passion' and love of music. I am well aware, and I would think so is Morrissey, of age-old stereotypes that brand Mexicans and other Latinos/as as 'passionate' and 'emotional' to a fault, as in the Latina spitfire and the fiery tempered macho. I don't think this is what he means, though it is important to identify this risk and work against these stereotypes in our analyses of fan cultures without evacuating their critical worth, and I would think Morrissey would agree. And, while it is fair to say that most Morrissey fans are indeed passionate and emotional about their man and his music, not just the Mexican and Latino/a fans in the US and Mexico, King's question to Morrissey about this particular fan base, and Morrissey's response ('I don't know'), captures the ineffable nature of what is often referred to as 'the Mexican-Latino/a Morrissey fan connection' on both sides of the US-Mexico border.

Morrissey's explanation ('they're passionate') resonates with many of the answers which have now become stock responses to the question: Maybe Mexicans and Morrissey of Irish Blood and English Heart go together because of the shared Catholic thing; maybe it's because we're all very melancholy, emotional, and expressive of our fierce passions. Maybe it's because Mexicans love sad songs about unrequited love sung by male crooners. For Mexicans in the US, perhaps it's the shared histories of immigration, displacement, and living as an outsider in a colonial relationship to the country we call home.

Then I remember: there are definitely important contexts and points of connection between Chicana/os (first-, second-, third generation of Mexican descent born in the US), Mexicans on both sides of the border, and a first-generation Irish singer born in England like Morrissey that illuminate these mutual affinities. As Trisha Ziff, co-editor of the important 1995 volume *Distant Relations: Chicano Irish Mexican Art and Critical Writing* (a big inspiration for this book) states, 'Irish people in Britain and Chicanos/ Latinos in the United States share a common experience of discrimination, politically, economically, culturally, and linguistically.'[4] Morrissey and fan communities in the Chicano-Latino borderlands bear these traces.

The Morrissey and Mexican-Chicana/o-Latina/o fan connection is legitimate, though very often misrepresented. This brings me to another reason why I was motivated to write this book. I was bothered by how the majority of existing media pieces (usually by white reporters not from LA) portrayed Morrissey fans, Chicana/o, Latina/o, and Mexican fans in particular. I saw characterizations of this fan base as inaccurate and pathologizing; words like 'fanatic,' 'strange,' 'unusual,' 'cultish,' 'depressive,' and 'obsessed' would creep up over and over again in articles that attempted to 'explain' the Mexican and Latino devotion to Morrissey. Or, fans were always objectified, exoticized, looked at as strange objects to be studied, like in the documentary *Is it Really So Strange?* (dir. William E Jones), or in Chuck Klosterman's 2010 essay '¡Viva Morrissey!'[5]

In my experience, Morrissey fans are not all objects or passive, depressed, sad, stunted, developmentally arrested people. The majority of fans are active, joyful, creative, and uniquely expressive in their fandom. They make art, design T-shirts, stickers, and jewelry; they form bands; they organize and produce events for other fans. They build community. They are active agents in the production and consumption of a special fan culture. It is the kind of fan I am and the kinds of fans I want to write about and shine light on.

Which then begs the question, why these particular fans? Morrissey certainly has fans all over the world, all corners of the globe, and he has lived in other places besides Los Angeles. He is hugely popular from Italy to Istanbul, Serbia to Seoul. Over the last twenty-eight years as a solo artist, Morrissey has gained, and continues to gain, new and young fans with every concert tour, with every sellout in venues from South America to Australia to East Asia. But no other set of fans, no other region of fans, has received the kind of media attention than have Morrissey fans in the US-Mexican borderlands.

Therefore, I offer this book as a way to view Morrissey fandom, particularly as experienced in Latino Los Angeles, less as a mystery and more as an illuminating study in transcultural fandom.

Welcome to Mozlandia, the Land of Moz.

Mozlandia

Morrissey Fans in the Borderlands

A book has neither object nor subject; it is made of variously formed matters, and very different dates and speeds. To attribute the book to a subject is to overlook this working of matters, and the exteriority of their relations. It is to fabricate a beneficent God to explain geological movements. In a book, as in all things, there are lines of articulation or segmentarity, strata and territories; but also lines of flight, movements of deterritorialization and destratification... Writing has nothing to do with signifying. It has everything to do with surveying, mapping, even realms that are yet to come.

Gilles Deleuze and Félix Guattari,
A Thousand Plateaus: Capitalism and Schizophrenia (1987)

The US-Mexican border *es una herida abierta* where the Third World grates against the first and bleeds. And before a scab forms it hemorrhages again, the lifeblood of two worlds merging to form a third country—a border culture. Borders are set up to define the places that are safe and unsafe, to distinguish *us* from *them*. A border is a dividing line, a narrow strip along a steep edge. A borderland is a vague and undetermined boundary. It is a constant state of transition. The prohibited and forbidden are its inhabitants. *Los atravesados* live here: the squint-eyed, the perverse, the queer, the troublesome, the mongrel, the mulato, the half-breed, the half dead; in short, those who cross over, pass over, or go through the confines of the 'normal.'

Gloria E. Anzaldúa,
Borderlands/La Frontera: The New Mestiza (1987)

INTRODUCTION

I Left the North, I Travelled South
Where is Mozlandia?

IN 1987, GLORIA E. ANZALDÚA PUBLISHED *BORDERLANDS/ La Frontera: The New Mestiza*, a foundational text in my field of Chicana and Chicano studies. That book is an inspiration for this book and its overarching themes. In 1987, Deleuze and Guattari also published *A Thousand Plateaus*, from which I take as one of this book's opening epigraphs about writing as a mapping project of what is here, where we are, and what lies ahead. In 1987, Prime Minister Margaret Thatcher and President Ronald Reagan were best buds, while Charles and Diana decided that year they were no longer meant to be. I was in junior high school in Whittier, California, where a magnitude 5.1 earthquake shook the ground beneath us, cracked the foundations in our homes, and toppled old brick buildings in historic Uptown. I survived that year by listening to Sinéad O'Connor, Terence Trent D'Arby, Duran Duran, Prince, and Run DMC. I had only heard of the Smiths, not yet knowing their songs, let alone having made the headfirst commitment of fandom. And speaking of the Smiths, in 1987, Johnny Marr left the Manchester band, breaking up the family, so to speak, before the release of what would be their final album, *Strangeways, Here We Come*. (Talk about *una herida abierta,* an open wound.) This rupture, this other '87 earthquake that was the Smiths' split, would spawn the solo career in the following year of one Steven Patrick Morrissey.

Morrissey is a famous international singer, a rankler of royals, a hater of Thatcher, a champion of the underdog. The former singer and unmistakable front man of the influential 1980s band, the Smiths, Morrissey has amassed a global fan following since his solo debut in 1988. He has released ten studio albums, several more live and compilation albums, and has toured the world extensively, playing to sold-out audiences all over the UK, Europe, North America, South America and East Asia for nearly three decades. Loved by his loyal fans and loathed by his detractors, Morrissey is arguably one of the most intriguing and popular, if not polarizing and controversial, iconic figures of popular culture.

But this book is not about Morrissey or even the Smiths; there are plenty of those already.

This book is about Morrissey fans, and more specifically, the Morrissey fan cultures and communities that are unique to the US-Mexico border region. *Mozlandia: Morrissey Fans in the Borderlands* maps the travels, people, and stories of Morrissey Smiths fan cultures through their transnational circuits of exchange, from Manchester to Los Angeles through the borderlands and back again. In doing so, the book sheds light on fans as active, creative producers of poetry, artwork, and other cultural objects that challenge stereotypes of fans as pathologically depressed and stunted people. It spotlights fandom's potential for enacting resistance and creating new spaces of belonging in places where we are told, too often, that we do not belong.

Travel Tips for Moztlán[6]: Morrissey in the Borderlands

Dictionary definitions of the word 'border' tell us that it can mean a few things. A 'border' is a line that separates political or geographical areas. These lines, such as those separating nations, are arbitrarily drawn, shift throughout history, and are policed mightily by armies and other machine-gun-carrying uniformed officers of the state. 'Border' also means an edge or boundary of something. Claims that we live in a 'borderless' world are made by people with the material and economic privilege of crossing them at will or leisure: surely, refugees from Syria or immigrants from Mexico would argue otherwise, that in fact we do not live in a borderless world. If we did, there would be no militarized patrols of national borders to reinforce the notion that borders exist and are defended at all costs to keep Them out of Our Country. In our current era of global capitalism, goods and money can flow freely across borders, while people—at least those who suffer the most from first world economic exploitation or do not have proper documentation—cannot. So to talk about 'borders' and 'borderlands' requires us to consider big questions: Which borders? Who can cross them and who cannot? Which nations, states, counties, towns drew these lines, and for what purposes?

The US-Mexico border we know stretches over 3,100 miles, from the Pacific Ocean in Southern California to the Gulf of Mexico in Southern Texas. This international border, which separates the US states of California, Arizona, New Mexico, and Texas from Mexico, was created in 1848 by the Treaty of Guadalupe Hidalgo. Between 1845 and 1848, large swaths of territory belonged to, and then didn't belong to, Mexico; before that, Spain. At one point, Mexican territory covered all of modern-day California to Oregon, all of Nevada, Utah, and parts Colorado and Wyoming, as well as the aforementioned the states to the south. I like Lalo Alcaraz's 2016 cartoon (Fig. 1), 'Mexico Paid For The Wall,' because it serves as a pointed visual aid and history lesson, salient in our current moment of a Donald J. Trump Republican presidential candidacy, to help us see how large Mexico was a hundred and seventy years ago. It also shows us that Mexicans have always been here and challenges notions of who and who does not belong within US borders: 'we didn't cross the border, the border crossed us,' as a popular immigration rights slogan reminds us.

These historical contexts must be part of any story of the US-Mexico borderlands, including ours. *Mozlandia: Morrissey Fans in the Borderlands*, takes Gloria Anzaldúa's definition of 'borderlands' as its main conceptual, material, and metaphoric framework. In her groundbreaking work, Anzaldúa theorizes the geopolitical area of the US-Mexico borderlands as a place of conflict, contradiction, emerging 'third' cultures, and cultural hybridity. She writes, 'A borderland is a vague and undetermined boundary. It is a constant state of transition. The prohibited and forbidden are its inhabitants. *Los atravesados* live here: the squint-eyed, the perverse, the queer, the troublesome, the mongrel, the mulato, the half-breed, the half dead; in short, those who cross over, pass over, or go through the confines of the "normal."'[7] Sounds like Morrissey and Smiths fans for sure.

While Anzaldúa specifically refers to the US-Mexican border region, her concepts can be just as productive in looking at any (violently contested) borderland area, such as the Northern Ireland-Republic of Ireland border. In the case of Morrissey, the English North-South divide comes to mind as his life's main organizing border: *I lost my bag at Newport-Pagnell*, a baggage service station that served as the unofficial dividing line between North and South that Morrissey sings about in the Smiths tune, Is It Really So Strange?[8] As a Northerner and border crosser himself, Morrissey has undoubtedly been shaped by the realities of borderland existence, one that reinforces the feelings of being the outsider, the other, even when ostensibly he is/we are home. It makes sense that Morrissey makes home, and has amassed his largest fan following, in the borderlands of the US and Mexico.

In this way, we can consider Morrissey as what Anzaldúa terms a 'border artist.' She writes,

The Mexico/United States border is a site where many different cultures 'touch' each other, and the permeable, flexible, and ambiguous shifting grounds lend themselves to hybrid images. The border is the locus of resistance, of rupture, implosion and explosion, and of putting together the fragments and creating a new assemblage. Border artists cambian el punto de referencia [trans.: they change the point of reference]. By disrupting the neat separations between cultures, they create a culture mix, una mezcla in their artworks.[9]

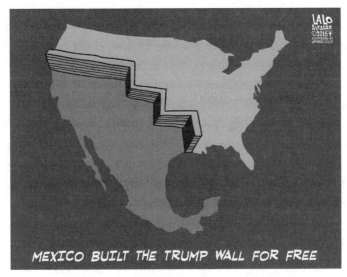

Go ahead, Trump. Build *this* wall, Pendejo!

Figure 1. 'Mexico Paid for the Wall.' Cartoon appears courtesy of Lalo Alcaraz and Universal Uclick. ©2016 Lalo Alcaraz. Used with permission.

Understanding Morrissey as a 'border artist' in Anzaldúa's terms compels us to recognize the complex and innovative ways in which he and his many US Chicana/o and Latina/o fans 'mix cultures' and 'change the point of reference' in a 'permeable, flexible, ambiguous, fragmented' borderland existence. We hear it when Gustavo Manzur, Morrissey's Texas Latino keyboardist of Colombian and Ecuadorian parentage, sings in Spanish during live versions of Speedway or on the *World Peace is None of Your Business* album. We hear it when Morrissey himself sings a verse in Spanish (albeit awkwardly translated) in a song like Don't Make Fun Of Daddy's Voice: 'No te divertes con papi, no!' We saw it when Morrissey and his band once came back for an encore dressed in Chivas kits—the Chivas de Guadalajara, a popular Mexican fútbol team. And we see Morrissey 'mix cultures' and 'change the point of reference' when he performs on stage with a Mexican flag draped on the monitors and sometimes draped around himself, as he has done recently in concerts around California, Texas, and New York.

Just look at the covers of this book. Morrissey as the Mexican La Virgen de Guadalupe, graphic by Rio Yañez, Chicano artist from San Francisco, California. Morrissey as a mariachi, taken from a greeting card series created by Vic Garry, a Manchester artist. These magnificent cover illustrations serve as fitting visual points of reference for the kinds of artworks and fan creations that we see elsewhere along the Moz fan landscape: we can find evidence across the borderlands of artists who imagine Morrissey as Frida Kahlo, or Morrissey as Vicente 'Chente' Fernández, or a cholo or vato loco.[10] In these ways, creative and sometimes gender-bending renderings of Morrissey as Mexican, Chicana/o, and Latina/o cultural icons attest to the salience of the singer as an 'image icon that refers to something outside of its individual components, something (or someone) that has great symbolic meaning for many people.'[11] Irish blood, English heart, Mexican soul.

What can we learn from these sorts of cultural appropriations of Morrissey by fans and in fan art, when he is imagined as significant feminine and masculine Chicana/o-Mexican icons like La Virgen, Frida, Vicente 'Chente' Fernández, or a mariachi? How do fans appropriate his words, his image, and make him our own, make him an acceptable Mexican and Chicano icon? Transcultural conditions account for much of this activity, yes, and so does a kind of fandom that helps us reimagine geographic and spatial relations between the global North and South, thereby challenging preexisting cultural and national hierarchies. Through Morrissey fandom, we reimagine our place in this world and recreate new ones.

Anzaldúa and other Chicana feminist theories of the border teach us to embrace the contradictions of living in the (US-Mexico) borderlands as racialized, gendered, classed, desiring bodies. We have visceral knowledge—our bodies and flesh know things that can't always be articulated but can be expressed in other ways. For Morrissey fans in the borderlands, and particularly for Chicanas/os, Mexicans, and Latinas/os, fandom is often a dynamic ethnoracial and gendered self-expression, a way of identifying as brown, immigrant, queer, other. We can be Morrissey fans without having to deny or repudiate our 'real' (whatever that means) Mexican, Chicana/o, or Latina/o cultural practices and identities. In effect, Moz fandom in the borderlands *is* an 'enactment of Latinidad,' a way of being Latino/a, in the US.[12]

This book explores some of those fan expressions that are distinctly rooted in US-Mexico borderland experiences.

¡Viva Morrissey! Of Chicana/o, Latina/o, and Mexican Fans

To discuss the US-Mexico borderlands, and racial/ethnic identity categories in the US more broadly, is to contemplate being—or being called—Mexican, Mexican American, Chicana/o, Latina/o, or the newest terms, Chicanx and Latinx.[13] Too often, these terms (Mexican, Mexican American, Chicana/o, Latina/o—the −a or −o signifying the feminine or masculine forms of words) are conflated, particularly in US discourse and especially in media portrayals of 'Mexican' or 'Latino' Morrissey fans. They don't all mean the same thing, they are distinct, and yet, they are related. Entire academic and artistic fields since at least the mid-1960s have been built on asking questions and debating about what it means to be Mexican American, Chicana/o, Latina/o in the US and Latin America.

While these terms are still debated and remain contested, most of us in these groups agree that such categories of ethnic and racial identity in the US arise from similar histories of European (Spanish, English, French) conquest, colonialism, invasion; US and Mexican nation-building; occupation, resistance, protest, revolution; systems of government bureaucracy and accounting; political motivations and institutional operations; and scientific constructs of racial 'difference.' So rather than dismiss the terms Mexican, Mexican American, Chicana/o, and Latina/o, as just more confusing 'labels' to eschew—because in the end, some would insist, we are all part of the human race and need to be loved, labels don't matter (or labels are divisive), let's just all unite with each other and get along (All Lives Matter!)—it is imperative to understand why these terms do matter for a more nuanced analysis of

Morrissey fandom, particularly as it exists in Los Angeles.

These terms and their distinctions matter especially because the question of Morrissey's Latino fans, and Mexican fans in particular, has engaged bewildered journalists, culture vultures, and media mavens for well over two decades. 'Why do Mexicans love Morrissey?' Sometimes the question is posed, 'Why do Latinos love Morrissey?' Scores of newspapers, magazines, documentary films, blog posts, scholarly essays, radio segments and television broadcasts from Los Angeles to El Paso, from Mexico City to Manchester, from one far off place to another, have inquired about the cultural phenomenon referred to as 'the Morrissey-Mexican connection,' also referred to as 'the Morrissey-Latino connection.' The headlines (and Morrissey's own public statements) say as much: 'Mexicans love Morrissey,' 'Latinos love Morrissey,' 'Morrissey's Latino Fans,' 'the Mexican Morrissey connection,' 'The 'love affair' between Latinos and Morrissey,' and 'Morrissey much loved in Mexico' are topics of any number of exploratory or explanatory write-ups. Even *The Times* of London ran its own article under the headline, 'Heaven Knows He's Mexican Now.' Furthermore, Morrissey himself is famous in these parts for saying, 'I wish I was born Mexican.' The world wants to know, tiresome as it is, *Why do Mexicans love Morrissey so much?* (Funny how no one asks about why Morrissey wants to be Mexican.)

What does it mean to ask that question? What are we asking, and why? When US or UK media outlets ask 'why do Mexicans love Morrissey,' do they mean newly immigrated Mexicans to the US, or do they mean people in Mexico? Or do they mean Chicanos/as, which are second, third, fourth generation Mexican Americans in the US? And when bloggers and reporters write about 'Latino Morrissey fans,' we have to ask, which Latinos are they talking about? Likely not New York Puerto Ricans or New Jersey Dominicans or Miami Cubans because, accurate or not, 'Latino Morrissey fans' as a descriptor has come to designate the mostly-Mexican-descent fan bases in California and throughout the US Southwest.

To clarify, we can begin by recognizing that Mexican, Mexican American, Chicano/a, and Latino/a are discrete categories of identity with particular histories that, generally speaking, refer to those groups of people of Mexican and/or Latin American descent. It is also important to know that these terms are specific to, and typically not used outside of, the US. In this book, I will focus primarily on the Chicana/o, Mexican American, and Latina/o Morrissey fan communities in the greater Los Angeles region and in reference to those groups of fans in the US-Mexico borderlands.

There's a world of difference between Mexicans in Mexico, born and raised in the country south of the border, and those of us born and raised on the US side, perhaps several generations removed from any direct ties to Mexico. These Mexicans born and raised north of the border likely grew up speaking English, or English and Spanish, perhaps a mix of 'Spanglish,' or just English as a first language, and their parents, maybe even their grandparents, are likely not immigrants. For our purposes here, I use 'Mexican' to describe fans in Mexico and to refer to the nation of Mexico; I will also use it to describe cultural practices on both sides of the border, as in the Mexican holiday of Día de los Muertos, celebrated widely in Los Angeles and other cities in the US with large Mexican populations. I also use 'Mexican' when fans I have interviewed self-identify as such, whether they were born on the US or Mexican side of the border; I will usually modify 'Mexican' with 'first-, second-, or third generation' in such cases.

The term 'Chicana/o' is a US-specific term that came into popular usage during the Civil Rights era Chicano Movements of the mid-1960s. It refers to a (leftist, progressive) politicized Mexican American. Chicana/o also means a person of Mexican descent born in the US, but not every Mexican American identifies as Chicana/o because of its radical, militant origins. In this book, I use 'Mexican American' and 'Chicana/o' to denote those fans born and raised in the US of Mexican heritage, who generally speak English as a first language, and generally did not immigrate to the US.[14] Morrissey, to his credit, understands the distinction of the term 'Chicana/o' as meaning US born Mexicans with some political consciousness and knowledge of race and class struggle. In his *Autobiography*, the English-born Irish man writes, 'Chicanos are my syndicates;' for my friend and fellow Moz Head, Morrissey autographed her DVD copy of the video collection, *¡Oye, Esteban!* with the following inscription: 'JoAnna, to my Chicana sister, Morrissey.'[15]

It is safe enough to say that in the US, all Chicanas/os are Latinas/os, but not all Latinas/os are Chicanas/os. 'Latino/a' is best described as an umbrella term used only in the US to describe groups from countries or who have roots in Latin America. This means that in the US, people from Mexico, Central America, and South America, and Caribbean countries like Cuba, Puerto Rico, and the Dominican Republic, can be called 'Latinos,' but in those countries, 'Latino' is not used as a self-identifying term. As poet and performance scholar Deborah Paredez reminds us, 'one becomes Latina/o only within the geographical and political economic borders of the United States.'[16] Here, I use 'Latina/o' to denote the broader fan base inclusive of those fans born and/or raised in the US of Latin American heritage, including Central America, South America, and Mexico. In some places, I also use it as a general descriptor, as in 'Latino Los Angeles' or 'Latino fans,' especially when I want to be inclusive, or when specific national origins are unknown.

Given all these terms and the lived realities that come with being/being called Chicana/o, Latina/o, Mexican in the US, we must consider Morrissey fandom, particularly as experienced in Latino Los Angeles, as less as a mystery and more as an illuminating study in transcultural fandom. In doing so, I follow fandom scholars Chin and Morimoto, who write,

> Transcultural fans become fans because of affinities of affect between the fan, in his/her various contexts, and the border-crossing object. [...] We eschew the term 'transnational,' with its implicit privileging of a national orientation that supersedes other—arguably more salient—subject positions. Rather, we favor the term 'transcultural,' which at once is flexible enough to allow for a transnational orientation, yet leaves open the possibility of other orientations that may inform, or even drive, cross-border fandom.'[17]

Chin and Morimoto's formulation of transcultural fandom sheds light on the particular ways in which Los Angeles and borderland Chicana/o and Latina/o fans of Morrissey express their 'affective investment' in the Manchester-born singer, and what such fan investments reveal about transcultural subjectivities in borderland contexts. 'Affect' is an operative term here as well, for it helps us recognize and access the critical power of what our bodies feel: affect relates to emotion, another word that appears in so many fan testimonies and write-ups. As affect theory scholars remind us, 'Affect...is the name we give to those forces—visceral forces beneath, alongside, or generally *other than* conscious knowing, vital forces insisting beyond emotion—that can serve to drive us toward movement.'[18] When applied to Moz fans, that affective movement—that feeling, that bodily knowing we get by being so affected beyond emotion by Morrissey and his music—could look something like hurling our bodies on stage to kiss, touch, and hug the man, or simply being moved to tears by his beautiful songs.

Likewise, the transcultural fandom lens helps us to see how Morrissey gives that love back to his fans. Morrissey's own declarations of affection and affinity for his 'Latino hearts' do not arise simply out of fondness: Morrissey's political and personal alignments with US Chicana/o, Latina/o, and Mexican communities befit a singer who has consistently championed the underdog and criticized social inequalities throughout his musical career.[19] The man performs with a Mexican flag draped on a stage monitor, Viva Mexico on display for all to see. And in the current political climate that sees a Donald J. Trump—a racist and specifically anti-Mexican Republican presidential candidate hellbent on 'building a wall' on the US-Mexican border—gain in voter popularity across the US, it means something affirming for a white UK-born global music icon like Morrissey to openly proclaim his love and support of Chicana/o, Latina/o, and Mexican fan communities on both sides of the border in his own not so strange ways.

No wonder the feelings are mutual.

This is not to suggest that this particular connection between Morrissey and his borderland fans is not unproblematic, or not without its complexities and contradictions. They're all over the place. I get the concerns around race (brown fans, white performer) and why his comments about Mexicans, while perhaps anchored in his genuine admiration, can come off as sounding flippant. Is Morrissey exoticizing Mexicans when he says he loves them for their good teeth and good hair? Is he romanticizing the Chicano gangbanger? And how could Morrissey admire UKIP Brexit leader Nigel Farage, a man who has stumped for Trump, the very same 'Thump' Moz has disparaged on his website and begged us please, don't vote for him, at his 2015 Los Angeles FYF show?[20] These are important and legitimate questions I've asked myself many times. But rather than view Chicana/o-Latina/o Morrissey fandom as simply an embrace of US notions of Anglo- and Eurocentrism, just another case of blind white man worship, I encourage an analysis of Chicana/o-Latina/o Morrissey fandom on its own terms in all its wonderful borderland complexities and transcultural formations.

From the Midlands to the Borderlands: Mapping Mozlandia

Mozlandia means Morrisseyland in Chicano Spanglish. The Land of Moz. Like how I grew up hearing Mexican relatives call Disneyland 'Disnelyandia.' Mozlandia. Like how Frida Kahlo, the iconic Mexican artist, famously called the United States 'Gringolandia,' or 'land of the gringos,' white citizens of the USA. The suffix '-landia' is a perfect Spanglish hybrid that denotes land or place, material and imagined space, a shifting landscape that can be mapped even in its fluctuations, its ephemerality. I use this hybrid word that takes Morrissey's nickname, Moz, and attaches it to a Spanglish word that designates 'land' somewhere else, somewhere on the other side, so close and yet so far off. I can't take full credit for the term's coinage. My bro-in-law came up with it in conversation and, in a true collaborative spirit, let me run with it.

'Mozlandia' is a symbolic term, my attempt to identify, theorize, and highlight the contours of Morrissey fanscapes, or landscapes of fandom, from the Midlands of England to the Borderlands of the US Southwest. Fanscapes form across time, place, and space; they are as earthly and material as much as they are imagined communities, states of mind. Morrissey fanscapes—like so many other global fanscapes for film series like Star Wars, book series like Harry Potter, sports teams like Manchester United—take shape around contours marked by race, class, gender, sexuality, age, nationality, and histories of conquest. The dance nights and discos, plays and performances, fashion, artwork, graphics, tribute bands, social media pages, and other modes of fan expression are all part of the Morrissey fanscape in Los Angeles and elsewhere.

There are many ways to veer off this beaten LA path, many other cities and communities one could potentially center in an exploration of fervent Morrissey fandom. Mexrrissey mastermind Camilo Lara called Los Angeles the 'motherland'[21] of Morrissey fans; we can think of 'Moz Angeles' as the 'capital' of Mozlandia. I chose Los Angles as our main region of exploration partly out of convenience (I was born, raised, and live here, and I'm an active Morrissey fan), but mainly because LA has a unique relationship to Morrissey. The sheer size of Los Angeles and its environs; its status as a global city; its historic ties to Spain and later, Mexico; its majority Mexican-Latino/a population; its status as the second largest Spanish language media market in the US; its relevance as a key Morrissey site (milestone performances, his residence); its large and active fan bases that emerged concurrently with Morrissey's solo career; and a host of other layered historical, cultural, social, and political contexts combine to give rise to 'Moz Angeles' as a rich and distinctive fanscape.

Morrissey's Los Angeles and Southern California fan bases reflect the highly diverse culture, economic, and racial makeup of this geopolitical mega region. This of course is not to say that all Chicanas/os and Latinas/os in LA are Morrissey fans, nor that the only Morrissey fans in LA are Chicana/o or Latina/o or even from LA. As Juliet 'Romeo Girl' Wong reminds me, there is a good-sized population of Chinese American, Filipino American, and Japanese American fans who run websites, attend events, and make art.[22] Yet, for all its diversity, Los Angeles is, has been, and remains an overwhelmingly Chicana/o-Latina/o-Mexican town. The culture of 'Moz Angeles' and the city of Los Angeles stands out in terms of its level of fan activity. There is a lot going on here.

I like to think of *Mozlandia* as a map book and storybook. Part field notes, part journal entries, part scholarly inquiry, *Mozlandia* is a collection of dispatches from the vibrant, lively Morrissey fan cultures that exist in and beyond Los Angeles. It is a book about love, maps, and Morrissey fans. The book mixes academic analysis with fanecdotes (fan anecdotes); it raises scholarly-like questions while providing insights from folks on the ground and in the mix, sprinkled with my personal insights as a fan and citizen of Moz Angeles. *Mozlandia* leads us from one end of Los Angeles to another, with detours in Manchester, England, where it all began. Chapter one, 'Playing Easy to Get: A Tour of Morrissey's Los Angeles,' is inspired by the Moz bus tours arranged by Craig Gill's Manchester Music Tours. Chapter one takes us through Morrissey's Los Angeles, routing us through the fan mecca that rivals Manchester in Moz cred. If Manchester holds the history of young, 1980s' Smiths-era Morrissey, Los Angeles shows us the artist who has evolved as a solo pop music icon in the 1990s and 2000s.

Chapter two, 'Boyle Heights, You Are Too Hot: Singing Your Life at MorrisseyOke,' focuses on the monthly singalong event that takes place at Eastside Luv Bar in Boyle Heights. As the only regularly scheduled event in the area that makes singing to Morrissey and Smiths songs all night the whole point of the show, MorrisseyOke showcases the strongly participatory foundation of the local Morrissey Smiths fan culture. Chapter three, 'When Your Gift Unfurls: Paying Tribute to Morrissey and the Smiths,' features the large and active tribute band scene in the LA area. There are more Morrissey and Smiths tribute bands in Los Angeles than there are for any other artist or band in the world. Chapter three examines the post-*You Are the Quarry* explosion of the LA tribute band scene and features interviews with several of the bands that formed after the release of *Quarry*, Morrissey's 'comeback' solo album and love letter to Los Angeles.

Chapter four, 'Our Weekly Appointment: *Breakfast with the Smiths, The World of Morrissey* on Indie 103.1,' spotlights the radio show that put Indie 103.1 on the Moz map. Hosted by LA's own 'Mexican Morrissey,'

José Maldonado, *Breakfast with the Smiths* represents a peerless display of transnational Morrissey Smiths fandom mediated by social media and routed through a Los Angeles Internet radio station. Finally, in chapter five, 'Written Words on Paper: Morrissey as Muse,' fans' written tributes take center stage. I focus on a Morrissey and Smiths themed poetry event in El Monte, California, as well as the world premiere of *Teatro Moz*, a Morrissey short play festival and playwriting contest held in Boyle Heights. Such poetic and theatrical offerings represent some of the most meaningful tributes to Morrissey, himself a lover of poets, plays, actors and writers. They are also important reminders of how fandom can be mobilized as a platform of creative expression.

After a brief Conclusion, the book ends with a short Epilogue, my fan letter to Morrissey. It is the first fan letter I have ever written to him, something that I should have written when I was seventeen or eighteen. Now, I write to thank him for his music and to reflect on the role he has played as a central part of my mind's landscape. From my days as a young fan, from when I first fell in love with the KROQ version of There Is A Place In Hell For Me And My Friends in 1991, to when, at age forty-one, I attempted to get my hair cut at Trumper's in London (only to be rejected on the grounds of my biology), my love and loyalty to Morrissey is both natural and confounding. I embrace it and grow with him and his music.

Fandom is personal, complicated, contradictory, affective, subjective, subject to all kinds of movements and shifts in the landscape. I like LA-based music writer Nikki Darling here, who says, 'Fandom is how community forms. It is a safe way to express desire. It is about identity, about finding your people and belonging, especially for those who don't quite fit in otherwise.'[23] Darling's comments show us how being a fan is an intensely personal thing, while at the same time it performs important social and community-building functions for us. How we show and practice our fandom says something about the people, places, and conditions of our lives: fandom facilitates our creation of alternate maps of the world across time zones and national boundaries with others through our fan connections to Morrissey.

Fandom is also sometimes difficult to sustain. It gets tested. It ebbs and flows. We break up and make up with our fan object. We get mad sometimes, and we want to hold our fan object accountable when they do or say some stupid shit, something confounding, something that goes against our own principles. Furthermore, active fandom, making fan investments, requires spending precious quality time and in some cases, limited resources like money and means, on the material objects (records, merchandise, concert tickets, T-shirts, memorabilia) and ephemeral experiences (attending fan conventions, disco nights, tribute band shows) associated with our fan object. Fandom is a condition of our late capitalist consumer world, where products and experiences are commodities. 'It is hard to be a fan sometimes,' writes Jack Halberstam, professor of English, gender, and feminist studies. 'Fandom is full of jeopardy and heartbreak, it is a jagged experience that confirms you and shatters you and often in the same location.'[24] Fandom isn't perfect, but it's fascinating.

From the Midlands to the Borderlands, this is Mozlandia, the land of Morrissey and his loving fans.

CHAPTER ONE

Playing Easy to Get
A Tour of Morrissey's Los Angeles

Sickened, I left England. The good life is out there somewhere. I found increasing strength as I purchased 1498 North Sweetzer Avenue in the West Hollywood zone of Los Angeles—the city of promises.

Morrissey, *Autobiography* (2013)

And what you came hoping to be cured with (which is what someone else came to be cured of—your sickness being someone else's cure) is certainly here, all here, among the flowers and the grass, the palm-trees, the blessed evenings...

John Rechy, 'The City of Lost Angels' (1959)

TO GET TO THE WEST HOLLYWOOD ZONE OF LOS ANGE-les from my hometown of Whittier, east of east LA, we have to take three freeways and drive thirty miles, usually for almost an hour and almost always in traffic. We take the 605 north to the 60 east to the 101 north, and we pass local landmarks like the red neon block letters of Rose Hills cemetery, visible throughout most of East LA and parts of the San Gabriel Valley. We pass the Montebello Town Center, the only mall on the Eastside. We speed through the predominantly Latino and Asian working class suburbs of South El Monte, Montebello, Monterey Park, and East Los Angeles before cutting through the interchange over to the 101 north where we slow to a crawl in the crunch of traffic through Boyle Heights, Downtown LA, Echo Park, and Silver Lake. When we finally exit on the famous Sunset Boulevard in East Hollywood, we keep driving for about four, five miles to West Hollywood.

On our drive to North Sweetzer Avenue from East LA, we pass fast food chains, hole-in-the-wall Thai and Vietnamese restaurants, Armenian auto repair shops, Chinese businesses, and Mexican supermarkets. We pass cheap motels, abandoned buildings, modest homes, some remodeled, many not, single family homes in name only as more and more of these little boxes house multiple families amidst too many gentrification developments and new chain stores. We pass tourist traps and LA landmarks like Olvera Street, site of the original Pueblo de Los Angeles, just across César Chávez Boulevard from the historic Chinatown District that used to be LA's Little Italy.

Stuck in downtown traffic, we can see Griffith Park Observatory and the Hollywood sign in the distance, but we aren't meant to see that the benign beige and gleaming glass buildings on either side of the 101 in downtown are an ICE (Immigrations and Customs Enforcement) detention center and the Twin Towers Correctional Facility, inmates and immigrants locked inside for the crimes of being poor and black and brown in the United States of America.

Across east and south and Downtown LA, chipped paint and sun-faded multi-unit apartment complexes with names like Tiki Terrace and Paradise Manor that were built in the 1960s sag next to swollen school buildings next to chain-linked empty lots in various phases of abandonment or construction. Cranes and cement trucks and endless orange cone construction zones signal the building of new structures that will soon be more totally unnecessary eat-shop-live high-occupancy high-priced urban enclaves, complete with their own Starbucks and Metro stations.

There are cars, cars, everywhere cars: on LA's notoriously congested freeways, new Benzes slide by aging Toyotas, oversized SUVs with moms and kids amble alongside tiny imports, shiny Lincoln limousines glide by rickety pickup trucks, lowrider vintage Chevys cruise next to rented

Kias with out of state plates, all duking it out with big rig trucks hauling cheap crap from China to the nearest Walmart.

And people. So many people in Los Angeles, population four million city and over ten million for the county: gente who've been here since it was Mexico and California Dream-seekers since the Dust Bowl and the ones who just got here yesterday from Korea or Honduras or Wisconsin. Economic and ethnic segregational patterns rooted in settler colonial histories put the wealthy white people, for the most part, on the west side of LA—near the beautiful beaches and good schools and healthy eating options and boutique medical cannabis dispensaries—and keep many other people out, scattering them throughout the working class suburbs in LA's east, south, and parts of the north.

Morrissey knows this Los Angeles, the city he formally called home between *Maladjusted* (1997) and *You Are the Quarry* (2004), and the city to which he inevitably returns, every time a homecoming. He reveals in *Autobiography* that before he settled into 1498 North Sweetzer Avenue, he lived in LA once before, in 1991, on Delresto Drive in the Hollywood Hills. There, near the posh Holmby Hills neighborhood north of the UCLA campus, Morrissey 'unwisely invest[ed] in a monstrosity where ten hours of fried-alive sun burns daily into each room.' He spent a lot of time in LA and across Southern California that year due to a series of marquee events from June to November in 1991 that hailed the arrival of 'Mozmania'[25] across Los Angeles and Orange County. These include Morrissey's US solo debut with shows in Costa Mesa (OC) and Inglewood (LA); his first US late night television appearance on *The Johnny Carson Show*; the debut of his new rockabilly-inspired touring band on live radio at the Capitol Records Building for KROQ; and the infamous UCLA concert at Pauley Pavilion that ended in a 'melee.'[26]

Indeed, Los Angeles proved to be too hot for Moz, who was seemingly hotter as a bona fide solo artist than as a Smith. He left LA before releasing *Your Arsenal*, and after stints in London and Dublin, Morrissey came back to 'Lost Angels' for good, or at least for seven long years, following the debacle that was the High Court Case that saw members of his former band sue him for back royalties: 'Sickened, I left England,' he writes, '[for] the good life' in LA. It is a funny thing to remember that LA is the city once derided by his buddy, Michael Stipe, who called it a 'lemming colony.'[27] Morrissey himself said on at least one occasion that he would never live in Los Angeles, telling one interviewer that 'Los Angeles is terribly nice but people once they get there cease to be real.'[28] Luckily for him and for many of his fans here, Morrissey changed his tune long enough to make home in LA, his sunny 'city of promises:' 'My Moz Angeles love affair is back on,' he assures us in *Autobiography*.

Though he eventually left Los Angeles for Rome and other far off places, Morrissey would return to make LA his home base of sorts. He comes back often, staying for long stints to live and work. He spent 2008 in Los Angeles recording *Years of Refusal*, and since then has returned annually to play milestone concerts, make late night television appearances and give rare interviews, as he did with Larry King in August 2015.[29] Upon returning from a recent epic South America tour, Morrissey was immediately spotted at some of his favorite local Los Angeles haunts.

Befitting a legendary global rock icon, Morrissey lived in the hills above the Sunset Strip among movie stars and the memories of Hollywood legends. He resided in West Hollywood, near the gays, tourists, and wannabe rock stars from Sunset Strip to Santa Monica Boulevard. He lived in *Hollywood*, that facsimile of LA life manufactured and sold by various entertainment industries, the Hollywood that lives in the global imagination as a superficial fantasyland full of movie studios, celebrity sightings, paparazzi hoards, hot nightclubs, shopping galore, venerable music venues, championship sports teams, overpriced amusement parks, celebrity chef restaurants, scenic surf beaches, endless traffic, and thousands of tourists.

Morrissey's Los Angeles is all this and more. When he wasn't cozy in some pub or record store somewhere on Sunset Boulevard, Morrissey 'also spent his free time in the city cruising the Mexican districts of East and South Central LA where the local gang culture would inspire First Of The Gang To Die and Ganglord.'[30] We can imagine Morrissey in his 'sky blue Jag' driving along, maybe on a 'drab Thursday' on one of his 'flits across the border,'[31] or perhaps to Northridge to see Al Martino, cruising the streets in the rich and the poor and the not very rich and the very poor parts of the city, composing song lyrics in his head, to say nothing of the barrio boy prison gang fantasies he was not so secretly harboring in his lustful heart. *Los Angeles, you are too hot.*

Our tour of Moz Angeles is inspired by Phill Gatenby's *Morrissey's Manchester* and Craig Gill's wonderful Manchester 'Mozbus' tour. We will make eleven stops along a roughly nine-mile route that runs from Silver Lake to West Hollywood, hitting up all the 'key Morrissey Hollywood landmarks' that Simon Goddard mentions under his 'Los Angeles' entry in the *Mozipedia*. In an effort to make this chapter a guide that someone might actually use, I've set up the tour in the most driver-friendly way possible, navigating back streets and freeways and tourist traffic that one will inevitably encounter in the heart of Hollywood. At the end of the chapter, I've included a list of additional Moz sites around greater LA for further exploration. Along the way, we will locate the name-dropped LA references that dot Morrissey's lyrical landscape, such as Cole and Cahuenga (I'm Playing Easy To Get), the Palms (All The Lazy Dykes) and the reservoirs (First Of The Gang To Die). These and other Morrissey sites make Los Angeles a city that rivals Manchester as a Moz fan mecca. If Manchester holds the history of young, 1980s' Smiths-era Morrissey, Los Angeles shows us the artist who has evolved as a solo pop music icon in the 1990s and 2000s.

This is Morrissey's Los Angeles, and this chapter is your guide.

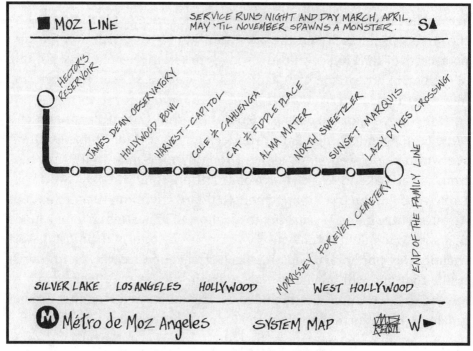

Moz Metro Map. Illustration by Michael Robinson, based on a sketch by the author.

1. Silver Lake Reservoirs

You have never been in love until you've seen the stars reflect in the reservoirs
And you have never been in love until you've seen the dawn rise behind
The Home for the Blind

Morrissey, First Of The Gang To Die

We know these lyrics by heart, the opening lines of First Of The Gang To Die, the song about a young Latino gang member who loses his life 'with a bullet to his gullet.' Goddard's *Mozipedia* informs us that Morrissey wrote the song 'after moving to Los Angeles,' a 'joyful requiem to a local young Latino criminal whose wayward lifestyle led him inevitably to an early grave.' Despite other possible interpretations of the song—Len Brown in *Meetings with Morrissey* cites a film character (a teacher named Hector played by Richard Griffiths) and one of Oscar Wilde's contemporaries (Hector Munro) as potential sources for the song—First Of The Gang To Die will always be synonymous with Los Angeles with its reservoirs and Home for the Blind.

The area of Silver Lake is hopelessly gentrified, property values around here through the roof, but the areas around the reservoirs—there are two, the large Silver Lake Reservoir and the smaller, adjacent Ivanhoe Reservoir—remain a popular destination point for many LA residents because of its scenic paths and dog parks that surround the water storage facility.

A bit of history: according to the Silver Lake website, the area was originally called 'Ivanhoe,' named by a Scotsman after his favorite Scottish novel. It's a nice Brit Lit inspiration and connection, which helps to explain the prevalence of Scottish *Ivanhoe*-themed street names in the area such as Rowena and St George. Around the turn of the last century, the area was renamed for the water board commissioner Herman Silver, a key figure in the development and construction of the reservoirs, which were completed in 1907.

Silver Lake's early history is also connected to the film and entertainment industry. Walt Disney built his first studio in Silver Lake, up on Hyperion Avenue and Griffith Park Boulevard, and several other studios, lots, and neighborhood areas were featured in old films: Laurel and Hardy's 1932 movie *The Music Box* may come to mind. As a result, many of Silver Lake's residents in the 1930s and the decades following included movie stars, producers, and directors. Around the 1970s, Silver Lake became a hotbed of gay leather subculture—the Eagle bar still exists not too far from here on Santa Monica Boulevard—and by the 2000s, gentrification tightened its stranglehold on the Silver Lake neighborhood, which is now home to a bunch of trendy boutiques, bars, restaurants, and other telltale signifiers of hipster invasion.

Silver Lake is bordered by Echo Park to the southeast, which is likely where Hector and his gang were from. On the northwest side is Los Feliz, where Morrissey guitarist Jesse Tobias is said to reside. Jesse is co-owner of the York, a bar in neighboring Highland Park, a Latino immigrant working class enclave in the midst of its own patterns of gentrification. Down the street from the York is Wombleton Records and Johnny's Bar, where Morrissey was once spotted shooting pool. From the *Los Angeles Times*: 'According to Elden Man, manager of boutique vinyl shop Wombleton Records, when owner Ian Marshall returns with an overseas shipment of Smiths related used vinyl, customers get starry-eyed when he tells them that the York is co-owned by Morrissey's guitarist and that Morrissey has shot pool at Johnny's Bar. Man says many make a block-long pilgrimage to have a pint on sacred ground.'[32]

Morrissey's 'Home for the Blind'—properly known as The Braille Institute of Los Angeles—is about three miles down the road from the Silver Lake Reservoir. We will bypass it on the way to the Griffith Observatory.

2. Griffith Observatory

From the Home for the Blind, we drive four short miles up Vermont Avenue to idyllic Griffith Park, home of the Griffith Observatory. The official website will tell us that 'when it opened in 1935, it was one of the first institutions in the US dedicated to public science and possessed the third planetarium in the US.' It is one of Los Angeles's most popular attractions for tourist, locals, and school kids alike, and features breathtaking views of the LA basin, the Pacific Ocean (on a clear day), and the famous Hollywood sign.

The Morrissey connection to the place is related to James Dean and his 1955 classic film, *Rebel Without a Cause*. James Dean filmed several key scenes here at the Observatory, including the planetarium inside and the manicured grounds outside. It was the first time that the Observatory was used as a film location. Since then, Griffith Observatory has been featured in countless commercials, films, and television shows.

Morrissey fans know of his deep admiration for James Dean, the good looking rebel immortalized by the very film that was shot here at Griffith Observatory, where Morrissey would be featured in a photo series for the April 1994 issue of *Q* magazine. Shot by British photographer of rock stars Andy Earl, the Griffith Observatory photos show Morrissey draped on a bench near the balcony's edge, sideburn-quiff profile-perfect as he gazes over his shoulder into the cloudy LA sky. Another photo captures Moz in a cheeky pose straddling and leaning forward on the balcony wall of the Observatory high above the bustling city below. He's clearly not afraid of heights like his idol, Dean, was.

Morrissey points of interest include the balcony bench in front of the TELESCOPE sign where he posed for the *Q* photo and a bronze bust monument to James Dean in the park outside of the Observatory.

3. Hollywood Bowl

The iconic and mythical Hollywood Bowl sits up in the hills off North Cahuenga Boulevard. From the Griffith Observatory, we will travel five short (though not quick) miles through Los Feliz—Jesse Tobias's neighborhood—and up the 101 to the Hollywood Bowl. The Bowl is historic and beautiful. It is one of my personal favorite places to be on summer nights. Buses from all over the suburbs bring locals hauling picnics of food and wine to summertime concerts under the stars. I have seen New Order, Björk, Grace Jones, countless jazz and Latin music shows, and Morrissey, of course, at this glorious venue.

Morrissey has played the Bowl on three occasions: two nights in October 1992 and one night in June 2007. The Hollywood Bowl is significant enough in Morrissey's career to warrant its own entry in the *Mozipedia*. Goddard writes, 'Morrissey is particularly proud of the fact that on 8 August 1992, the 35,000 tickets for his two nights at Los Angeles' Hollywood Bowl on 10 and 11 October that year sold out in twenty-three minutes, smashing the previous record held by the Beatles.' Morrissey would return to the Hollywood Bowl fifteen years later on 8 June 2007 during what was called his 'Greatest Hits Tour.'

I went to that show. I had just passed my PhD qualifying exams in San Diego and moved back home to LA. That night at the Hollywood Bowl, Morrissey roared onto the stage to the opening song, The Queen Is Dead. My heart pounded and tears spilled out of my eyes as I beheld Morrissey live on stage for the first time in fifteen years. I clutched my sister, Monica, who was there with me, and we jumped up and down as we cheered and screamed: *OH MY GOD THERE HE IS MORRISSEEEEEEEYYYY! AAAAHHH!* We couldn't believe our friends were running late and missing all of this. It was pretty magical and totally memorable.

Too bad Morrissey didn't think so at the time. He will write in his *Autobiography* the following:

> By Friday we play the Hollywood Bowl, and Mikey [Farrell, Moz's keyboardist] presents a personal guest list long enough to encircle the city, and I reject it since the eye-crossing cost of it is ultimately subtracted from my pension fund. Mikey sulks at the rejection and this creates backstage tension. Filmed as we walk on, we all look uncharacteristically unhappy.

4. Capitol Records Building

We drive back down the hill to Vine Street to see the iconic Capitol Records Building. Steps away from Hollywood Boulevard and directly in the path of the Hollywood Walk of Fame, the famed white cylindrical tower stacked like records with a spire on top can be seen from all over Hollywood and by anyone who drives through on the 101 freeway. (Fig. 1)

The Capitol Records Building was built in the mid-1950s when the British record label, EMI, bought Capitol Records. Scores of music industry stars have worked and recorded at the storied building, though no one else, save for maybe Tommy Lee, has cavorted on its roof with Baywatch babe Pamela Anderson like Morrissey has. He did so for the promotional spoken word video for his single, Earth Is The Loneliest Planet, from his 2014 effort *World Peace is None of Your Business*. The

Figure 1. Capitol
Records Building
on Vine Street in
Hollywood, CA.
Photo by the author.

album was released on Harvest Records, an imprint owned by Capitol, which no longer has any business distributing Morrissey's latest work. Morrissey ripped the label for failing to support and promote the *World Peace* album—recall the 'Fuck Harvest' and 'Crapitol Records' T-shirts donned by the band members during select *WPINOYB* tour dates.

In the video for the title track, Morrissey and Anderson, an avowed animal rights activist and PETA member, saunter around the rooftop over a hazy pre-dusk Hollywood afternoon. I remember driving back from Santa Barbara one day and seeing helicopters hovering above the roof and to the side of the Capitol Records Building. In the distance on the roof, two or three small figures, a couple people doing who knows what up there and someone else filming them. I thought maybe they were shooting an episode of *The Bachelorette* or some other unnecessary reality show. Then a few months later on the twitters and various fan posts on social media, I see something about a new Morrissey video with Pamela Anderson in it, and it was shot on the roof of the Capitol Records Building. I immediately remember that drive back home from Santa Barbara on that cloudy day, and all I could think was *Holy shit, that was MORRISSEY up there filming the video for Earth is the Loneliest Planet! And that was no Bachelorette, that was Pamela Anderson!* It had to have been! I like to think that I had witnessed a bona fide Moz Angeles moment that day while driving south on the 101.

Nearly twenty years before Morrissey and Pamela Anderson prowled around the roof, our Mancunian singer marked an important career milestone inside the Capitol Records Building. There, in November 1991, Morrissey debuted his brand new touring band composed of strapping rockabilly lads from North London—Boz Boorer, Alain Whyte, Gary Day, and Spencer Cobrin. The session, hosted by expatriate British DJ Richard Blade, produced the EP *Live at KROQ,* now a collectors' item, and featured three tracks from *Kill Uncle*: Sing Your Life, My Love Life, and a rocking version of the piano ballad, There Is A Place In Hell For Me And My Friends. During the live session, Morrissey took phone calls from adoring fans who professed their love for him.

Sadly, while the building is not open to the general public, Moz fans will still appreciate the views of the iconic building and other related sites along Hollywood and Vine. For example, on the sidewalk just outside of the Capitol Records Building, the stars of recording arts luminaries such as the Beatles (John, Paul, George, and Ringo each have one), Tina Turner, Roy Orbison, Buddy Holly, and many others align on the Hollywood Walk of Fame. Moz fans can even recreate the photo that Morrissey took while sitting at the top of Steve Cochran's star, which is just a few steps down on Vine. And across the street from Capitol Records is the historic Avalon venue, formerly the Palace, where the annual Los Angeles Smiths and Morrissey convention is held.

Figure 2. I'm Playing Easy to Get: Cole Place and in the distance,
Cahuenga Boulevard on Sunset Boulevard looking towards the
Arclight Cinemas and Amoeba Music. Photo by author.

5. Amoeba Music/Cole &Cahuenga

A short walk down Vine and over to Sunset will bring us to Amoeba
Music near Cole and Cahuenga, where Morrissey apparently plays easy
to get. Indeed, many fans have been lucky enough to score autographs
and photos with Morrissey at Amoeba Music, one of the better-known
Moz Angeles landmarks.

Amoeba Music is a San Francisco Bay Area institution, known for
its massive selection of new, used and rare vinyl and CDs. The famed
record store has locations on Haight Street in San Francisco, and the
original flagship store opened in 1990 on Telegraph Avenue in Berkeley,
just down the street from my alma mater. In addition to its unmatched
selection of music, Amoeba is also known for hosting free in-store
concerts that feature both established and up-and-coming artists.

In 2001, Amoeba proclaimed on its website that it 'opened its biggest store yet,' right here in the middle of Hollywood. It spans an entire city block on Sunset Boulevard between Cahuenga and Ivar; Cole is on the other side of Cahuenga (Fig. 2). So when Morrissey sings, 'When you see me between Cole and Cahuenga, I'm just plain desperate' in his song, I'm Playing Easy to Get, we know he must mean he's been at Amoeba and walking down Sunset towards the Cat & Fiddle...

6. Cat & Fiddle (former site)

Urban Morrissey legend tells us that the Cat and Fiddle pub (Fig. 3a) was the best place to find the singer when he lived in LA. For thirty-two years, until it fell victim to greedy property owners who sold the venerable watering hole to make room for God-knows-what, the Cat and Fiddle's beautiful courtyard patio and pub serving pulled pints and British fare attracted a mixed crowd of music industry types, UK expatriates, and Hollywood locals. Morrissey found some semblance of home there when he visited LA and would make the Cat and Fiddle, proudly Hollywood's only British pub, his favorite local while he lived here. Moz was a regular frequenter of the pub and made himself at home there, so much that he was even known to hand over his iPod of music to the DJ, who would dutifully plug it in and play nothing but music from Morrissey's personal playlists for the entire pub.

Many LA fans have told me their stories of meeting Morrissey at the Cat and Fiddle, and the themes are familiar: he is either out on the patio or in one of the back rooms; he is usually accompanied by friends or members of his band; he is usually drinking a bottle of Corona or something with vodka; and he always kindly obliges the shy and excited fan who eventually approaches him. Many got him to sign a limb for subsequent tattooing, or maybe just a CD or a napkin, snap a photo, get a hug, say I love you. Albert Torres, an LA native and big Morrissey fan who goes by the name 'Hapie-ssey,' told me his story of when he met the singer at the Cat and Fiddle. Upon spotting Morrissey, Torres approached him at the pub and was actually invited by Moz to sit with him in his booth and chat over a pint. 'He was so nice,' says Torres of our singer. After a chat and a drink, Torres asked Morrissey to sign his leg; he got it tattooed the following day. To this day, 'Hapie-ssey' keeps a photo of him and Morrissey together from that night at the Cat as his social media profile picture.

Another LA fan, Liz Hernández, told me about her Morrissey Cat and Fiddle encounter. She and her friend had tried a few times to see if they could meet their idol at the pub, but to no avail. Finally, one day, it happened. When it did, she was mortified because mid-bite into a beefy burger, she spotted Morrissey entering the pub. 'He was right across from me when he walked in, and he still smiled at me though, but I was totally embarrassed,' she said, because meat is murder.

These stories are the stuff of LA fanlore, the dream of meeting Morrissey at the Cat and Fiddle. Sadly, like the Palms, the Cat and Fiddle is no more, and Morrissey will have to find another pub with another back room in which to sit, ponder a pint of bitter, and greet knowing fans. (Word on the street is that Morrissey's new LA spot is AGO Restaurant, a fine Italian dining establishment on Melrose co-owned by Robert DeNiro. Moz is A-list now.) When the Cat and Fiddle announced it was closing in December 2014, many fans met each other there one last time to toast Morrissey and hang out where he did so many times, sharing memories and tributes and folklore about the Hollywood pub that forever binds Morrissey to LA. (Fig. 3b.)

In true form, Morrissey posted these elegiac words on True-to-you. net about his favorite watering hole:

23 October 2014
The earth dies screaming

A large part of me dies at news that the pillowy bosom of the Cat & Fiddle is to close down on December 15th, making the universe all wrong. A beacon of light will soon be a headstone, and where will we now go to chew each other's fat? Yes, life is fragile and we all end up as worm chow, but the Cat And Fiddle is one of the Great Drinkers of The 20th Century, and is as stable and rooted a part of the Strip as number 77. We are all orphaned.

with funeral pace
Morrissey
Florence, Italy, 22 Ottobre 2014.

7. Hollywood High School

A short half mile away, 'basically Crawling distance from the bosom of the Cat & Fiddle,' as Jesse Tobias describes,[33] is the famed Hollywood High School, site of Morrissey's milestone *25Live* homecoming concert, a celebration of his twenty-fifth year as a solo artist. Located at the intersection of Sunset and Highland, Hollywood High School stands amidst the tourist traffic and television studios not too far from the Hollywood and Highland shopping district. The school's official website boasts a long list of luminary alumni, over five hundred, most of them actors and singers like Carole Lombard, Judy Garland, Ricky Nelson, and Laurence Fishburne. In 2012, the high school was added to the National Register of Historic Places. For these reasons, perhaps it becomes clear why Morrissey chose to perform his milestone concert here in these hallowed Hollywood walls.

I remember being stuck in class when tickets went on sale, 10am on some random Tuesday in the middle of the semester. In his *Autobiography,* Morrissey writes that his March 2, 2013 show at the Hollywood High School Auditorium quickly sold out 'in eye-crossing style.' It was one of those shows that was announced at the last minute, long after many of us already had tickets for the previous night's Staples Center concert with Patti Smith supporting, itself the makeup show from the one Morrissey canceled the previous November when Iggy Pop was supposed to open for him. I never scored tickets to the Hollywood High concert. On the night of the show, I drove by Hollywood High to gawk

Figures 3a and 3b. The Cat & Fiddle, before and after it was forced to shutter. Photographs by author.

at the crowd, enviously witnessing the line of Latinas and Latinos and a few outliers, young and old, waiting to be let in to see Morrissey in such an intimate setting. My homegirl Karla, who graduated from Hollywood High as a theater student in the early 1990s, would tell me later: 'Dude, you shoulda told me, I coulda snuck you into that show. I know *all* the secret spots in that auditorium.' Alas. I, like many others, would have to settle for watching the *25Live* film on a big screen during its short theatrical release in the summer of 2013.

Morrissey sites include the front stairs of the school, where a seemingly younger Morrissey was photographed jauntily bouncing down the front stairs near the Liberal & Household Arts building. (Fig. 4a) Those of us who have seen the cover image on the DVD packaging for *25Live* will recognize the school's edifice and its carefully-trying-not-to-be-racist image of its "Sheik" mascot. Turns out the mascot was inspired by a 1921 Rudolph Valentino film. (Fig. 4b) There is Morrissey, on the *25Live* cover, standing on the football field, too cool for school in a pale ivory and pink suit, shades on, lips puckered, pointing to something off in the distant, just like on the cover. Hello, Hollywood.

Figures 4a and 4b. Hollywood High School front steps and rear edifice.
Photos by the author.

8. 1498 North Sweetzer Avenue

We arrive at Los Angeles's answer to 384 Kings Road in Manchester.
(Fig. 5a) 1498 North Sweetzer Avenue was Morrissey's residence from
1998–2005. (Fig. 5b) 'I had no idea then that seven years would pass
without a new label,' writes Moz. 'But I have a real home with hardwood
floors, and I am momentarily free from the petty wars of England. Palm
trees range around each window of 1498, a house steeped in Hollywood
history since 1931.'

The house was built by Clark Gable for his wife, Carole Lombard, in
the hills above the famous Sunset Strip and has since housed famous
authors, actors, and directors. The BBC Channel 4 cameras 'burst into
Morrissey's life' at this house to film the 2002 made for television
documentary, *The Importance of Being Morrissey*, showing viewers
back home the ample evidence of his fabulous Los Angeles living. After
Morrissey left LA for Rome to record *Ringleader of the Tormentors*, his
A-list neighbor Johnny Depp, would buy the house from Morrissey in
2005 'for use as a guest annex.'

In the 1990s and 2000s, to catch Morrissey at home, to meet him at

Figures 5a and 5b. A Tale of Two Houses. 1498 North Sweetzer Avenue, West Hollywood, California, and 384 Kings Road, Manchester, England.
Photos by the author.

his doorstep, was the ultimate intimate Los Angeles fan moment. There is documentary film footage of fans meeting Morrissey outside his front door or catching him as he drove out of his driveway in his shiny luxury vehicle, only to disappear into Sunset Boulevard traffic. In his collection of fan stories, *The Day I Met Morrissey*, Dickie Felton profiles a fan who drove from Houston, Texas to Los Angeles to see where Morrissey lived. The fan scored a meeting, chat, and autographs when he drove up to the house and caught the singer outside waiting for a ride.

I recently visited 1498 North Sweetzer for the first time with two fellow fans, both first-generation Mexican fans from the San Fernando Valley. Both of them shared fond memories of coming up here with a group of eight or ten people; they would park in the tiny cul-de-sac and serenade Morrissey, hoping he was there listening, even if he did not come out to greet them or part the curtains from on high to make eye contact with them. 'One of us would bring an acoustic guitar, and we'd all just be together right there (points to the cul-de-sac in front of then-Morrissey's garage) singing his songs, see if he'd come out,' shares one of the fans, known as Clover Dean. I imagined it like a mañanitas serenade, very Mexicano, and Morrissey would have probably loved it.

As I listened to Clover's story, I imagined what it would be like for Morrissey to see a group of beautiful brown fans singing his songs to him. I looked around the property, went up the stairs as far as the locked gate would permit me, and I took it all in. I was struck by the feel of the place: lush, like paradise, the green palm trees looking down apathetically from the surrounding hills, like something the great LA writer John Rechy would describe.[34] The weather changes up there. It smells good, and you can breathe. Something about North Sweetzer also felt like Disneyland. (Then, in the yard next door, I heard the waterfall amidst the palm trees and imported lushness, and I imagine Johnny Depp as the Disneyland pirate captain at home.) Seeing the house, though, Morrissey's former residence, made my heart skip and my skin tingle. He *lived* here, and there's a part of Morrissey that will forever remain at 1498 North Sweetzer Avenue. You can feel it.

Though the man hasn't lived there for over ten years, the Sweetzer residence remains part of Morrissey's LA lore: fans continue to make their way up the narrow, steep, curvy street to the last house in the cul-de-sac, the one with the concrete stairs leading up through the iron gate to the whitewashed mission style home with its red Spanish tile roof amidst the thick vegetation and privacy shrubbery that has never been very good at its job.

9. Sunset Marquis Hotel and Spa

I am leg-ironed in my villa at the Sunset Marquis and
I watch it all unfold on the nightly news.[35]

Since 1991, the year he sat leg-ironed in his villa watching news of the infamous concert riot he allegedly instigated at UCLA, the Sunset Marquis Hotel and Spa has been Morrissey's home away from home. (Fig. 6) He lived at the hotel before he moved to the house on North Sweetzer, and he continues to return to stay during his LA visits.

Located less than a mile down the road from 1498 North Sweetzer Avenue, the Sunset Marquis is located on Alta Loma Road, a steep

Figure 6. Entry denied. Author in front of the hotel.
Photo by Clover Dean. Used with permission.

residential street between Sunset and Santa Monica Boulevard. Though only steps away from the jungle of the Sunset Strip, the hotel and its grounds, featuring Mediterranean style villas, are venerated for the relative seclusion and privacy it offers its clientele. There is also a recording studio on site where many a Grammy-award winning song has been recorded.

The Sunset Marquis opened its doors in 1963 and has been the unofficial home of rock stars and touring bands gigging their way through LA's historic music scene for over fifty years. The hotel website boasts of the celebrities who have called the hotel home and hangout over the decades, and in 2013, the hotel began selling a souvenir coffee-table book called *If These Walls Could Rock: 50 Years at the Legendary Sunset Marquis Hotel,* documenting the storied hotel's famous rock star reputation. Morrissey joins the likes of the Who and James Brown and Guns N' Roses and so many others have left their marks on this hotel. Hole singer Courtney Love immortalized the hotel in a 2010 song: 'Follow me back to the Sunset Marquis / Lock ourselves into the room / Gamble it all / And lose it on me,' lines we can perhaps hear Morrissey sing.

The Sunset Marquis looms large in the collective imagination of Morrissey fans. It even inspired a short play, 'Sister, I'm A...,' that uses the hotel as a setting for a not-so-chance fan meeting. The only Sunset Marquis Morrissey story I have is not really mine. A former student told me that she met Morrissey in an elevator at the Sunset Marquis. After I screened Morrissey's Suedehead video on the first day of my Desire in Literature and Culture class, the student approached me afterward and said, 'I met that guy.' *You met Morrissey?* I asked, ready to give her an A+ for the class. Yes, she said, and explained that her father works in the music industry and stays at the Sunset Marquis all the time. One day, in the lobby, he pointed out Morrissey to her as 'the guy from the Smiths, some eighties band,' before they all ended up in the elevator together. She was very pleased when she saw my face light up. I wanted to ask all sorts of questions like what was Morrissey wearing? Did he say anything to them in the elevator? Where was he going? Did he smell good? I reeled in the stalker-fan questions and thanked the student for making my day, and I vowed that one day, I would go to the Sunset Marquis when Moz is in town and try to meet him in the elevator. Alas, I found out the hard way that not anyone can just walk into the hotel. It is strictly guarded by beefy brown bouncers who will only let you in if you can show proof of registered guest status.

One is better off heading to nearby Book Soup, one of Morrissey's favorite local spots and where he stopped upon returning from his 2015 South America tour to autograph copies of *Autobiography* and *List of the Lost.* Down the street on Sunset is Mel's Diner, where Moz once sat with Arthur Kane of his beloved New York Dolls.

10. The Palms (former site)

All the lazy dykes/Cross-armed at the Palms...

From the Sunset Marquis, a quick jaunt down Santa Monica Boulevard will land us at the site of the former famous dyke bar that Morrissey name-checks in his 2004 song from *You Are the Quarry*. Sadly, the bar is no longer here, and so we can only pass by its former site on the way to Hollywood Forever Cemetery.

The Palms was an historic lesbian bar for nearly fifty years, and the last remaining one in the area, when it closed its doors at the end of pride weekend in 2013. Often mistaken by hetero couples for a fancy steakhouse called the Palm, the Palms welcomed neighborhood regulars and celebrity lesbians alike, such as Ellen Degeneres, k.d. lang, and Melissa Etheridge. In *Mozipedia*, Simon Goddard describes how 'the singer recalled how he would often pass by admiring its "absolutely fascinating" clientele of female bikers and other "very, very strong women,"' lesbians who would make the drive from all over LA to be themselves, see themselves here at The Palms. The sight of strong lesbians hanging around the club inspired Morrissey to write All The Lazy Dykes, 'a plea to a married woman in denial about her true sexuality to 'free yourself, be yourself, step into the Palms and see yourself.'

I have some fond personal memories of going to the Palms as a young just-out dyke in the late 1990s and early 2000s. It was the only dedicated lesbian bar around, and it rivaled the (also now closed) Lexington Bar in San Francisco in lesbian lore as a must-go, must-see bar. Women were hot, you might see someone famous, you might hook up, you might be the willing guinea pig for one of the straight girls who just wanted to see what it was like. The Wednesday night before the Thanksgiving holiday at the Palms was always steamy and packed.

When I saw that Morrissey had a song on *Quarry* called All The Lazy Dykes, I was annoyed at first. I wanted to walk up the street, find Morrissey at the pub, and tell him, 'C'mon man, why do you gotta call us lazy? Not cool, Morrissey.' And when I saw that he repeats the 'lazy dyke' statement in his *Autobiography*, I rolled my eyes. There it is again, we're all just lazy dykes I guess and all the boys are just too-good-looking race car drivers. But despite my annoyance and imaginary conversation, I found a way to listen to the song—I'm a fan first, but that doesn't mean I can't be critical—and learned to appreciate it for its shout-out to closeted women and lesbians everywhere. And on his Los Angeles album, *Quarry*, it especially was nice to see some lesbian West Hollywood representation for an area of town that all too easily is just about the boys. Props for that one, Mozzy. I forgive you.

These days, when I hear the song, I rejoice because in the end, Morrissey has done his part to immortalize the Palms as an important countercultural marker of queerness that so many of us not-always-lazy cross-armed dykes remember well.

11. Hollywood Forever Cemetery

We drive east down Santa Monica Boulevard through gay West Hollywood en route to the final stop of our tour, the Hollywood Forever Cemetery, which will one day be Morrissey's final resting place. (Fig. 7) Los Angeles locals show up in droves for Cinespia's summer movie screenings under the stars at the cemetery, and even more attend the annual Día de los Muertos festival (AKA LA Day of the Dead), held inside the cemetery since 1999.

Opened in 1899, the cemetery is one of the oldest memorial parks in the country and listed in the National Register of Historic Sites. Located on Santa Monica Boulevard, the cemetery was built on the rear lot of Paramount Studios just behind the cemetery on Melrose Avenue. It is LA's answer to, say, Paris's Père Lachaise cemetery: tourists from all over the world come to Hollywood Forever Cemetery to visit the graves of Douglas Fairbanks, Jayne Mansfield, Rudolph Valentino, and Toto the dog from *Wizard of Oz*.

Morrissey was photographed at least twice here: once, lying on his side in front of the large tomb of SMITH in 2004, and again in 2009 at

Figure 7. The other Cemetry Gates: Hollywood Forever Cemetery.

Figure 8. One day goodbye will be farewell: Johnny Ramone's gravesite, Hollywood Forever Cemetery, Día de los Muertos, 2015.

Photos by the author.

Johnny Ramone's gravesite. (Fig. 8) 'I sat there for a very long time, and I felt quite good about it. I felt it was a nice position, and it was nice that his bones were under the soil that I was sitting on,' said Morrissey.[36]

One day goodbye will be farewell, and on that day, we will find Steven Patrick Morrissey's gravesite next to Johnny Ramone's in Hollywood Forever Cemetery across the reflecting pool and the big lawn where Lila Downs sang about mezcal and Mariachi Manchester played Smiths and Morrissey songs one year at the Día de los Muertos main stage.

Additional sites: Why don't you find out for yourself?

It is impossible to know or list all the places in and around LA that Morrissey ate, shopped, drank, sunbathed, shot pool, scratched on postcards, and the like. We do know there are potentially dozens of Moz-related places that could be part of this tour, and dozens more if we consider other cities and locales across California where Morrissey has either performed in concert, name-dropped in a song, or written about in his *Autobiography*. For those fans who find themselves enjoying an extended stay in Moz Angeles and have the means to travel around the region, here is a list of off-tour sites that may be of interest. For example, Pasadena can have its own extended entry. Alain Whyte is said to live there; Boz and Lynn Boorer have stayed at a friend's home there; Morrissey has passed time there. My lists are no means exhaustive, and I welcome additions. Our list will keep growing the longer Morrissey and some of his band mates call the Los Angeles area home.

Greater Los Angeles area concert venues where Morrissey has performed, in no particular order:

* The Forum (Inglewood, South Los Angeles)
* Santa Monica Civic Auditorium
* Pasadena Civic Auditorium
* The Hollywood Palladium
* Pauley Pavilion, UCLA Campus
* Galen Center, USC Campus
* Henry Fonda Music Box (now The Fonda Theatre)
* Shrine Auditorium
* Los Angeles Sports Arena
* Staples Center
* Hollywood Bowl
* The Greek Theater
* The Shrine Auditorium

* Fox Pomona Theater
* Hollywood High School Auditorium
* Coachella Valley Music and Arts Festival
* Gibson Amphitheatre (formerly Univeresal Amphitheatre)—demolished in 2013 to make way for the Harry Potter attraction at Universal Studios Hollywood.
* FYF Festival at Los Angeles Sports Arena and Coliseum grounds
* Santa Ana Observatory, Santa Ana (Orange County)
* Pacific Amphitheatre, Costa Mesa (OC)
* Arrowhead Pond, Anaheim (OC)
* Irvine Meadows, Irvine (OC)
* Bren Events Center, Irvine

Other Morrissey-related sites:

* Conway Studios (*Quarry* and *Years of Refusal* recording sessions, 2004–09)
* The York, Highland Park (co-owned by Jesse Tobias)
* Johnny's Bar (Highland Park)
* Lucky Baldwin's Pub (Pasadena)—often visited by Boz Boorer and Lyn Boorer when they stay in Pasadena. Boz and Lyn are local favorites. They host their Vinyl Boutique pop-ups at local records stores like Kaos in Covina, as they did in the winter of 2015. Boz has also played guest DJ at Club Underground at the Grand Star Jazz Club in Chinatown. Many fans have met and posed for photos with Boz and Lyn, who are always very friendly, generous and approachable to fans. We love Boz and Lyn!
* Espacio 1839 (Boyle Heights). Clothing, music, and bookstore where certain Morrissey band members have been spotted purchasing Boyle Heights and East LA themed T-shirts for their singer.
* Saks Fifth Avenue (Beverly Hills). Morrissey was photographed by a fan shopping at the men's fragrance counter around the time of this 2015 New Year's Eve concert in Los Angeles.
* AGO Restaurant (West Hollywood)

CHAPTER TWO

Boyle Heights, You Are Too Hot
Singing Your Life at MorrisseyOke™

Sing your life
Walk right up to the microphone and name
All the things you love
All the things that you loathe
Oh, sing your life
       Morrissey, Sing Your Life (1991)

OUR TOUR OF MOZ ANGELES SHOULD REALLY BEGIN here in Boyle Heights, at a building on the corner across from the historic Mariachi Plaza. Painted on the side of the building facing the Metro Gold Line stop and 1st Street Bridge is a shadowy face of a graying guitar-playing mariachi, the mural a tribute to the neighborhood's Mexican musical heritage. (Fig. 1) Across the top of the building, letters in mirrored script on a rusty iron plate spell out *Eastside Luv*, a neighborhood bar holding it down *gentefication* style. The chainlink gates are locked, the sidewalk outside still quiet in the early hours of evening. A lone taco truck parked across from the bar awaits hungry pre-partiers and post-work Metro commuters. It is Thursday, the first one of the month. The sun sets over the historic LA River bridges, the downtown skyline, and the ocean beyond.

A few hours from now, someone nice and beerbuzzed will be up on stage singing Unloveable or Suedehead or Sheila Take A Bow, sometimes in Spanish, maybe even in Japanese, usually in their best Morrissey English manner. Most of the capacity crowd will be cheering, clapping, and singing along, and others will be chatting, paying no mind, or pushing their way towards the bar that also serves as a catwalk for the weekend burlesque dancers.

A few early arrivals chill in the rear patio and enjoy a smoke or a clandestine toke. Others mingle near the front of the stage, eagerly anticipating the arrival of our exuberant host, Alexis de la Rocha, and her clipboard of sign-up sheets. They all want to be the first one on the list: the night's leadoff singer gets a drink on the house. Later, a line of regulars, newcomers, and a few stray hipsters forms around the corner under the watch of the graying mariachi. They will text friends and tag themselves on social media while trying to smooth-talk The Barrio Dandy (a.k.a. John Carlos de Luna) or any one of the staff of burly brown bouncers who guard the entrance with a shiny click-counter in one hand and the other hand stretched out like a traffic cop saying stop.

The door to Eastside Luv swings open and the sounds, sights, and scents of a typical first-Thursday night spill out onto the sidewalk and echo throughout Mariachi Plaza. The Smiths' classic This Charming Man bounces out of the DJ's speakers and a shy singer on stage croons along on the mic while most of the crowd sings along, some louder than others. On a screen at the rear of the bar, the classic Los Angeles Chicano music film, *La Bamba*, plays on a loop, and Alexis calls for the next singer who climbs up on stage, clumsy and shy. On cue, the new singer sways with her eyes closed behind thick glasses and curved shoulders and starts to sing. She whips the mic cord like Moz. *I'm so sorry,* she sings, letting loose, and suddenly it sounds like someone turned up the volume on the happy crowd.

Whiffs of floral pomades and perfumes rise from goodlooking Latinas and Latinos who pack the small corner bar for the monthly merriment. On most nights, the crowd is diverse enough, reminiscent of the generations-deep histories of working class immigrant Mexican,

Japanese, and Jewish peoples who made this neighborhood, named after an Irishman immigrant settler called Andrew A Boyle. But, like the rest of LA, the MorrisseyOke crowd is still majority Chicana/o and Latina/o. They have driven from near and far all over the greater Moz Angeles area—El Sereno, Whittier, Lynwood, Huntington Park, Downey, Santa Ana, Pacoima, Pomona, even Bakersfield and Barstow, the halfway point to Vegas—to experience the event that is unlike any other Morrissey fan party around. Morrissey fans visiting Los Angeles from as far away as Brooklyn, New York and Birmingham, England, have made the required pit stop in Boyle Heights to check it all out. Welcome to the one and only MorrisseyOke, a quintessential Moz Angeles Morrissey fan party and monthly ritual of singing along to the songs that save our lives.

In what can often feel like a saturated LA Morrissey/Smiths club and bar scene full of tribute band shows, disco nights, and DJ sets, fans can afford to be discerning about where to go to get their fix. A Moz-themed event must stand out in some way (and appear on the right social media feeds) to keep drawing crowds and appealing to fans. In addition to the weekly, monthly, annual, and holiday-time rotation of regularly scheduled events, there are also the occasional Morrissey Smiths related events such as poetry readings, art shows, photography exhibitions, book release parties, even academic panels. While each of these events offers a distinct fan experience, nothing quite stands out like MorrisseyOke for the camaraderie, community, and range of fan experiences it provides.

Since its founding on Morrissey's birthday in May 2011, MorrisseyOke (or MozOke) has developed into a scene in and of itself, a unique Morrissey fan scene and sub-subculture with its own rules, etiquettes, and practices. The hybrid singalong/DJ dance party/hosted night of live entertainment that celebrates Morrissey's music continues to lure capacity crowds every month as it has for over five years. As the only regularly scheduled dedicated karaoke-type event in the area, one that makes singing to Morrissey and Smiths songs all night the whole point of the show, MorrisseyOke showcases the strongly participatory foundation of the local Morrissey Smiths fan culture. The regulars, newbies, and steady flow of monthly attendees, the local celebrity host, its storied

Figure 1. Exterior shot of Eastside Luv Bar y QueSo, located at the corner of 1st and Bailey Streets in historic Boyle Heights, East Los Angeles. Photo by the author.

Eastside Luv home, and the surrounding Moz Angeles culture that sustains it, all contribute to the success of MozOke as a living, shifting, and layered image of a particular brand of Morrissey fandom expressed in Los Angeles. Sure, not everyone who goes to MorrisseyOke is necessarily a Morrissey fan, but even so, one can't help but be mesmerized at the ones who are and who do get up there to sing their lives.

Walk Right Up to the Microphone
Singing Our Lives at MorrisseyOke

TONIGHT
"Be Your Best Morrissey" contest at Midnight & win a pair of tickets to Morrissey/Iggy Concert... Winner determined by Audience (loudest Cheers or Boos... simply loudest response). So, BRING YOUR OWN

FANS to cheer for YOU. Arrive early. FREEjoles EventO. Hostess Alexis de l.a. Rocha & DJ BeeSyde

MorrisseyOke Facebook post, August 2012

The night was an instant hit, and it's easy to see why. Young or old, female or male, gay or straight, white or Latino, everyone who grabs the mic instantly channels, whether through outright mimicry or in subtler ways, Morrissey's enigmatic persona: defiant, wounded, bitchy, droll and earnest all at once.

Andy Hermann, *LA Weekly*, September 2014

'There are two rules of MorrisseyOke.'

It is just before ten p.m., and Alexis de la Rocha steps up to greet the crowd and welcome everyone. Before calling up the first singer of the night, she reminds everyone of the ground rules at MorrisseyOke. 'Rule Number One, no booing. If you boo, you'll get booted out onto Mariachi Plaza. And Rule Number Two, have fun! There are backup mics for your friends to come on stage and sing along with you and every beautiful person in the audience will be singing along, too. Now before we begin, you know I have to ask, how many virgins do we have with us tonight? Don't be shy, the veteranos and veteranas will show you how it's done! So let's have some fun, tip your bartenders well, and say hello to our DJ Jess Funk!' DJ Jess cues the Super Morrissey Bros.' version of This Charming Man[37] in all its 1983 video game 8-bit glory and thus begins another edition of the popular Morrissey singalong night.

On a typical MozOke night, the first hour is usually a warm-up. The bar is still filling up; some people are drinking for a buzz while others figure out which song to sign up for. In the next three to four hours, Alexis calls up singers one by one. One of the regulars usually kicks off the evening with his Spanish rendition of This Charming Man, sometimes Suedehead. On rare occasions, a brave 'Virgin,' or MorrisseyOke first-timer, will kick off the night. Those that follow often go more than once, putting their names in multiple slots. Others get shy and cross their name off the list, and still others will only get on stage with a friend or group to lead a singalong to favorites like Girlfriend In A Coma and Irish Blood, English Heart. Some veterans have been known to bring their own guitars and play acoustic versions of songs while someone else provides vocal accompaniment. Once in a while, a burlesque group such as Mozsexxy will perform their sultry dances in between karaoke sets.[38]

Well into the night, Eastside Luv is packed. The bar's small and narrow shape invites patrons to get up close and personal to the singers and each other. By midnight, most people are a few drinks in, socially lubricated, and ready for action. Alexis calls up the next singer. Roger, a regular, jumps up the small metal staircase and begins dancing like Elvis to the opening chords of Sing Your Life. A big light-eyed dude with a perfect pompadour, pressed vintage bowling shirt, and impeccably cuffed Levi's 501s over two-toned wingtips, Roger saunters up and down the catwalk, moving like Morrissey in the video as he sings in the mic. I join an excited group of people making their way up to the stage to be backup dancers for Roger, who unexpectedly grabs my hand and starts showing me how to swing step. I'm buzzed and giddy, so I go along with it.

There we were, a boy-and-butch dancing pair, hand in hand, arms swinging in a big arc along the beat to Sing Your Life because you can't help but sing *and* dance to this song. The video of a skinny Morrissey in a baggy white suit on stage, flanked by handsome North London rockabilly musicians as he swings along to the music, plays in our collective imagination. From the stage, we see brown bodies moving rhythmically in the small, steamy confines of Eastside Luv. When the song is over, I thank the cute rockabilly Chicano for the song and dance. Cheers, whistles, and dancing breaks out in the crowd and eventually, the next singer is up.

Scenes like this one with Roger and the dancers highlight the joyfully communal activity that makes MorrisseyOke unique among fan events and offerings around town. It is also a prime example of the ways in which fans respond to particular songs, which songs get the crowd going, and which ones send people to the bar or out to the patio for a smoke. Sure, there are the requisite anthems like How Soon Is Now or There Is A Light That Never Goes Out that usually succeed in generating crowd-pleasing moments of togetherness. Other singers make it their mission for the night to sing the lesser-known tunes. One veteran, Geoffrey, likes to pick unsuspecting Morrissey solo tracks, deep cuts along the line of The Harsh Truth Of The Camera Eye or Oboe Concerto; such song choices puzzle the crowd, save for the one or two serious Moz fans who know the song and which album it comes from. But songs like First Of The Gang To Die and Sing Your Life have a certain kind of resonance with the MorrisseyOke faithfuls. First Of The Gang is a hometown favorite, and, like at a soccer (football!) match, many people will join the singer in belting out the last line: 'he stole all hearts awaaayy!'

Along with the others mentioned, Sing Your Life ranks high on the list of fan-favorites, as Roger's moment demonstrated. The rockabilly styled anthem has a special place in the Morrissey solo oeuvre as 'the first Morrissey record to distantly gyrate in the general direction of fifties rockabilly.'[39] The song's invitation to come on stage and sing echoes Morrissey's own teenaged sentiments: '[I] reached a point where I could no longer be a member of the audience. I had to be on stage and I think a lot of people do feel that.'[40] The song even made *OC Weekly* editor Gustavo Arellano's 'Top Most Mexican Morrissey/Smiths Songs of All Time' list, clocking in at number eight behind Glamorous Glue and Mexico. In Sing Your Life, according to Arellano, 'Morrissey expresses the fierce individualism that has characterized his career, the fierce individualism also praised in Mexican song and in the Mexican character—a fierce individualism that society always tries to smother or rob.'[41] No surprise that the song's title decorates license plate frames and car windows of youthful twenty- and thirty-something Chicana/o and Latino/a fans on the streets and freeways of Moz Angeles. My sister, Melinda, has a bumper sticker on her minivan: *Sing Your Life*. It is a slogan, a theme borrowed by club promoters and event organizers for nights such as the annual Sing Your Life Art and Music Morrissey night at Mal's Bar in Downtown LA, or the Sing Your Life Sundaze dance party at Footsie's Bar in Highland Park, hosted by DJ Rosie Bojangles. It has become a motto, a mantra, Morrissey's mandate to us, and the foundation of MorrisseyOke: walk right up the microphone and have the pleasure of meaning what you sing.

Now is Your Chance to Shine
Fulfilling *Fantasies* at MorrisseyOke

I am off-key, but I do my best.

Morrissey, *Autobiography* (2013)

To sing on stage in front of an audience is to bear one's soul, to make oneself vulnerable. It is to tell a story, to express emotion, to invite participation in the co-creation of a moment in time that will not and cannot be experienced in exactly the same way ever again. To sing on stage in front of people is also to entertain, show off, be a ham, tease and titillate those there watching and listening. It is to shine, if even just for the length of the time of a pop song. For those with the desire to sing on stage and express oneself through song, karaoke remains an ideal way to do it. It is accessible, egalitarian, and ubiquitous. You don't need formal training in the arts to get up there and sing: all you need is a favorite song and a shot of courage. There's karaoke at bowling alleys in the rural Midwest, in suburban dive bars, at fancy cocktail lounges in Asian enclaves of large urban metropolises. Wherever you find it, karaoke generally means group fun and memorable merry-making for both singers and audience members. The added dimensions of desire, fantasy, and fandom make MorrisseyOke a special kind of karaoke-inspired experience.

MozOke has roots in the popular global phenomenon of karaoke, a Japanese word that means 'empty orchestra.' Karaoke as many of us know and experience it has come a long way from the first 'singalong machines' that originated in Japan and the Philippines.[42] Los Angeles has a particularly rich history of karaoke as a multifaceted space of cultural practices along national, ethnic, and class lines. USC English and gender studies professor Karen Tongson, whose forthcoming book *Empty Orchestra* theorizes karaoke as a cultural practice in the US, articulates the 'abject' associations of karaoke that make it a global phenomenon even while it carries associations of 'slightly risqué,' uninhibited displays of emotion. She writes,

Karaoke is a mass cultural activity, but one that still carries with it the frisson of doing something slightly risqué (hence its frequent overlap with inebriation)... And yet karaoke as a mass practice can't quite broach the mainstream, because of its various 'abject' associations with immigrant communities, aspirational everymen longing to be idols, isolate geeks who only interact with the outside world through their computers, drunkards, gaggles of girls group-singing to Madonna, queens bereft of the piano bar's liveness, slumming with an electronic delivery system for their show tunes, and other such 'sad' spectacles.[43]

Much like how tribute bands are often derided as unoriginal copies and the refuge of failed rock stars, Tongson shows us how karaoke is often viewed by mainstream culture as being 'derivative,' 'debased,' and in reality show contexts, used as 'shorthand' for negative judgment and 'condemnation.' And yet it is precisely the cultural form of karaoke that invites and makes room for—and is fiercely appropriated by—seemingly 'abject' groups such as immigrants, 'drunkards,' 'geeks' and 'queens' to inhabit spaces that would otherwise be inaccessible to such groups in the mainstream. It comes as no surprise then that Smiths and Morrissey fans, often seen by others (if not self-described) as outsiders, misfits, nerds, queers, 'abject' in their own ways, would take to a style of karaoke as the ultimate form of celebratory self-expression.

In this way, we can also understand karaoke as a democratic form of empowerment for these groups. Following Roland Barthes, scholar Stephen Royce Giddens reads karaoke as a performance of human nature: 'the karaoke performance—song selection, performance technique, and singer-crowd interaction—is another form of human expression. In this view, karaoke is not any different from any other singing or artistic performance. Popular songs tell our stories, and, by selection, we have a hand in the writing: *the presentation of the self as karaoke life.*'[44] Participants in MorrisseyOke engage in this kind of 'presentation of the self' as fans through their song choices, in their performance styles, and in their reactions and interactions with the audience.

The opportunities to 'present the self' in these ways have everything to do with design and content of MorrisseyOke. MozOke's format can be best described as 'mock-karaoke,' which accounts for a large part of the event's appeal. Unlike traditional karaoke, there are no lyrics on a screen at MorrisseyOke, no cheesy instrumental backing tracks. Accordingly, singers have to know the lyrics by heart, or they cope by bringing their phones on stage and reading the lyrics that way, though such a practice usually makes for distracted and half-hearted singing. The best performances are from the singers who know the song in their bones: they strut on the stage, sing with hands over hearts, arms outstretched, eyes closed, on one leg, and tongue out, being like Morrissey if even for a moment. They sing by heart, lyrics memorized as in the mariachi performance tradition.

Thankfully, unlike many karaoke settings, where would-be singers' song choices could be limited by what's only provided by the host in beer-stained binders, MozOke's DJ Jess Funk has the world wide web at his fingertips. Singers can choose any song in the Smiths or Morrissey catalogue that can be accessed in any number of online sources, from YouTube to iTunes. With practically unlimited song choices, MorrisseyOke singers can truly customize their 'presentation of the self' through the karaoke performance. Therein lies the primary distinction and allure of MorrisseyOke—singers get to sing to the actual Smiths or Morrissey songs. Who wants to listen to some phony instrumental version of Smiths or Morrissey when you can sing and dance to the real thing? (Fig. 2) When a singer is called, DJ Jess Funk cues the song and lowers Morrissey's vocals, thereby clearing space for the participant to sing over (or with) Morrissey to the original recorded track. In this way, the singer effectively 'becomes' Morrissey—one better than filling in the vocals over the 'empty orchestra' karaoke version of the song.

For many participants, MorrisseyOke offers an inviting and sanctioned space for acting out fantasies of 'being' (like) Morrissey. As a regular participant, observer, and occasional host of MorrisseyOke, I can say that this fantasy gets played out often at MozOke, especially by the lead singers of area tribute bands who show up to take the stage and 'show off' their best Moz. In the throes of fandom, these singers attempt performed embodiments of Morrissey by mimicking his signature stage moves and vocal inflections. There is a kind of freedom in the uninhibited exhibition of sentiment, feeling, and love that comes with singing a favorite song on stage, in front of others who can sing along with you at an event created expressly for such a purpose.

For others, 'being' Morrissey, donning 'Moz' through clothing, hairstyle, affect, or attitude is a way to solicit admiration, attention, approval, and love. There is also a level of play-acting between the singer and audience. I have seen members of the MorrisseyOke audience reach out for a handshake or even climb up the stairs and hug the singer as fans do at actual Morrissey concerts. For those whose goals do not necessarily include wanting to 'be' or 'become' Morrissey, MozOke serves as a vehicle for expressing other kinds of fantasies and desires: of transgression and/ or belonging, of fitting in while standing out. Here is one example that serves as a fitting case in point.

It was one of those nights at MorrisseyOke: loud, crowded, too many repeat singers, all of them dudes. Then seemingly out of nowhere, a young-looking Asian singer took the stage solo. She stood out among the largely Latino T-shirt, jeans, slick hair-wearing crowd with her beanie cap, tunic-style dress, and white velcro sneakers. She went over to the DJ, then to Alexis before she took the mic, her song cued. The familiar guitar intro to This Charming Man filled the bar to whoops and applause. She opened her mouth and began to sing, but suddenly the crowd quieted down, puzzled. She was singing in Japanese. She displayed confidence in her moves and singing voice, and the crowd perked back up, dancing and cheering her on during the song's familiar refrain. This singer would take the stage again later that night, this time singing a duet in English with her friend, 'Alma' (Fig. 3), to enthusiastic cheers and applause. After she sang, I went to meet her. She introduced herself (I'll call 'Hazel'), and I asked her if she had ever done that song before. Hazel shared the following:

> I've been here a few times with my friends. It's cool to hear some people
> sing in Spanish or bring a guitar on stage and play along. I was inspired
> by the guy who sang This Charming Man in Spanish. I thought, I could

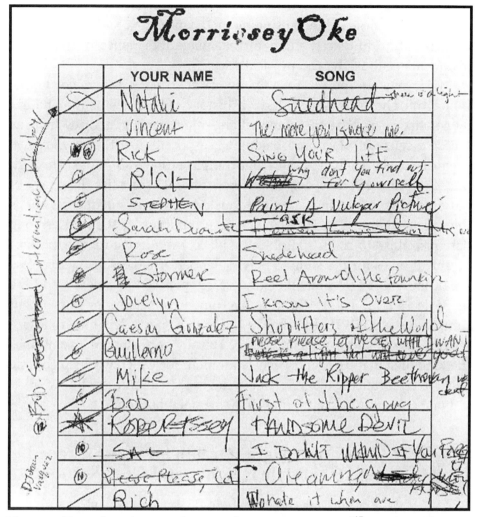

Figure 2: 'To perform is to speak your voice, to cast your vote.'[45] MorrisseyOke sign-up sheet. Provided to the author by Alexis de la Rocha. Used with permission.

do that in Japanese. I worked on it and tonight was the first time I got to sing it in Japanese.

Of all the MorrisseyOke nights I've attended and hosted, this remains one of the most memorable moments. I'm pretty sure it was a

MorrisseyOke first, someone singing in Japanese to a Smiths song, and yet a beautiful full circle moment that made total sense in this space historically, culturally, and musically.

Music has the power to help us claim a place and make home. When you and your people have a history of displacement—whether by colonizers or settlers or gentrifiers—music and memories help us access a sense of place and belonging, especially for those who have been displaced or pushed out from the place they call home. Through music, we can reclaim space and make it ours. Therein lies the power of not only Morrissey's music, but of fans' creativity in making his songs their own—literally, as Hazel's Japanese rendition of the Smiths song demonstrates—to claim space, find a place, even if just for the amount of time it takes for the song to play. Such performances also compel us area Chicanos/as to remember that yes, Japanese folks also lived here in Boyle Heights before the US government sent them to internment campus during WWII, and they're as much as part of its history as are Mexicans. But more than anything, Hazel's performance exemplifies the kind of signature MorrisseyOke moment for which we keep coming back: to celebrate the diversity of our fan expressions and, while we're at it, build community in a rapidly changing neighborhood.

Why Do You Come Here? Or, I'm So Very Sickened MorrisseyOke, Boyle Heights, and *Gentefication*

> Why do you come here? And why do you hang around?
>
> Morrissey, Suedehead

Hazel's performance, Roger's impromptu dance party to Sing Your Life, and so many others of these MorrisseyOke cross-cultural, intercultural expressions of Moz Smiths fandom, represent the kinds of cultural moments that emerge from, and are made possible by, a confluence of social and historical forces. MorrisseyOke, a great Moz Angeles fan party, is very much a product of its time, place, and people. It is a product of nearly two decades' worth of lavish media coverage—an archive, really—

Figure 3. MozOke singers
'Hazel' and 'Alma.'
Photo by the author.

on the so-called Latino (or Mexican) Morrissey fascination. Finally, MozOke, in some ways, is also a by-product of gentrification.

Since its founding in May 2011, many mainstream, public, and independent radio, film, television, and Internet news crews have been dispatched to Eastside Luv to document, film, and report on MorrisseyOke, its creators, and its patrons. Los Angeles based reporter Leslie Berenstein Rojas was the first to report on MorrisseyOke in December 2011 for the local public radio station, 89.3 KPCC. A Latina Morrissey fan who grew up in the nearby working class neighborhood of Huntington Park, Berenstein Rojas covered the event in a segment that aired on the daily news show hosted by award winning broadcast journalist, Madeleine Brand.[46] Two years after *The Madeleine Brand Show* covered MorrisseyOke, the trendy 'alternative' rag *LA Weekly* ran a story on the event.[47] Since then, there have been nearly a dozen feature articles, Internet 'news' items, local television shows, and mini-documentaries on MorrisseyOke. It is typically covered as a consummate Los Angeles Morrissey fan event—and one more for the 'Latinos and Morrissey' file.

The media attention given to MozOke has certainly contributed to recent hype around this special homegrown fan product. Such hype can have both positive and unwelcome effects that say more about the trend of gentrification than it does about fandom. For as much as the 'Latinos and Morrissey' theme is a part of the media coverage of MorrisseyOke, so is gentrification a part of the background story of the event, its venue Eastside Luv, and Boyle Heights more generally.

Boyle Heights, like Silver Lake, Highland Park, and Echo Park before it, represents the next frontier of new development by outsiders. This immigrant, blue-collar historic Eastside neighborhood is the latest target of outside investors and developers who want to build new housing units, art galleries, a shopping center, and a Starbucks—the ultimate symptom of the social malady that is gentrification. Like the constructions of the East LA freeway interchanges in the 1960s and 1970s before it, the construction of the Metro Gold Line through East LA and Boyle Heights, as well as the Metro station at Mariachi Plaza in the 1990s, displaced longtime low-income residents, pushed out day-laboring mariachis, and changed the landscape of the historic neighborhood.

Founded in the 1870s, Boyle Heights was named in honor of an Irish émigré, Andrew A. Boyle of County Mayo, who owned the land previously inhabited by Indians, then Spaniards, then Mexicans, before it was settled by white European migrants. Irish blood, Mexican land. Too perfect. At the turn of the twentieth century, the ethnic and racial makeup of the town was considerably diverse until the 1930s and 1940s, when the communities of Japanese, Jewish, Russian, Italian, and other immigrants who called Boyle Heights home started to move out of the neighborhood, and out of East LA more generally, though not for the same reasons. This exodus of Asian and European working class immigrant groups created what historian George J. Sánchez describes as a more 'high-density Mexican residence' in Boyle Heights and its environs. In his important study, *Becoming Mexican American: Ethnicity, Culture and Identity in Chicano Los Angeles, 1900–1945*, Sánchez writes, 'Since integration of the Mexican immigrant population with American-born Chicanos contributed to the creation of a distinct barrio culture, both Belvedere and Boyle Heights became important settings for the definition of Chicano life in California during the twentieth century' and 'a locus of Chicano cultural development.'[48] To this day, Boyle Heights remains a predominantly Mexican American and immigrant neighborhood and cultural center that attracts locals and visitors to its street fairs, markets, restaurants, and art spaces.

The bar that is now home to Eastside Luv used to be called The Metropolitan Bar, an old neighborhood watering hole since the 1940s. In its heyday, The Metropolitan reflected the diversity of this working class enclave east of the LA River: 'Celebrations from all walks of life... Jewish, Japanese, Italians, Russians, Mexicans, and others have occurred in this little joint,' says Eastside Luv's website about its watering hole predecessor. In the early 2000s, Boyle Heights native Guillermo (Willie) Uribe bought the bar with his wife, Arlene. At that time, it was just an old rundown cantina that had seen better days. With his background in construction engineering, Uribe renovated the bar and reopened it in 2006 under its new name, Eastside Luv. Promoted as a wine bar, Eastside Luv quickly became a 'cultural mecca' that attracted 'young Latino professionals, artists, musicians, politicians, teachers, curators and even a fellow engineer or two,' says the *LA Times*.[49]

Since it opened a decade ago, the bar has hosted film shoots, community fundraisers, Bernie Sanders rallies, and annual Día de los Muertos celebrations. It is also regarded as a premiere Eastside live music and performance venue; bands such as Grammy-winning local heroes, Quetzal, groups like the Mozsexxy burlesque troupe, and up-and-coming Mexican-fusion rock trio, ¡Aparato!, have all graced the stage at Eastside Luv. Accordingly, Uribe's bar has become a formidable presence in the local community. It is also a symbol of the changes— for better or for worse, depending on who you ask—brought on by the expansion of the Metro Gold Line rail station at Mariachi Plaza and the rising profile of the neighborhoods just east of Downtown LA.

The neighborhood remains contested territory for the grassroots community groups, immigrant rights groups, developers, city planners, 'urban revivalists,' and would-be gentrifiers who are all currently engaged in the battle for Boyle Heights. Some local efforts aimed at preventing, or at least stalling, the transformation of a cultural gem like Mariachi Plaza into another chain-store mall have been successful.[50] However, some critique has also been aimed at Eastside Luv, and a few of its neighboring businesses, as evidence of what has been termed 'gentefication.'

From the *New York Times* to the America Ferrera-produced web series, *Gente-fied*, Boyle Heights is most recently portrayed as the Los Angeles neighborhood experiencing a wave of 'gentefication.' Uribe is generally credited as the one who coined, or at least made common, the term that derives from the Spanish word 'gente,' or people. Berenstein Rojas defines 'gentefication' as 'the process of upwardly mobile Latinos, typically second-generation and beyond, investing in and returning to the old neighborhood.'[51] The example of Eastside Luv as an effect of 'gentefication' and of MorrisseyOke in particular as a trademarked, signature product of the bar point to the contradictions at play in the creation of this particular space by and for economically better off second and third generation Chicanos at the expense, some would say, of the less well-off immigrant communities who live in Boyle Heights. It also takes us back to questions of place and space: for whom, by whom, accessible to whom, belonging to whom.

Uribe maintains a critical eye towards gentrification as unfettered outside, non-local investment for white palatability and profit, and instead, promotes a philosophy of *gentefication*. As he tells *Los Angeles Magazine*, 'If gentrification is happening, it might as well be from people who care about the existing culture. In the case of Boyle Heights, it would be best if the gente decide to invest in improvements because they are more likely to preserve its integrity.' In Uribe's case, his choice to open a wine bar was partially motivated by the lack of 'legitimate night life' in the area for residents who generally went elsewhere—Downtown, Pasadena, Alhambra, Whittier—for a night out. Other children and gente of Boyle Heights followed suit, returning to the neighborhood to make investments and open small businesses. Eastside Luv's neighbors on 1st Street, a main thoroughfare, include a 'Chipster' (Chicano hipster) taco stand that serves tacos with traditional and non-traditional ingredients, like kale; a theater house and performance space; an art gallery; a book store that also houses an Internet radio station and a clothing boutique that specializes in Boyle Heights swag; and a coffee shop, all owned by a new generation of Chicanas/os and Latinas/os who have roots in the historic neighborhood. *A rush and a push and the land that we stand on is ours.*

MorrisseyOke is easily the most popular night at Eastside Luv. Its formula for success must be understood within these historical contexts of Boyle Heights and in light of its more immediate designation as a site of gentefication. It also helps to know a little bit about its founder. MorrisseyOke is the brainchild of Alexis de la Rocha, who also works some nights as a bartender at Eastside Luv. A second-generation Latina born in Los Angeles to a Cubana mother and Chicano father, de la Rocha grew up in the east of east LA suburbs of Whittier and La Habra, California.[52] Full disclosure: Alexis and I go way back. I have known her since she was in high school and best friends with my youngest sister, Monica. I know that her Morrissey cred extends back to her early fandom in the 1990s, when she and Monica would drive around listening to *Kill Uncle*, especially King Leer, a song Alexis will occasionally sing at MorrisseyOke. Years later, Alexis would find herself working as a television host at *LATV*, a Latino news and entertainment network, when it aired an exclusive Beto Cuevas-led interview with Morrissey in 2007.[53] De la Rocha is also a working musician, actor, and puppet-maker. She is best known as a dynamic and captivating front woman, first as the lead singer of the experimental Los Angeles area Latino-alternative rock outfit, Beatmo (2004–2009), and now as the ethereal lead vocalist and leader of LEX, a dreamy all-woman David Bowie-in-*Labyrinth* electro/synth/dance/jazz/pop group produced by Peter Franco of Daft Punk fame.[54]

De la Rocha was working at Eastside Luv one night when the idea hit her. She tells *LA Weekly* that she was inspired by the Eastside

Luv's mariachi singalong night, a signature event at the Boyle Heights bar where singers belt out rancheros, boleros, corridos, and mariachi classics backed by a live mariachi band. A Morrissey and Smiths fan since her high school days in the late 1990s, she was also keenly aware of the thriving Moz fan scene in LA, especially in historically Mexican and Chicana/o areas of East LA. May was coming up, Morrissey's birthday month, and she thought the bar would be a great venue for a Morrissey-themed event. MorrisseyOke as an idea was an easy sell to Willie, the bar's owner and a son of Mexican immigrants who grew up down the street listening to mariachis and Morrissey.[55]

On Morrissey's birthday in 2011, MorrisseyOke debuted to a capacity crowd. The event became so popular—the local celebrity host, the bar as a local hot spot, and the built-in Moz Angeles fan base all contributed to its immediate success—that it found itself on the bar's packed calendar for the first Thursday of every month. MorrisseyOke as a concept has since spawned other 'Oke' nights devoted to the likes of Selena, Juan Gabriel, Depeche Mode, and postpunk bands like Siouxsie and the Banshees and New Order, all iconic musicians and bands that are also culturally significant to Eastside Luv's mostly second and third generation Chicana/o-Latina/o clientele. For Morrissey Smiths fans, MorrisseyOke provides a welcome addition to the roster of dance parties, tribute band shows, and DJ nights that give Moz Angeles its name. For de la Rocha and Uribe, MorrisseyOke represented something else, a signature event that would not be copied. Before long, Uribe, always an enterprising and business-minded individual, trademarked the name of his bar's exclusive event. By definition, the trademark endows MorrisseyOke™ with a special status in the Morrissey fan marketplace as a 'mark (secured by legal registration or, in some countries, established by use) used by a manufacturer or trader to distinguish his goods from similar wares of other firms.'[56]

As a trademarked brand, MorrisseyOke™ becomes recognized as a distinctive and marketable product. In the large LA/SoCal Morrissey fan market, this distinction is key to profit and survival. Branding is a way to claim valuable space in the marketplace. I use 'brand' not without chafing a little, well aware of the risks of commodifying, essentializing, and homogenizing this community, the fans, and their events. I also have to pause when considering the 'down side' of gentefication's impact. As Boyle Heights native and guitarrón-playing member of Mariachi Manchester, Gloria Estrada, tells me, 'Even places like La Monarca (an LA-based Mexican-style bakery and coffee mini-chain), while owned by Mexicanos, they still participate in the displacement of people who have called this place home long before it got trendy. I remember when all of 1st Street and Mariachi Plaza was packed with all these men in full charro dress carrying instruments and looking for gigs, playing in the restaurants here. Now, you don't see that many. Who knows where they all ended up.'[57]

Such complicated relationships to neighborhood and place are brought into sharp relief by the contradictory nature of 'gentefication.' While local activists and residents understandably have grounds to criticize or withhold their business from places such as Eastside Luv or any of the 'gentefied' Boyle Heights businesses owned and run by the new generation, I cannot be so quick to condemn. I like that Latinos/as and Chicanos/as who were born and raised in the area come back to invest in it, rather than having some gringo from Brooklyn throw down money to build the next hot thing. When I feel conflicted about 'gentefication'—glad that La Monarca is there, but also mindful of who had to be kicked out so it could be built—I have to remember that we are all walking, living contradictions, and I have to hold both things as a child of the borderlands. I go back to what I learned about Dodger Stadium. I know that deep, violent injustices were perpetuated by Brooklyn Dodgers team owner Walter O'Malley and his LA cronies in the late 1950s. I know they lied to Mexicans and forcibly evicted them from Chavez Ravine only so they can build a new baseball stadium on that land, bring the Dodgers to LA from Brooklyn. Hell, even the acclaimed Los Angeles based Latino comedy and performance troupe, Culture Clash, wrote and performed a play, *Chavez Ravine*, about this fiasco. But I grew up a Dodger fan, and 'Los Doyers' are in my blood. I'm also not a Boyle Heights native. I was born in Montebello, a few miles west, but like many second and third generation Chicanas and Chicanos, I have family roots on the Eastside—City Terrace, East LA, and by extension, Boyle Heights. And I'm a Morrissey fan. At the end of the day, I love MorrisseyOke because of what it has given us fans: a home, a place to gather, a space to celebrate the singer we love. That doesn't mean I can't be critical of some of the social and economic forces that spawned it and the other 'gentefied' businesses in town.

A Place in Boyle Heights for Me and My Friends Welcome Home

'place, n.1: The amount or quantity of space actually occupied by a person or thing; the position of a body in space, or in relation to other bodies; situation, location.'

Oxford English Dictionary

A good number of Morrissey and Smiths songs share the common theme of finding, and taking, one's place in this world. Where something is, who gets access to it, what politics and histories are behind it, who 'we' are, what is 'ours,' which individuals and communities have brought it into being and thus claim it as their own, all matter in thinking about any particular place in any particular context. Who created this place and for whom? And why here? Since its first uses some thousand years ago, 'Place' has meant many things that are related to the use and design of land and space: a public square; an open place in town; a marketplace; a small residential square or side street; a battlefield; ground contested by opposing forces in battle; and a person's home. (*OED*) It implies stability at the same time it reminds us of impermanence, conflict as well as harmony. In all of these ways, Eastside Luv Bar and MorrisseyOke are such places.

Another reason I, and so many MorrisseyOke regulars, love it is because of the sense of home we get by being there. Every month, before she calls up the first singer of the night, Alexis reminds us all, 'Eastside Luv is our home. This is your home, your bar, your night. You, the fans, make this happen every month.' There have been spans of time, maybe three or four months, where I did not attend MorrisseyOke for whatever reason. When I did go back, it's like I never left. Same bartenders, same DJ, same host, same owner, same music. MorrisseyOke is comforting, and it provides a cozy, familiar home in an otherwise sprawling and impersonal Los Angeles.

If the bar feels like 'home' to the mostly Chicano/a clientele, that is because Uribe designed it that way. Aesthetically, Eastside Luv's décor and design pay homage to the community's deep Mexican and Chicano heritage. The design choices reflect the vision of a self-described Chicano 'pocho'[58] (Americanized Mexican, historically a derogatory term) in terms of its ethnic, class, and cultural symbols, 'like you're in someone's house,' says Uribe. Glowing velas, the tall colorful candles that are mainstays on Mexican altars everywhere, line the bar next to the bottles of beer and wine on display. Art and photography by local and regional Chicano/a artists hangs on walls covered with deep red and black velvet wallpaper. Chicano slang, other clever Spanglish plays-on-words appear as alternative spellings on event fliers ('Free-joles EventO' as in 'free event,' a play on the Spanish *frijoles* for beans) and other bar announcements. Vintage Mexican film posters, dim lighting, a stripper pole (a cheeky disguise for drainage hoses) at the end of the catwalk complete the look of this proud pocho bar[59] that is home to MorrisseyOke.

In these ways, the venue itself contributes significantly to the 'homey' atmosphere and meaning of MorrisseyOke. The people, the gente, the good ol' reliables who show up every month move around and take ownership of the place as if it is their home. Veteranos ('regulars' in MozOke speak) welcome virgins, fans make way for newbies or casual fans who only know How Soon Is Now or the double decker bus song. Like any home, the atmosphere is not always harmonious. Not everyone always gets along, and some folks are downright territorial. But generally speaking, the vibe of a comfortable and secure place of shared fandom and goodwill is there for anyone who seeks it out.

One veterano, a good MozOke ambassador, attends pretty much

every month. His name is Oscar, but he goes by the nickname Chato. I see Chato around the LA Moz fan scene, and he often performs with some of the local Smiths Moz tribute bands in the area, playing acoustic guitar wherever he's needed because he 'loves the music.' Occasionally, he will bring his guitar to MozOke and accompany a singer, as in the photo opposite, with another MozOke veteran and fixture of the scene, Clover Dean (Fig. 4). I've asked Chato about what keeps him coming to MorrisseyOke besides his fandom and love for the music. 'It feels like family here. Everyone is here for the same reason, because they love Morrissey and the Smiths. We all feel a special connection to the music, and we can all celebrate that here together.'[60] On another night, I spoke to Anita and Omar, MozOke 'virgins.' They shared this:

> We came here from Sylmar. We've been hearing about this bar that does all Morrissey karaoke, and we love him, so we wanted to come and check it out. It's awesome. It's the perfect place if you're a Morrissey fan and just wanna hang out and sing with other people who love the songs as much as you do.[61]

Chato's sentiments are shared by many of the veteranos/as I have spoken to. However, when a couple of virgins can also express something similar on their first night means there is something special about MorrisseyOke. The community vibe, the sense that Morrissey Smiths fans are at home there all speak to the importance of a place like Eastside Luv in forging fan community spaces like MorrisseyOke. Like any 'home' or 'family,' MorrisseyOke is rife with the petty personal politics and bullshit behavior of some of its goers. I have my own critiques of some of the things that can and do go on in that space, but it's certainly not the only Mozfan space in town that is prone to hypermasculine heteronormative homophobic aggression from attendees. (Apparently, some of these dudes forget whose music they're there to sing and listen to.) But in general, I find MorrisseyOke to be an inclusive and queer-friendly space. It's my home, too.

78

Figure 4. Veterano MorrisseyOke duo: Clover Dean singing to Chato's version of a Smiths classic. Host Alexis de la Rocha stands against the wall with her clipboard. May 2015.
Photo by the author.

On the rare first-Thursdays that Alexis has another commitment, she will ask me to host MorrisseyOke. I have had the pleasure and privilege of hosting it five times. Alexis has always said that MorrisseyOke is her 'baby,' something she helped create, nurture, and bring to full being, and she trusts me to take care of it when she has to be away. She told me once that it's really because of me that MorrisseyOke exists. 'You were the OG fan in my life. You totally influenced Monica who introduced me to Morrissey. I only knew of the Smiths from some girl in my PE class, but I came to love Morrissey because of you,' she told me once at dinner. All I could do was stay quiet and shed tears. This was very kind and generous for Alexis to say (true to her nature), and while I'm flattered to take a tiny bit of that credit, I know that MorrisseyOke is bigger than me, her, Willie, the bar, any single one of us. It's ours. It is as a community space by fans, for fans.

The few times I have hosted, I see what Alexis sees every month. I have a new appreciation for the graceful juggling act she has to do sometimes when the same singers, drunker as the night goes on, want to keep signing up to sing. It is the job of any good host to keep the night moving along, to keep the singers happy, to be fair to everyone who signed up and wants to sing. If too many people want to sing Suedehead, There Is A Light That Never Goes Out, or any other song, the host must gently suggest alternatives so as to avoid repeats. My favorite part about hosting is the view from the stage, the joy I see in the faces in the crowd when someone is up there singing a song everyone loves. I can't help but sing and dance myself, mic in one hand and clipboard in the other. I *love* these songs. I love seeing other fans react with excitement when DJ Jess cues Tomorrow, or First Of The Gang, or Paint A Vulgar Picture for the next singer. I am reminded of why we do come here and why we hang around, as we have for over five years.

On Morrissey's fifty-seventh birthday, 22 May 2016, MorrisseyOke celebrated its fifth anniversary. Mariachi Manchester, LA's newest Morrissey Smiths tribute band (see chapter three), were the guest performers there to celebrate our man's birthday and the MorrisseyOke milestone. At once an homage to the bar's and to Boyle Heights' mariachi heritage, and a testament to the popularity of mariachi style Morrissey tunes with these fans, Mariachi Manchester's renditions of hits like First Of The Gang To Die, Girlfriend In Coma, Ask, and The More You Ignore Me, The Closer I Get got the crowd singing, dancing, and bonding over the music.

The best parts of the performance were the moments when the band would play a traditional standard mariachi song—say, the Mexican classic La Negra, with its signature trumpet and string introduction, or El Mariachi Loco, which local Dodgers fans recognize as Mexican first baseman Adrián González's walkup song—and transition in the middle of the mariachi tune to a well-known Smiths Moz song. For example, Miguel Pasillas, trumpet player for Mariachi Manchester, will play the opening notes of La Negra, a song that begins slowly, anticipatory, as if building up the excitement, tapping into those memories of our Mexican grandparents. After a few bars of the classic Mexican instrumental, the rest of the band joins in and, like magic, the song becomes First Of The Gang To Die. 'You have never been in love,' sings fake-mustachioed Moises Baqueiro to the rhythm and beat of La Negra. The crowd, as they say, went wild.

Any given first-Thursday at Eastside Luv can be filled with these kinds of moments that bring me and others there so much joy. It's why we keep going back. I love that fans of all body types and skin shades, from

Figure 5. Author on stage at MorrisseyOke, May 2015.
Photo by Alexis de la Rocha. Used with permission.

various backgrounds and neighborhoods, take the stage to sing their favorite songs, affecting a range of Morrisseyesque movements, from the awkward crooked dancing of early Smiths-era Moz, to the stately stalking and impeccably timed mic cord whipping of mature solo Moz. I love witnessing the many gender and racial transgressions (female bodies 'being' Moz, brown bodies inhabiting a white Anglo singer's persona), expressions of liberation, and fan fantasies playing out and channeled through singing (over) Morrissey on stage. I love the allure of exhibitionism and voyeurism that the stage set-up begs: bars, straps, poles, a runway, and not just for the occasional performances by the local Smiths Morrissey tribute burlesque troupe. These are transgressive spaces in which desires are fulfilled, social norms are challenged, and new ways of being are imagined and lived out, if only for the length of a song, if only once a month at MorrisseyOke.

CHAPTER THREE

When Your Gift Unfurls
Paying Tribute to Morrissey and The Smiths

tribute (n.): an act, statement, or gift that is intended to show gratitude, respect, or admiration

New Oxford American Dictionary

When your gift unfurls, when your talent becomes apparent
I will roar from the stalls, I will gurgle from the circles

Morrissey, Lucky Lisp

THERE ARE MORE MORRISSEY AND SMITHS TRIBUTE bands in Los Angeles than there are for any other artist or band in the world. I imagine that no other city in the world has as many tribute acts devoted to one artist or band as does Los Angeles for Morrissey and the Smiths.

At last count, there are seven active Morrissey and Smiths tribute bands in LA, and if we include the rest of California, we can add three or four more to the mix. As if there were not enough homegrown LA tributes to Morrissey and the Smiths to fill club promoters' coffers and bar owners' cash registers, several out-of-area tribute bands have come to Moz Angeles to play for excited fans who want to hear and see what other bands from other cities sound like. The annual Smiths/Morrissey Convention presented by London Calling and the World Famous KROQ is often the best place to see out-of-town Smiths and Morrissey bands from places like San Francisco, San Diego, even Dublin and Liverpool. May, Morrissey's birthday month, is by far the busiest month for area Morrissey Smiths tribute bands; other high-frequency times of the year include the Halloween and Día de los Muertos season, Christmas through New Year, and St Valentine's Day. Anytime Morrissey plays a show in the greater Los Angeles area, including Orange County, we can count on at least one after-party headlined by a local tribute band. The plethora of Smiths Moz tribute bands and the regularity with which they perform—not every band performs every weekend, of course, and some play more regularly than others—means that on any given Thursday through Sunday night all year long, there will be at least one Morrissey Smiths tribute band playing at a club or bar somewhere. From North Hollywood to Santa Ana to Riverside to San Diego, Southern California Morrissey Smiths fans who want their live music fix will almost always have somewhere to go.

Tribute bands are unlike any other form of fan expression. Anybody can show up to karaoke and sing something s/he may not know so well and still get away with it. Anybody with a laptop or iDevice can tune into a radio show. Anybody can show up to a club and dance the night away. But to find and organize a group of like-minded musicians, then find the time that works for everyone to rehearse, then practice a lineup of songs for months and months before feeling confident enough to finally book a gig, then book said gig (itself a task that can take time), then promote the show, get bodies in the door, get paid a few hundred bucks, and then do it all over again for the next gig who knows when: that takes something else, another level of fandom, an undying love for the music, a disciplined commitment to the work of playing these songs in a band. And yes, it also involves a little bit of ego. Forming a tribute band requires all that and more: it demands pure *ganas*—the desire, the drive, the want—to get up there for the joy of playing the music and making other fans happy.

This is not to suggest that every single member of every single tribute band is a die hard Morrissey Smiths fans, or that they want to all make other fans and audiences happy. Some are up there to get paid, others are up there because they're filling in for someone else; people play in tribute bands for many different reasons that don't always have to do with fandom. However, I will venture to say that in every single tribute band, there is at least one die hard Morrissey Smiths fan, if not a core group of die-hards. And this fandom, this profound connection to and love for the music, is the battery that powers the band.

So why Morrissey Smiths tribute bands? What compels people to form them? What do they contribute to fan scenes and communities? What sustains all of them in a fairly concentrated region? I offer three points of consideration: 1) the 'long fetch' of LA Mexican American history; 2) the undeniable impact and influence of British pop music in the US more generally, and LA more specifically; and 3) Morrissey's 2004 release of his Los Angeles album, *You Are the Quarry*. I explore these items first before moving on to profile some of the Morrissey Smiths tribute bands from the Los Angeles area.

The Long Fetch of Moz Angeles

The sheer number of Morrissey and Smiths tribute bands in LA is one thing. The atmosphere here kind of invites it. The fact that nearly every one of these bands is all-Mexican/Latino would be something else if we were not in Los Angeles or the US Southwest, so let's start with that. American Studies scholar George Lipsitz frames popular music through what he calls the 'long fetch of history.' In his 2007 work *Footsteps in the Dark: The Hidden Histories of Popular Music*, Lipstiz describes popular music as an important 'repository for collective memory' that also contains 'hidden histories and long fetches.' Lipsitz borrows the term 'long fetch,' defined as 'the distance between a wave's point of origin and its point of arrival,' from historians Marcus Reddiker and Peter Linebaugh, who compare the trajectory of history to the ocean's waves. To our eye, waves rise and fall in a short matter of time even though they 'begin their journey thousand of miles out at sea.' Lipsitz continues,

'Their form, size, and shape come from the speed of prevailing winds in the atmosphere, the power of currents hidden beneath the sea... Waves appear abruptly and immediately, but they have a long hidden history before the human eye notices them.'[62]

Imagining history as an ocean wave (a very nice image) and acknowledging the role that popular music plays in marking the present as history by 'helping us to understand where we have been and where we are going'[63] puts the fact of Morrissey Smiths tribute bands in Los Angeles into clear perspective. To do so means to realize that things which seemingly come out of nowhere or cannot be immediately explained, such as the so-called 'Latino-Mexican Morrissey love affair' and the proliferation of all these tribute bands, actually have been in the making for some time through the forces of history's pushes and pulls. With Lipsitz's help, I point to two specific historical moments that comprise part of the 'long fetch' of this big wave of Chicana/o-Mexican-Latina/o Moz Smiths tribute bands in Los Angeles.

The first is to look at LA's pop music history since the post-WWII era of the 1950s and 1960s, what Chicano historians call the Mexican American generation. The 1950s saw the birth of rock'n'roll music, so-named by a white Cleveland radio disc jockey named Alan Freed. He called the new mix of music he played on his show—black musical forms such as jazz, rhythm and blues, gospel along with white country and rockabilly—'rock & roll,' thus christening a new popular music phenomenon and making history. This period of the 1950s and early 1960s also shows us the multicultural, multiethnic makeup (not just Mexican) of the dance-hall bands that were popular in the working class agricultural communities across the San Fernando and San Gabriel Valleys to the north and east of Los Angeles.

Accordingly, second and third generation Mexican youth who grew up in the area speaking mostly English as a first language and listening to rock'n'roll as opposed to their parents' Mexican music have always formed rock'n'roll bands as a form of cultural expression. As Los Angeles race and labor historian Matt Garcia writes, 'Inspired by Valens and other Los Angeles bands, many local Mexican American youths formed

85

rock 'n' roll groups to emulate their heroes, play music, and create homespun sounds.'[64] What Valens, Ricky Nelson, and Elvis Presley were to 1950s-era LA Mexican Americans, and what the Sex Pistols and Ramones were to the next generation of Mexican American punk rockers, so the Smiths and Morrissey are to the generations of English speaking Mexican Americans who grew up in the 1980s and 1990s. Emulation is a form of tribute. In these ways, we can see how generations of Mexican Americans in the region have built their own localized histories of making and claiming public space through forming bands, playing the popular music of the day, and going to see these bands play live.

This brings us to the second point about why so many Moz Smiths tribute bands—and several others that fall under UK new wave/ postpunk—not only exist, but thrive in LA. Georgina Gregory, a UK-based music scholar, describes the impact of British music on the American cover band scene since the 1960s and 1970s. In her 2012 book *Send in the Clones: A Cultural Study of the Tribute Band*, Gregory writes, 'The fact that British bands made infrequent visits to the US only served to heighten enthusiasm for cover acts capable of offering UK pop in their repertoire and demand was further accelerated by the "British Invasion" following the arrival of the Beatles in New York.'[65] Cover acts filled the gap in the absence of the 'real' bands that were booked too infrequently or perhaps not at all.[66] Gregory also cites the high price of tickets and impersonal atmosphere of 'stadium rock' with its massive venues, crowds of over 50,000 people and distance between the artist and audience. She writes, 'The appearance of tribute acts helped to draw fans back to the small, friendly local environments of small theatres and live music venues, environments which were struggling to attract pop and rock fans by the late 1970s.'[67] This point speaks to the important social and economic role that tribute bands play in creating community by providing local spaces for shared experiences of fandom around a particular band or singer.

We cannot underestimate the powerful, culture-infiltrating influence of British music on the US popular music scene. Whether it was the Beatles and the rest of the so-called 'British Invasion' bands, British

Popular music hit hard Stateside in the 1960s and 1970s. Our parents were smitten with bands like Eric Burdon and the Animals, Herman's Hermits, the Yardbirds, the Who, the Rolling Stones, the Beatles, and Fleetwood Mac. By the time the 1980s came around, my generation of the 'modern rock' KROQ variety clung for dear life to bands like the Cure, Depeche Mode, Pet Shop Boys, Erasure, and of course, the Smiths and Morrissey; then came the 'shoegaze' rock of the nineties: I loved bands like Cocteau Twins, Ride, Slowdive, My Bloody Valentine, Lush, Catherine Wheel, bands I heard about by listening to KROQ and working at a local music store in the early 1990s. LA had a homegrown 'shoegaze' band, Mazzy Star, fronted by our local East LA Mexican American singer, Hope Sandoval. British music, for better or for worse, is in our blood, mixed in with all the 'Mexican' music, jazz, rockabilly, R&B, Chicano brown-eyed soul, and other formative musical styles that saturated the airwaves in our homes, cars, and at our backyard house parties from Los Angeles, California to Corpus Cristi, Texas.

We can definitely place the Smiths, and thus Morrissey, within this 'long fetch' of the 'British Invasions' of the US pop music since the 1960s. Another important context for considering the proliferation of Smiths Morrissey tribute bands in LA is the current popularity of 1980s UK pop/postpunk music more generally. Los Angeles enjoys a thriving 'eighties' scene that celebrates the era of what locals remember as 'KROQ' and 'Power 106' music. The two radio stations loom large in the collective imagination of LA's suburban, working class people of color communities. Those of us who remember this decade well think of 'The Eighties' in terms of Depeche Mode, the Cure, the Smiths, New Order, and other British postpunk 'new wave' music we heard so often on KROQ 106.7FM, *and* 'The Eighties' of Madonna, Michael Jackson, Prince, Lisa Lisa and the Cult Jam, Babyface, and other pop, dance, and freestyle created by people of color in the US that we heard on Power 106 and KIIS FM. I'm painting a broad picture here to illustrate the roots of LA's thriving nostalgia scene that celebrates the pop music and culture of 'The Eighties'—alive and well in clubs all over the San Gabriel Valley and Southeast LA.[68] These 'eighties' bars and clubs regularly host Smiths

Morrissey tribute bands, along with tributes to other UK eighties bands like New Order, Siouxsie and the Banshees, Depeche Mode, and the Psychedelic Furs.

Thus far, we've covered some of the 'long fetch' of pop music history, from the advent of rock'n'roll in the 1950s and the rise of the post-WWII Mexican American generation, through the current popularity of 'eighties'-themed bars and club nights, all operating to set up Los Angeles for the emergence of the many tribute bands devoted to the Smiths and Morrissey. There is one more key component, the aspect of historical preservation that tribute bands enact with every performance. According to ethnomusicologist John Paul Meyers, tribute bands contribute to the preservation of rock and pop music by treating the music of the past with 'historical respect and legitimacy.'[69] I will say more about the historical preservation element of the tribute project in the conclusion of this chapter, but I mention it here to drive home the following point: tribute bands, for the most part, celebrate the music of the past in the present. When we consider that many tribute bands first formed in the 1970s after the original bands broke up, or when a popular singer passed away, we can understand their role in resurrecting the music of these bands for the continued enjoyment of fans and audiences of the original. After all, tribute bands run on nostalgia, shared memories, and fan passion for the songs being performed. They also rely on cultural memory and the audience's sense of history with the original bands. Tribute bands represent a reincarnation of bands like the Smiths, whose members are all alive and well but who are, as a band, dead (at least in the eyes of Morrissey, who swears he will never reunite with Johnny Marr, Mike Joyce, and Andy Rourke).

All of which brings us to our third and final point for considering LA's Moz Smiths tribute band scene: the post-*You Are the Quarry* popularity of Morrissey in Los Angeles, a hotbed of Moz fan activity. If, following Meyers, we understand that tribute bands' role in preserving and recreating musical history, particularly in bringing 'dead' bands back to life for a night, then Smiths-only tributes make sense in this light. Certainly, tribute bands that only play the music of the Smiths exist; consider Liverpool's the Smiths Indeed, which do not perform Morrissey's solo music. Nostalgia for the Smiths runs deep in the band's UK homelands. But if you want to see tribute bands play the music of the Smiths *and* Morrissey, or sometimes just the music of Morrissey, then you have to come to Moz Angeles. The very fact of paying tribute to Morrissey, a singer who is alive and well and remains active as a touring artist, means that tribute bands perform more than just an historical function of preserving or resurrecting defunct bands: they reimagine and recreate Morrissey's music for the here and now.

We can see why a band like the Smiths, mythically defunct and never to be reunited if we are to believe our Morrissey, lends itself so fittingly to tribute band projects. But Morrissey, alive and kicking despite being 'slowed down' by recent health issues,[70] plays shows in the greater Los Angeles and Southern California area at least once a year. Fans here get to see 'Real Morrissey' often enough. And yet, plenty of insatiable fans want more. It is rare for a living, active, new-music-making rock star to be the focus of a tribute band in her/his lifetime. Morrissey, as usual, is an exception to this unwritten tribute band rule. But even in Moz Angeles, what can possibly warrant seven tribute bands? And how do all these bands distinguish themselves in the plethora of tribute bands in the LA and Southern California Moz fan scene? A look at the post-*You Are the Quarry* landscape will help us see some of the less-obvious conditions for the emergence and proliferation of all these tribute bands.

For many years, the only band on the scene was Los Angeles based Sweet and Tender Hooligans. Established in 1992, they are the elder statesmen, so to speak, of the Smiths and Morrissey tribute band circuit. Along with front man José 'the Mexican Morrissey' Maldonado, the Hooligans are Danny García on drums, David Collett on lead guitar, Joe Escalante on bass, Art Barrios on rhythm guitar, and Thomas Lennon as 'honorary' rhythm guitarist. The Hooligans were named by *LA Weekly* as one of the best tribute bands in the area, and they enjoy an especially high profile among Morrissey and Smiths fans outside of LA as one of the few touring Moz Smiths tribute bands. In her book *15 Minutes with*

You, London fan Julie Hamill notes that the Hooligans 'have sold out concerts in Los Angeles, Orange County, San Francisco, San Diego, Seattle, Boston, New York, Austin, El Paso, Monterrey, Tijuana, London, Leeds, Manchester and Glasgow.'[71]

The band continues to play shows around Los Angeles and Orange County, with occasional trips back to San Diego and El Paso, Texas. The highlight of the Hooligans' calendar is their annual Morrissey birthday show every May 22. No matter which day of the week Moz's birthday falls, the Hooligans' Morrissey birthday show always draws a packed house, whether at Anaheim's House of Blues or Hollywood's Henry Fonda Theater, where Morrissey once played. They pull out all the stops for this annual birthday bash: guest musicians (Mikey Farrell, Morrissey's former keyboardist, has joined them onstage), mariachis, long set lists, birthday cakes. Another of the Hooligans' standout performances took place in July 2014, when the Sweet and Tender Hooligans took the stage outside of the Pasadena Rose Bowl for a big soccer pre-game show. The game? Manchester United versus the Los Angeles Galaxy, of course.

The Sweet and Tender Hooligans are what I like to call a first-generation Smiths and Morrissey tribute band. They are the first and, in many fans' eyes, the best ones out there. But now, in 2016, they are not the only ones out there. The Hooligans dominated the Moz Smiths tribute scene for well over a decade until the excitement of Morrissey's Los Angeles album, *You Are the Quarry*, spawned a new generation of tribute bands. *Quarry*'s release in 2004 was hailed as the artist's comeback, 'true to form' and 'arguably the best thing he's done since *Vauxhall & I*,' after many years without an album or record deal.[72] Die hard fans, who had never lost track of Morrissey even in his so-called 'lost' years following 1997's *Maladjusted*, finally had new songs to listen to and a tour to look forward to. For other fans whose enthusiasm for Moz was dormant, *Quarry* reignited their love, with some fans even claiming that the album with Irish Blood, English Heart and First Of The Gang To Die 'made them a Morrissey fan again.'[73]

My sense is that *You Are the Quarry* was the catalyst for the surge in fans' demand for more tribute bands. Their insatiable hunger for live performances of Smiths and Morrissey songs grew, exceeding even what the venerable Hooligans could offer a few times a year. Word on the street is that fans, too, wanted an alternative to the Hooligans, or perhaps just new blood, while other fan-musicians in the area wanted to try their hand and offer their versions of the familiar songs. The vibrant and active fan culture in greater LA and SoCal is over three generations in the making, providing fertile soil for the growth and sustenance of multiple tribute bands. But even this soil requires tilling every so often. So between 2004 and 2015—during which time Morrissey himself returned often to Los Angeles, played many concerts, and marked significant career milestones as in his *25Live* Hollywood High School show in 2013—Smiths and Morrissey tribute bands seemed to sprout up everywhere around California, and particularly in Los Angeles.

The release of *Quarry*, fan demand for more Morrissey (and Smiths) music, and a combination of other cultural factors spurred the next generation of post-Hooligans Morrissey and Smiths tribute bands throughout the US. In 2004, Compton and South Whittier gave birth to These Handsome Devils, A Tribute to Morrissey and the Smiths; These Handsome Devils formed a full twelve years after the Hooligans burst onto the scene, making them the first post-Hooligans tribute band in LA. After These Handsome Devils came San Francisco's This Charming Band in 2005. 2006 saw the debut of two Smiths and Morrissey tribute bands, New York City's Sons and Heirs and San Diego's Still Ill. The Handsome Devilz formed in Chicago, Illinois in 2009, while Panic, A Tribute to the Smiths and Morrissey would put Dallas, Texas, on the tribute map in 2012. During this time in Los Angeles alone, at least seven more bands would form. Some are now defunct or perpetually in hiatus (Kill Uncle, Louder Than Bombs), but many others are alive and active. In addition to the Sweet and Tender Hooligans (1992) and These Handsome Devils (2004), other bands currently make their rounds around Moz Angeles include Strangeways (2008), Maladjusted (2012), Nowhere Fast (2012), Mariachi Manchester (2014) and Sheilas Take A Bow (2014). All of these bands, in their own ways, play the music of Morrissey and the Smiths.

Paying Tribute
Five Bands Give the Gift of Moz

With such a wide selection of local tribute bands, LA area fans have several options for enjoying a night of live Smiths Morrissey songs. In the next section, we will meet five of these bands from the LA area: These Handsome Devils, Maladjusted, Strangeways, Mariachi Manchester, and Sheilas Take A Bow. Here, I present interviews and conversations with at least one representative from each band: their stories, their words about what it means to be part of such a vibrant scene and what it means to give fans the gift of live Moz Smiths songs performed in intimate club settings. Rather than compare them to each other or rank them, we would be better to recognize each band's unique contributions to the scene and the different gifts they offer to the Moz Angeles fan community. If a tribute is 'an an act, statement, or gift that is intended to show gratitude, respect, or admiration,' then these five bands represent the many ways in which it is possible to pay loving tribute to Morrissey and the Smiths in true Los Angeles style.

Here they are, in chronological order of their formation.

THESE HANDSOME DEVILS, A TRIBUTE TO MORRISSEY AND THE SMITHS: These Handsome Devils (not to be confused with The Handsome Devilz Smiths and Morrissey tribute from Chicago) were the first post-Hooligans, *Quarry* inspired tribute band to form in LA. Founded in 2004, their dozen-plus years on the scene make them the second longest running tribute band in the land next to the originals, Sweet and Tender Hooligans. Current members of These Handsome Devils include Daniel Alcocer (vocals), Eddie Stephens (keys, guitars, upright bass), Julian Solis (bass), Juan Frausto (drums), and Omar Alcocer (lead guitar).

The band was founded by two brothers, a cousin, and a friend in the Willowbrook neighborhood of Compton, California. While Compton is often invoked as a predominantly black neighborhood, the home of West Coast gangsta rap and groups like NWA, the working class south Los Angeles suburb these days is more racially and ethnically diverse than some would imagine. It follows that the musical soundscape of Compton, and of south central Los Angeles in general, is a heterogeneous reflection of its residents: sounds of homegrown rap, Mexican banda and norteño music and Central American cumbias mingle with seventies rock, eighties new wave, and popular top forty music.

When I first saw These Handsome Devils, they were playing for two bucks a head at the Santa Fe Springs Swap Meet as they do regularly. I have seen them at other venues, but nothing quite matches the crowd and energy of one of the Devils' swap meet shows. Situated just off the 5 freeway near the border of LA and Orange County, minutes from Knott's Berry Farm and Disneyland amusement parks, the Santa Fe Springs Swap Meet is a huge venue that attracts hundreds of working class, mostly immigrant families from all over southeastern Los Angeles County and north Orange County. With rows and rows of booths selling everything from Mexican snack foods to cell phone covers made in China, the Santa Fe Springs Swap Meet also doubles as a well-known regional music venue for tribute acts and original bands of all stripes. 'Come for the bargains, stay for the fun!' is the motto of the place, and plenty of people do. Local bands like Tierra, the classic Chicano rock outfit, and area tribute bands such as such as No Duh! (tribute to No Doubt) and of course, These Handsome Devils, will play to several hundreds of people on any given Friday or Saturday night.

The band's slick logo (Fig. 1) shows a graphic of a tommy gun spraying gladioli instead of bullets. The tommy gun of course is a visual reference to the one Morrissey holds on the cover of *You Are the Quarry*, while the gladioli represent what Morrissey would wield on stage in his early days with the Smiths. The logo marks the year of the band's formation, 2004, the same year as *Quarry*, indicative also of the band's Morrissey solo leanings.

I spent the most time talking with Eddie Stephens, a Whittier resident and musician's musician who joined the band in 2010. Eddie now serves as These Handsome Devils' primary contact, social media promoter, and musical director. His first love is Elvis Presley, and he tours as a bass guitarist for nationally known Elvis tribute acts. A talented multi-instrumentalist, Eddie has performed with musicians such as Bo Diddley and Thee Midniters, and he also works as a sound technician for touring bands across the US. Eddie's Elvis fandom easily crosses over into Morrissey and the Smiths, particularly when it comes to some of the more 1950s inspired rockabilly tunes that the band will often play as part of their big three-set shows at the Santa Fe Springs Swap Meet, where they are the resident Moz Smiths tribute band. Over happy hour beers and burgers in Whittier, I had a chance to meet with Eddie and ask him a few things for this book.[74] We discussed Morrissey, the Handsome Devils band, the crowds at their shows, and his sense of what makes a tribute band successful. Here are some highlights of our conversation, in Eddie's words.

On fans' expectations of tribute bands, and of tribute bands offering a service to fans

'People are paying for the service one way or the other, so we gotta give them the product. And These Handsome Devils strive to put out a top product every time we take the stage. Moz fans are picky, especially about the tribute bands. Morrissey as the original artist can do no wrong, but a tribute band can almost do no right. We have to live up to *that*, what fans have in mind when it comes to Morrissey and the Smiths. As a tribute band, if we can remind you in any way of them, if we can bring back memories and remind you why you love this music, give you an experience that feels good, then we have done our job.'

On These Handsome Devils and how they deliver their tribute product:

'Musical excellence. Holding each other accountable. For us, it's an investment in mind, heart and soul, and we have to protect our product.

Figure 1. These Handsome Devils band logo. Image appears courtesy of Eddie Stephens. Used with permission.

I know I can be a bit hard on Daniel, our singer, but that's because the Morrissey guy has to be on point. If you're gonna do it, do it right, or don't do it at all. That goes for all of us, but even more so for Daniel or anyone who plays the Morrissey part.'

On Morrissey and the Smiths:

'I think Andy Rourke is the unsung hero of the Smiths. Johnny Marr is a genius. I love Morrissey, I love the music. Of course there are parallels with Elvis—the sideburns, the hairstyle, the suit Morrissey wore during the Oye Esteban tour that was like Elvis's black suit from 1968, even (the Elvis song) His Latest Flame with Rusholme Ruffians. As a bass player, I love it when I can bring out the upright and play The Loop, Sister I'm A Poet, Sing Your Life, and Rusholme Ruffians. But Jack The Ripper is my favorite Morrissey solo song to perform.'

On audiences:

'At shows, you have the usual range of fans. There are the casual fans all the way to the die-hards. A lot of times you get the 'I'm so sorry/ Double decker bus' crowd. They just wanna hear the hits, so we better play Suedehead ('I'm so sorry') and There Is A Light ('Double decker bus'). You also get the die hard fans, the picky Moz fans who want to hear other songs, the deep cuts, and they'll stand in front of the stage with their arms crossed and dissect everything. We have our trolls, a lot of harshness directed at us, and it kills us, and I know other bands get shit, too. Pues get up here then, if you think you can do it better, get up here and do these songs yourself, you know? People don't realize it's hard to do these songs and do them well. We love the music, too, we respect it, and that's always behind what we deliver. I can tell we're doing something right when I see people in the crowd singing along, happy. I love watching the faces of the fans at our shows.'

STRANGEWAYS, A TRIBUTE TO THE SMITHS AND MORRISSEY: Keep the music of the Smiths alive. Introduce these magical songs to a new generation. Play these songs with passion. These are the main driving forces of our next band, Strangeways, A Tribute to the Smiths and Morrissey.

Fittingly, the seeds of the band were planted when co-founders and longtime friends, Julian Ricardo (voice) and Ralph Paredes (guitar), went to see Morrissey at the Hollywood Palladium during the singer's memorable ten-night engagement in October 2007. Ralph and Julian met back in 1993 as students at Rio Hondo College in Whittier, California. At the time, Ralph was shooting video for the Sweet and Tender Hooligans, while Julian was an aspiring actor. Shared musical interests, especially the Smiths, would make them fast friends. Ralph would go on to work on postproduction teams at Warner Brothers as a graphic designer, while Julian landed roles in commercials, short films, and television series. They forged their friendship by playing music in their free time; Ralph would play guitar to Depeche Mode and other eighties 'KROQ' songs, while Julian would sing. But it wasn't until fourteen years later, inspired by seeing Morrissey in concert at that Palladium show in 2007, that the idea to form a tribute band would take hold.

A few months after that fateful Morrissey show, Ralph and Julian recruited Rawl, Ralph's brother, to play bass. The trio played their first gig with a drum machine in April 2008. They called themselves 'Strangeways' after the Smiths' last album. Shortly thereafter, they added a friend, Joe Espinosa, on drums; the foursome would play local gigs through 2008 and 2009, until Joe moved out of state. The band's Facebook page tells the rest of the story: in 2010, Strangeways added a good friend, John Arrieta, on rhythm guitar, and in 2011, their lineup was completed with the addition of Jorge Arroyo on drums. Now in their fifth year with this current group of musicians, friends, and superfans, Strangeways continues to excite audiences with their rockin' style and energetic performances of Smiths and Morrissey hits.

I saw Strangeways on television before I saw them perform live. The band were featured in a segment on ABC 7's *Vista LA,* a weekly news show in Los Angeles that spotlights Latino/a cultural happenings around the city. Strangeways were part of a feature about Latino subcultures and the popular eighties new wave music scenes at bars like The Hully Gully in Downey. The episode aired in May 2011, and it was just the profile boost the band needed to put themselves on the Moz Angeles map of tribute bands. Since then, Strangeways, based in the eastern San Gabriel Valley cities of Covina, West Covina and La Puente, California, has steadily cultivated its own set of fans and followers. Their rise is due mainly to regular performances at the popular Rock It! nights held at Carnaval Nightclub in Pomona, not too far from where Morrissey played at the Fox and Johnny Marr at The Glass House. Strangeways have played memorable shows with Depeche Mode and New Order tribute bands, and they joined Liverpool's tribute, the Smiths Indeed, and This Charming Band from San Francisco, in the their biggest show yet: the 2016 annual Smiths/Morrissey Convention in Hollywood, California, hosted by Richard Blade.

I first met the band after a 2012 gig at Spike's Bar in Rosemead, California. I was immediately drawn to Julian's unique stage style. Clearly, this guy was a performer, and he connected with the songs he sang in a way that I hadn't seen since José Maldonado of the Hooligans. Julian sang, danced, and did his own thing: here was a tribute band singer who was not trying to 'be' Morrissey, not trying to be derivative. No flowers, no thick black glasses, no crooked dancing. Just pure, uninhibited joy that comes when a singer truly loves and feels the music. I saw Strangeways again the following year in Pomona, and I followed that up with a meeting with singer Julian to talk music, fandom, Smiths vs Morrissey favoritism, and our shared queer connections to the songs that saved our lives. A few months later, Julian and I found ourselves as co-judges (along with MorrisseyOke founder, Alexis de la Rocha) for the 2014 Teatro Moz theater festival. It would be another two years before I had the chance to catch up with the band, fresh off their marquee performance at the 2016 annual Smiths Moz Con. The following comments are taken from various conversations with Julian over the course of four years.[75]

Unless otherwise indicated, all quotes are attributed to singer Julian Ricardo.

On being a fan:

'I was a Smiths fan first, then a Moz fan. KROQ and my friends were my sources for music. One day, a friend gave me *Meat is Murder* and I heard I Want The One I Can't Have. I was hooked. It wasn't so much the song as it was the lyrics. I thought, this guy [Morrissey] is singing to me. The lyrics hooked me because I wanted to sing it to my friend, the one who gave me the CD [of *Meat is Murder*], but I was afraid because I had these feelings that I was never able to express. I grew up lonely and confused, and the Smiths were my solace. I paid attention to Morrissey because he was different.'

On forming Strangeways, A Tribute to the Smiths and Morrissey:

'We weren't intentionally starting a Smiths cover/tribute band. We just jammed a lot of eighties Brit new wave, and it turned out the guys said I sounded most like Moz than any of us when we'd do those songs. So it happened. We played our first show as Strangeways in 2008 and have been playing ever since then. We said if we were going to play all Smiths and Moz songs, not bunch of eighties songs, then we have to do this right and with sincerity. We love [the music] and want to give it back to those who love it. *I* love it so much, I *feel* the music, and that's what I want people to feel when they see us. That's our goal, to keep the spirit of the music alive for the longtime fans and the new generations who are just coming into their Smiths and Morrissey fandom.'

[*From drummer Jorge:*] 'We have that responsibility, to play the songs as everyone knows them in the best way we can. If a band isn't around anymore, like the Smiths, we have a responsibility to give the audience an experience of what it would be like to see them and hear these songs live. We're passionate musicians and we love the music, and it comes through in how we express it on stage. These five guys—we're definitely all fans and that propels us to be the very best we can be when we get up on stage and do these songs. Every show is the same commitment.'

[*From guitarist Ralph:*] 'I have nine years in this band; all of us are close friends, some of us are family—Rawl is my brother. The friendship and our closeness definitely helps us. There are no revolving members, just us five. And this combination of guys is magical.'

On being the lead singer:

'My favorite song to sing is Irish Blood, English heart. It's forceful, direct, pointed, very masculine, a punch in the face, a *rock* song. I find that when I'm up there, I gotta move to the music and give it back to the people there. This music gives me chills. There's this incredible feeling and affect it gives you. The music moves me, and it's how I want to engage the crowd as the lead singer. It involves performance, movement, eye contact, singing to people, feeling it. It's also about a shared experience with the fans in the crowd, an exchanged between singer/performer and the audience/fans. It's not my music, I'm not giving away my product, but we're giving you a shared, collective experience of this music that we have a real love for.'

On the band's favorite songs:

'We have about sixty Moz and Smiths songs in our repertoire, and we try

Figure 2. Strangeways Tribute. L–R: John Arrieta (guitar), Ralph Paredes (guitar), Julian Ricardo (voice); Raul 'Rawl' Paredes (bass); and Jorge Arroyo (drums). Photo by María Vásquez, courtesy of Strangeways band. Used with permission.

to play the songs as they're recorded. Our strength as a band is playing the Smiths songs, the more rock'n'roll ones like Bigmouth, versus the ballads and slower songs, whether Smiths or Moz. We like to rock out and usually assemble an upbeat, up-tempo set list. We find that our rock'n'roll versions of Smiths songs go over well; the live energy of the songs get us all going. Jorge on drums is a powerhouse! How can you not feel it? That's the magic of the original Smiths songs.'

On playing the 2016 Smiths Morrissey Convention in Hollywood, California:

(Ralph and Julian): 'One of the goals for the band was to get to the Convention. It's something every Moz Smiths tribute wants to do. Who wouldn't want to play on that stage at that marquee fan event, that historic venue? We knew Ray from Chaos Records (one of the Convention's organizers) since high school. Back in October 2015, Ray asked the band if we'd play at the Convention in April. Yes! It was always a goal of ours. We knew what a big show it would be, definitely our biggest one to date. We'd be playing for hundreds of die hard Moz Smiths fans who were there specifically because they're fans. This was the Convention! This wasn't a gig in an 80s club. We knew there'd be people there wondering who we were, asking "who are these guys, why are there here, do they deserve to be here?" We put in many extra hours for rehearsal. We had to step up our game. Just being there and doing the Convention show was exciting. There was even a green room! The energy from everyone got us going. We got great feedback after the convention, and we're getting ready to do our next show at Rock It! in Pomona. But that Convention show was definitely a high point for us.'

On the next generation of fans:

[*From guitarist John:*] 'A lot of our audience is a little younger. What I'll say about the tribute band is that a big part of what we get to do is introduce the new generation to this music. We keep the music of the Smiths alive for all the fans who come to see us, but to introduce it to new or younger fans, to give them the experience of hearing these songs live, maybe for the first time, is a great honor and responsibility.'

MALADJUSTED, A SINCERE AND HUMBLE TRIBUTE TO THE MUSIC OF MORRISSEY AND THE SMITHS: Maladjusted call themselves 'a sincere and humble tribute to the music of Morrissey and the Smiths.' They formed in 2012 from the remnants of two other Los Angeles area bands: the short-lived all-Morrissey solo tribute outfit called Kill Uncle, and the on-again, mostly off-again Louder Than Bombs. After some personnel changes, members of Kill Uncle would disband and form yet another band in 2012, Nowhere Fast, while the singer of Kill Uncle, Edgar Zermeno, would team up with Chuy Michel, the guitarist from

Louder Than Bombs: add Chuy's younger brother, Ivann Michel on drums, and a childhood friend, Willie Castillo on bass, and Maladjusted is born in the southeast Los Angeles city of South Gate.

The first time I saw Maladjusted, it was unintentional. I was at the 2013 Smiths Morrissey Convention in Hollywood, and I went with the intention of seeing These Charming Men, the Smiths Morrissey tribute band all the way from Dublin, Ireland. The very special guest on the bill that night was Spencer Cobrin, former drummer in Morrissey's 1990s-era band. I also saw the name 'Maladjusted' on the bill, though at that point, I had never heard of them. Was this another tribute band, maybe an all-Morrissey solo act? Were they from LA or somewhere else? I ventured to think they must be pretty good to be playing at the Convention, a yearly event that tends to book the best Smiths Morrissey tribute bands from all over.

I thought These Charming Men were great, so much that at the end of their set, I made my way to the stage to run on and hug their 'Morrissey' front man, Dave. These Charming Men finished their set, the raucous crowd delirious with having seen a band from Morrissey Smiths ancestral lands. Whoever this next band was, whoever had to follow *that* act from These Charming Men from Dublin, had better be good.

When Maladjusted took the stage, the first thing I noticed was their all-Latino lineup. A few songs in, Spencer Cobrin took over the drums for three songs to wild cheers and applause. His thunderous and expert drum playing immediately elevated the sound of the band. There was an original Moz solo band mate up there, playing drums, with that band! By the end of the set, I was a full-fledged fan. Maladjusted's performance blew me away, and not just because Spencer from Moz's old band joined them. Who were they? Where did they come from? Many months later, I would find out that this Convention gig was only Maladjusted's second live show. Ever. For a band this new to play the Smiths Moz Convention, the largest and most high-profile annual fan event in LA, was pretty big. Many tribute bands never make it to Moz Con, never even get asked.

Soon after, I began to look for announcements and fliers for Maladjusted's next performance. I was drawn to them for their attention to Morrissey's solo music, starting with the name of the band, the only one around with a Morrissey-specific name. They played Moz songs that not a lot of the other bands did, and the singer was effective at evoking the masculine subtlety, the style, of mid- to late-career Morrissey. Edgar Zermeno's Morrissey is not the frenetic flower-wielding frontman of the Smiths. It was a nice change for me.

Since that epic convention performance, I saw Maladjusted several more times at venues ranging from the Museum of Latin American Art in Long Beach to my local hometown nightclub, Sage Lounge in Uptown Whittier. I got to know some of the members of Maladjusted the same way I met and got acquainted with members of the other tribute bands featured here: by approaching them after their gig, introducing myself as a fan and researcher, and thanking them for a wonderful night of live Smiths Morrissey songs. However, Maladjusted was the first band I got to see during rehearsals, and doing so gave me a unique insight into how they prepare for gigs and their strategies for pleasing the audience.

I joined Maladjusted during rehearsals one night in September 2015 as they prepared for an upcoming gig. In November 2015, I sat down with singer Edgar, a US Marine and cross-country big rig driver, to further discuss his band and its genesis. During this conversation, Edgar shared some of his methods and strategies for learning the songs and fronting the band, as well as some highs (performing with Boz Boorer in Las Vegas and Spencer Cobrin at the MozCon) and lows (finicky audiences and bar owner/club promoter politics) of being one of many Moz Smiths bands in the area. I have culled together the following highlights from my conversations with the band and Edgar from September through November 2015.

On Malajusted's background:

All of the band members hail from traditionally working class, Mexican immigrant neighborhoods across south- and northeastern Los Angeles, such as Huntington Park, Lincoln Heights, and Pico Rivera. Sixteen years separate the eldest band member from the youngest. Each of the members brings a deeply personal connection to the music to their performances with the band. Lead guitarist Chuy Michel is a prolific guitarist who plays in his original band, Pastilla, and occasionally with the San Francisco Smiths Moz tribute, This Charming Band. Chuy's skills are in high demand when other bands need a fill-in guitarist, but Maladjusted is his band and Johnny Marr his man. Maladjusted's star lead guitarist once held his own next to Boz Boorer when Morrissey's main man and long time musical director joined the tribute band on stage at a gig in Las Vegas. When he is not busy playing guitar for a living, Chuy records other bands in his state of the art home studio. He and his brother Ivann play in The Furs, a tribute to the Psychedelic Furs, while Edgar sings in an eighties cover band called The Walkmans with members of Sheilas Take A Bow.

On the band's unorthodox rehearsal methods:

Maladjusted prepares for gigs not by having a prepared set list of songs, but by calling out random Morrissey and Smiths songs as they go. As Edgar tells me, 'We usually come into the gig with a set list, but we are also prepared to mix it up, go with what we're feeling, what the audience is into or not. We make a lot of on the spot decisions about what we play.' Such a strategy keeps the band members on their toes and keeps the crowd happy. Granted, a band can only do this if each member is confident, skilled, and well-practiced. It also needs to have a significant amount of songs under their collective belt, ready to go at any time.

Part of Maladjusted's strategy is to always open with popular songs, the big hits like Suedehead, Irish Blood English Heart, This Charming Man, sometimes First Of The Gang. 'Then,' says Edgar, 'we feel it out. We might play some of the B-sides, deeper cuts like Seasick, Yet Still Docked or Life Is A Pigsty. But mostly we go with what the audience wants, what they're feeling,' explains the singer. With over one hundred Smiths and Moz songs (and counting) in their repertoire, a talented guitarist like Chuy ('he can play anything, and he plays every note,' marvel his bandmates), and superfans like Ivann and Willie in the rhythm section

Figure 3. Members of Maladjusted have fun on stage at Sage Lounge in Uptown Whittier, March 2016. Photo by the author.

who know the music and can pick it up quickly, Maladjusted can adjust well to their audience's desires, while playing songs that the band members themselves love.

On how singer Edgar prepares for a gig:

To prepare for his role as singer of a Morrissey Smiths tribute band, Edgar studies Morrissey. The Maladjusted singer watches lots of live performance clips of Morrissey, listens carefully to each song, absorbs the nuances of the vocal deliveries. He does his homework. Says Edgar, 'I study him, I pay close attention to what Morrissey does during songs, his gestures, actions, certain things he does for certain songs. It takes more than getting a little fade, pompadour, waving dead flowers around on stage. I think of dress, costumes, even if I have to make my own shirt or piece. I gotta sell it. And it's also an outlet for me because I love the music. I feel the song. If you're not having fun in the audience, then I'm not doing my job.'[76] Later, I think of what Edgar said here as I read the following from Georgina Gregory's *Send in the Clones*, in which she describes the 'dramaturgic challenge' in playing Morrissey: 'This is because playing Morrissey requires a respectful and sensitive approach, where care must be exercised to avoid falling into the trap of lampooning or parody.' Edgar takes to heart this 'dramaturgic challenge' of giving us a heartfelt and sincere Morrisseyesque performance each time he takes the stage with Maladjusted.

On the Mexican connection to Morrissey:

'The white people love the Smiths, and all the Mexicans want to hear the Morrissey stuff.' At the rehearsal I sat in, Edgar half-jokingly made this remark, and at least three other Maladjusted members chuckled in agreement. While this comment is a generalization that risks oversimplifying fans' race-based preferences, if they even exist, I couldn't help but nod in some kind of affirmation that yes, it's probably true what they say, 'Mexicans love Morrissey,' because one rarely hears it the other way: we never see the headline, 'Mexicans love the Smiths.' Just Morrissey. And yet, from their gigs in Las Vegas, Salt Lake City and all over Los Angeles, Maladjusted has also found some truth in that statement—we can look to the Mexican all-star tribute outfit, Mexrrissey, for some confirmation of this fact: their debut album, *¡No Manchester! Mexico Goes Morrissey*, is a collection of Mexified solo Morrissey songs, none from the Smiths.[77]

On their own fandom:

'We are fans first,' say members of Maladjusted. They listen to plenty of other bands, singers, and genres of music: Edgar favors Mexican crooner and icon, Luis Miguel, while Chuy loves Pink Floyd. Maladjusted's members all grew up in the LA area on a healthy mix of alternative rock en español and US/UK rock from the 1970s and 1980s. Bands like Depeche Mode, Psychedelic Furs, and Café Tacuba are all-around favorites. But Smiths and Morrissey top the list, as they must. Each band member expresses their fandom in their own personal ways. Edgar prefers the slow, dramatic ballads of Morrissey's solo years; Life Is A Pigsty is a personal favorite. Chuy, a serious guitarist, admires Johnny Marr and relishes playing Bigmouth Strikes Again. My favorite comment came from bassist Willie Castillo, whose first language was Spanish. 'I learned English listening to the Smiths and Morrissey. I love them!'

EL MARIACHI MANCHESTER: Morrissey and mariachis go way back in Chicano/a and Mexican Mozlandia imaginings. For years at Cinco de Mayo and el Día de los Muertos events around Los Angeles, vendors have sold T-shirts, posters, and other folk-art fan-made objects with graphic designs of Morrissey represented as a mariachi. There's Morrissey in a photo-shopped mariachi sombrero on a promotional flier for a 'Cinco de Moz' party. There's Morrissey represented as Vicente 'Chente' Hernández himself, tall, manly, and sharp-looking in his full *traje de charro*, or 'Mexican cowboy suit.' Mexicans and non-Mexicans alike have an easy time imagining the strapping, handsome singer from Manchester as a charro-suited crooner of the musical style most synonymous with Mexico: see the band Mexrrissey, who perform wearing mariachi style charro pants, or the back cover of this book, illustrated by an artist from Manchester who has never been to Mexico or Los Angeles.

Many of us Moz fans around LA are used to seeing the image of Mariachi Moz on T-shirts, fliers, posters for sale online, at swap meets, and specialty Chicana/o-Mexican boutiques; many of us own some of these items, wear them with pride, display them in our offices or bedrooms, post them to our online profiles. If we can see Morrissey as a Mexican Mariachi, and we also hear the Mexican in Morrissey's music: we hear the corridor, ranchero, cumbia, the mariachi ballad in songs like First Of The Gang To Die, Everyday Is Like Sunday, and This Charming Man. It was only a matter of time before someone, inevitably, would bring Morrissey Smiths songs to life, mariachi style. It happened in East Los Angeles in 2014, when a group of Mexican musicians living in Los Angeles—a Tejano (Texas-born Mexican), an East LA Chicana, a Mexican born in DF (Distrito Federal, the capital city of Mexico), a 'Mexican Johnny Marr' born in South Gate, and a Chicano from California's Central Valley—formed El Mariachi Manchester.

El Mariachi Manchester represents a new kind of tribute band that is rooted in older traditions. The ensemble grew from collaborations among alternative Latino/a musicians, music teachers, and college professors who are part of vibrant music and cultural scenes across Los Angeles, Texas, Mexico, New York and Washington, DC. Vocalist Moises Baquiero joined forces with UCLA ethnomusicologist, Alexandro D. Hernández-Gutiérrez, on vihuela (a small guitar-like instrument); USC jazz graduate and multi-instrumentalist, Gloria Estrada, on bajo sexto (bass guitar); UCLA mariachi member and high school music teacher, Miguel Pasillas, on trumpet; and guitarist extraordinaire, Chuy Michel, on acoustic guitar. (Fig. 4) Together, they form the world's first and only mariachi tribute to Morrissey and the Smiths.

The band explains the genesis of the group in the following bio, taken from El Mariachi Manchester's website. They write,

> Mariachi Manchester represents the nexus of Moz Angeles and the ever-adapting mariachi tradition in Los Angeles. Mariachi Manchester croons like the Mozzer in union with Juan Gabriel or Pedro Infante. They are at times playful in their reinterpretation of the Smiths/Morrissey and mariachi, but grounded in a serious foundation of both branches. Their mash-ups of Smiths/Morrissey songs with mariachi sones and rancheras display how relatable the emotion, themes, and sounds of these musics truly are. ¡Ajúassey!'

In this way, El Mariachi Manchester constitutes a tribute band, though not in the typical style of one. They do not play the songs as originally recorded by Morrissey Smiths, nor do they sound or look like the originals in ways that other 'proper' tribute bands aim to do. Rather, El Mariachi Manchester reinterprets, reimagines, and rearranges Smiths Morrissey songs as mariachi 'mash-ups,' playing them as Mexican-style favorites while maintaining the structure and melody of the original songs. And in doing so, they simultaneously reimagine mariachi music, an adaptable musical form that represents an amalgam of styles: El Mariachi Manchester takes the rural form of nineteenth century Mexican music and transposes it to perform songs from the urban landscape of twentieth century Manchester. The results are an unmistakable borderland expression of Los Angeles Mexican meets Manchester North England/Irish cultural hybridity, the songs of the Smiths and Morrissey giftwrapped in mariachi strings, trumpets, and trajes de charro.

I attended El Mariachi Manchester's debut show, held in December 2014 at La Cita Bar in Downtown LA. The roomy bar was packed with many familiar faces from the Moz fan scene around LA. Many of us had seen the other tribute bands many times, but there was something anticipatory about waiting for these mariachis to take the stage and play these songs. This was new, different, and definitely something we haven't seen in LA, and yet, totally expected: many of us have waited for a mariachi style Morrissey Smiths band to come out because it just seemed like a natural next step in Moz Angeles.

It was an unforgettable debut gig. People sang along to practically every song. Happy tears streamed down my face as I locked arms with the people next to me to sing and sway along to El Mariachi Manchester's renditions of First Of The Gang and many others in the Moz Smiths canon. We let out Mexican-style gritos (cries or yelps of excitement and joy during songs or other celebratory moments) that punctuated each song's end, or sometimes we'd let one out—ay-ay-ay!—in the middle of a song during an interlude. The mariachi experience elicits this kind of participation, especially at an LA Mexican bar like La Cita, where mariachis and modern rock commingle and clash. We smiled, danced, and sang along in an outpouring of emotion, while El Mariachi Manchester

Figure 4. El Mariachi Manchester. L-R: Miguelessey (Miguel Pasillas); Gloriassey (Gloria Estrada); Alexandrossey (Alexandro D. Hernández-Gutiérrez), Moisessey (Moises Baqueiro); Chuyssey (Chuy Michel). Photo by Erika Michel. Flier design by Gloria Estrada, April 2015. Image appears courtesy of El Mariachi Manchester.
Used with permission.

played on, their musical renditions simultaneously reminding us of our grandparents' music and 'our' music: we grew up with both.

They were a hit before they even began.

Since then, El Mariachi Manchester's profile has risen quickly. They have performed at marquee events in Los Angeles, such as the 2015 LA Day of the Dead celebration at Hollywood Forever Cemetery headlined by Mexican songstress Lila Downs and others, while headlining their own shows at venues like The Globe. El Mariachi Manchester has also attracted publicity and press coverage in media outlets like *NPR*, *The Huffington Post*, *Pocho.com*, *Latino Rebels*, and *AJ+*. They are currently at work recording their first album of mariachi-esque Moz Smiths songs. I sat down with 'Alexandrossey,' 'Moisessey,' and 'Gloriassey'[78] to discuss the cinematic history of modern mariachi music, Smiths and Morrissey fandom in Mexico and the US, and the 'natural' fit of Moz Smiths songs with mariachi classics.

On how Mariachi Manchester formed:

[*Moises:*] 'I was born and raised in DF, Mexico City. When I was twenty-five, I moved to the US with no intention of becoming a musician, but I found myself in the rock en español scene in LA. This was in 1995. There was also a lot of British music, the kind my older brother liked growing up in DF. The Smiths' music attracted me. It was dramatic, melancholic, and I liked the chord progressions. I started writing music when I got to LA. Then I joined Los Abandoned (an alternative bilingual rock band from Los Angeles) in the early 2000s. I played bass guitar. I can say that Mariachi Manchester came out of Los Abandoned. We had a song that sounded like Everyday Is Like Sunday, and from there, we thought oh, let's do an all mariachi Morrissey band. My ex-wife always wanted to hear the Morrrissey song, I Know It's Gonna Happen Some Day, as a mariachi song, and we thought, why not? Then Los Abandoned broke up around 2007, but the mariachi Morrissey idea was still there. It was timing, really. I met Alexandro and Miguel, our trumpet player, who had no idea who Morrissey was! He never heard of it. Gloria is the fan. She's the one who pushed it, to do the band. The timing for all of us to come together was finally right, so in 2014, Mariachi Manchester was established.'

On the origins of modern mariachi music:

[*Alexandro:*] 'Mariache music, with an e, is peasant music. Before the 1930s, it was associated with rural, indigenous, and African musical traditions throughout parts of Mexico. Mariache basically was a fandango, a gathering of musicians playing traditional son forms. Then in the 1930s through the 1950s, the Mexican film industry gave us the mariachi as it's popularly known now. Those films were part of the época de oro, or Golden Age, of Mexican cinema. That's where you see the trajo de charro costumes, the big hats, the horns and other markers of the modern mariachi look and sound. From around the 1940s and onward, we see the mariachi as a national symbol of Mexico. This way of imagining the music, the image of the mariachi cowboy in full traje de charro—which was the uniform of the landed classes—was about raising the class image of this music and those who performed it. Mariachis and mariachi music in this period was a romantic image of Mexico, and also about urbanizing, or bringing rural music to DF, making this kind of music suitable for the urban audiences. The mariachi had to look and sound more formal than its rural, fandango origins. This music was in the communities before it was on stage. The emphasis on the singer and the ensemble also comes out during these Golden Age movies to show Mexico as a unified nation with a national identity; the "Mexicanness" is highly regarded during the época de oro. You get the mariachi and Mexican crooner figures around this time, which was a construct of the Mexican music industry. The ballet folklorico, the featured lead singer, were all put together for show purposes. The mariachi becomes commodified. The pop idols come out of the innovations made during this period. Luis Miguel, Juan Gabriel, Chente. They are products of the recording industry. Of course, Morrissey fits into that tradition.'

On Morrissey Smiths and mariachi music in LA:

[*Gloria:*] 'Music is a documentation of what's happening. Around LA, mariachi music is part of the culture and scene, in restaurants especially, at parties. I immediately think of the Irish pub and Mexican cantina connection, the connection through social class. And mariachis play everything. That's their job. They play everything, even pop. They're human jukeboxes. So it's not an abnormal concept for us to play Smiths and Morrissey songs, especially here in LA. I grew up in Boyle Heights, and mariachis were all around me. It's the epicenter of mariachi music. And at Roosevelt High School, where I went, people loved Smiths and Morrissey. To me, the fusion of mariachis and Morrissey made sense. It took me back because playing the music is more about the feeling and less about the musical aspect. The emotion of both mariachi and Morrissey Smiths music—the words, phrases, lyrics all resonate deeply. It's a nostalgia project for me.'

On adapting Smiths Morrissey songs into mariachi music:

[*Alexandro and Moises:*] 'We maintain the song's structure and melody. We don't change it, so when we start to play a song like Ask or Girlfriend In A Coma, you'll recognize it right away. We sing all the songs in English, and we keep all the original lyrics, except in Panic, where we change the lyric to "Panic on the calles del Cabo," panic on the streets of Cabo. That panic is different, you know, like deportation, the panic of being without papers. Different from the panic Morrissey sings about, but yet it fits.

For us, doing the songs are about translations and transculturalism. We like to blend some of the songs, fit one inside the other. For example, when we do First Of The Gang, it begins with Miguel on trumpet playing those opening notes. It sounds beautiful. Then somewhere in the middle of the song, after a couple of verses, we will go into La Negra, a classic mariachi song that features a similar trumpet melody line. We play a verse or two of La Negra before returning to First Of The Gang. We do the same with Ask and Please Please Please Let Me Get What I Want. When we do those famous traditional mariachi songs within a Smiths or Morrissey song, people go nuts. They sing it all. There's something very comforting about it all.'

SHEILAS TAKE A BOW: AN ♀DE TO MORRISSEY AND THE SMITHS:

> It's good to hear a woman's voice singing these songs.
>> Latina student at California State University,
>> San Bernardino 'Manifesta' event[79]

> Sorry, boys. You've monopolized the tribute band scene for too long.
>> Monica Hidalgo, bassist of
>> Sheilas Take A Bow, in *L.A. Weekly*[80]

Shakespeare's Sisters? Pretty Petty Thieves? Queen is Dead? International Playgirls? What would an all-woman/all-gurl[81] Morrissey Smiths tribute band be called? Like all good Moz Smiths tribute band names, the name would be a direct reference to a song, album, a spin on a recognizable title. Most importantly, we wanted people to know we were an 'all-girl' band by our name. It was the primary way we would distinguish ourselves from all the dude bands.

Before I go any further, full disclosure: I am the singer in Sheilas Take A Bow, the first and at this point, the only all-woman tribute to Morrissey and the Smiths. I was a little shy to include my band here; I was afraid it would come off as self-interested, self-promoting, self-indulgent, just bad form to write about the band that I sing with in my own book. Compared to the other tribute bands here, we haven't even been around that long. But then my publisher encouraged me, convinced me that I *had* to write about Sheilas Take A Bow in this chapter. We are just as much a part of this story as the others. I thought about it and realized that even if I was not in this band, if my sisters were not in this band, I would still most certainly include the 'all-girl' Moz Smiths tribute band in this chapter. I just happen to have co-founded this one.

We began not so innocently enough. My sister Monica and I grew tired of all the manspreading we'd encounter in the Moz Smiths fan scenes around LA, particularly where tribute bands, live performance, and karaoke were involved. A lot of dudes taking up space, and a few women, too, but not in the same ways. The dudes were the ones putting their names all over the MorrisseyOke sign-up sheets to sing multiple times; the dudes were the ones forming the tribute bands. Where were the women up there, playing instruments, rocking these songs, holding space for the fans with two X chromosomes? My sister and I wanted to see something we haven't seen yet: we wanted to see women up there playing those songs that we love, too. Why not us?

The idea of starting an all-grrrl Moz Smiths tribute band had been brewing in our collective minds for a while. Both my sisters and I have always been inspired by other women who cover all-guy bands, like the venerable Iron Maidens and the Bitchfits. Plus, we all loved Morrissey and the Smiths since I practically converted them back in the 1990s: I was seventeen, Melinda was fifteen, and Monica almost eight. Formative years. The best part is that both my sisters were already musically trained, and Monica already had years of experience playing in bands and navigating the local scene's politics of getting gigs and playing shows. I never had any musical lessons or training whatsoever, but the three of us figured that my longtime Morrissey fandom, my deep love of his songs—they've been in my bones for over twenty years—and my hammy karaoke persona could somehow translate and be enough to front a tribute band. (Not necessarily, as I found out.)

At first, I did harbor some doubts about jumping into the crowded LA Moz Smiths tribute band scene. Did we really want to enter the fray? We weren't so sure, either, that the world—that Los Angeles—needed another Morrissey Smiths band. But Monica and I kept thinking, we could do this. We should do this. We have all the essential components: fandom, musical skill, connections to the scene, *ganas*. So one day in February 2014, a few days shy of my fortieth birthday, Monica and I decided to play through some songs, test the waters. Ask, The Last Of The Famous International Playboys, Panic, Shoplifters Of The World Unite And Take Over, First Of The Gang To Die. It was shaky, but it was a start. That night at Monica's house, we took the first steps to forming Sheilas Take A Bow, An Ode to Morrissey and the Smiths. Monica would play bass, I would sing, and we would recruit Melinda, our other sister, to play keys. We just needed a guitarist and a drummer, and surely in Los Angeles, we could find a female drummer and guitarist who were Moz Smiths fans enough to consider joining a tribute band.

From that first foray in February, it took us until September, October of 2014 to complete our band. First, we found Melody 'Mellowdee' Moran, our rhythm guitarist, who was a colleague of Monica's husband, and Mellowdee soon after found our drummer, Toni Santoyo. The Sheilas were complete, and after about three months of playing together and learning enough songs for a short set, we were ready to make our mark on the Moz Angeles tribute band circuit. We played our first gig at Sage in Uptown Whittier in January 2015. A few months later, Liz Gómez would join us on lead guitar. Since May 2015, Sheilas Take A Bow have performed at clubs, college campuses, and bars around Los Angeles and Orange County with 'Toni the Poni' on drums, 'Moni Rourke' on bass, 'Mindy Keys' on keyboards and rhythm guitar, 'Lizzy Marr' on lead guitar, and 'Méllissey' on vocals. (Fig. 5)

The following comments are taken from an interview with members of Sheilas Take A Bow for a forthcoming fanzine.

*On the starting the first all-female tribute to the Smiths
and Morrissey:*

[*Moni:*] We all love the music so much. Our love for the music is first. Secondly, we wanted to represent and claim space within the Moz scene for women, as musicians and fans of the music. We also wanted to show that women can do it too, and even better than some of the guy tribute bands. We work hard to play the music as the fans want to hear it, while also giving our own interpretation of it since we are not men. We definitely pride ourselves on being the best musicians we can be and respecting the integrity of the music. We also feel that we make each other better musicians, and playing these songs makes us better musicians.

*On calling themselves 'An Ode to Morrissey and the
Smiths':*

[*Méllissey:*] An ode is a lyrical poem that is usually addressed to someone or about something in particular, and an ode is meant to be sung. I also like 'ode' as another way to say 'tribute.' I knew going into it that if I was going to be the singer, I was never going to sound and look like Morrissey in the way that guy singers can, just on the basis of biology. I can't sound or sing like him, but I can sing *to* him, *with* him, sing to other fans, sing his songs like the poems they are. So 'ode' here is very apt. It became our way of naming the kind of tribute we would offer as female-bodied musicians up there performing these songs. Plus, I liked that we could make the 'O' in 'ode' to look like the female symbol ♀ if we wanted.

On how the band chooses songs:

Figure 5. The mujeres de Sheilas Take A Bow, An ♀de to Morrissey and the Smiths. L–R standing: Monica 'Moni Rourke' Hidalgo (bass); Toni 'the Poni' Santoyo (drums); Liz 'Lizzy Marr' Gómez (guitar); Melinda 'Mindy Keys' Hidalgo Carrillo (keyboards, rhythm guitar); crouching: Your Author, Melissa 'Méllissey' Hidalgo (vocals). Flier by Clover Dean for Sheilas Take A Bow. Used with permission.

[*Mindy, Liz:*] We usually have Mel tell us what songs she feels comfortable singing. A lot of the songs are too low for her, so she'll either pick songs she can do in that same register that Morrissey sings in, like Piccadilly Palare and Interesting Drug. She's taking vocal lessons and she's improving, so that also gives us a wider range of songs to pick from. Once in a while, if it's a song we all want to do but that may be too low for her, then we work on changing the key, moving it up a step so Mel can reach the notes. We've done that for Hector (First Of The Gang To Die) and Sunday. But everyone has their favorites. Liz likes to do a lot of Smiths songs, and Monica and I like a lot of the rockabilly or early Morrissey solo songs from Kill Uncle or Your Arsenal. Toni loves the songs from Bona Drag. We all love to hear her play The Queen Is Dead. She nails it every time! We also have to be aware that people want to hear the popular songs, but we also want to play songs that not a lot of the other tribute bands play, like Staircase At The University. So we try to balance it. We always play our theme song, Sheila Take A Bow.

On being women musicians today:

[*The band:*] For all of us, this is an opportunity for us to live our passion and to contribute to the scene. Although we all came to music in different ways, this experience has been awesome and it has shown us that it is important for us to take time for ourselves to do what we love to do. In terms of being women musicians in the Morrissey/Smiths scene in LA, it has been challenging. We feel that the scene has been good to us, and we have met a lot of good people who love Morrissey and the Smiths as much as we do. A lot of the guys in the other bands have been really helpful and supportive of us. However, we know the bad part is that most of the time, we are looked at more critically than our male counterparts. It seems that many people dismiss us before actually listening to us play because we are female. Or, people will say they don't need to come out and see us again because they've "already seen the all-girl band." Well, how many times have those same people seen the guy bands? No one thinks twice about going to see one of the other all-guy bands again and again. It's a reflection of the larger societal attitude, the sexism. As women, we feel that we have to work that much harder to be accepted and respected as one of the many tribute bands here in LA, like everywhere else.

The Roar From the Stalls: Concluding Thoughts

These Handsome Devils. Maladjusted. Strangeways. Mariachi Manchester. Sheilas Take A Bow. The bands' stories speak for themselves. They provide clear portals into the diverse, eclectic, international, intergenerational, and very personal dimensions of Moz Smiths fandom as embodied and expressed in the US-Mexican borderlands. But most importantly, all of these bands, like so many others from Sweet and Tender Hooligans to Still Ill, This Charming Band to These Charming Men, give the gift of the tribute in their own ways. At their very best, these bands are as much a tribute to the music of Morrissey and the Smiths as they are to the fans: gifts of memory, experience, and live performance that transport us to a time when we were there, watching the Real Thing, or at least helping us to experience what it could have been like to see the Smiths, to remind us why we keep going to see Morrissey.

I'll never forget the first time I saw Sweet and Tender Hooligans. It was March 2009. I never saw the Smiths in concert, and at that point, I had seen Morrissey in concert a mere three times (well, two and a half: my first Moz show was in 1991 at UCLA, aborted after barely two and a half songs. Melee ensued.) When the Hooligans burst onto the stage at the now-defunct Detroit Bar in Costa Mesa, they gave me chills. I closed my eyes and thought, *this is what it must have been like to see the Smiths*. It was as close as I and everyone else there were going to get to watching the Smiths; it was as exciting as watching Morrissey himself. And therein lies the main contribution of tribute bands to any fan scene: they want to deliver a live performance experience that's as close to the real thing as possible, pleasing casual and committed fans alike. Or, as in the case of Mariachi Manchester or Sheilas Take A Bow, bands who do not aim to reproduce a facsimile of the Smiths or Morrissey but who do offer unique, culturally informed interpretations of the songs, they give the audience new ways to hear, listen to, and imagine these familiar songs.

Most tribute band members would agree that it is a pleasure and privilege to play the music of the Smiths and Morrissey for other fans. That's not to say that ego does not get in the way some times. I've seen more than my share of tribute band performances that were ruined by wasted, overconfident singers or noodling, show-off lead guitarists who sank an otherwise very good show, or who ruined what otherwise could have been a sincere and selfless tribute to Morrissey Smiths had it not been for the distraction of egos. And every tribute band, no matter how seasoned or how long they've been at it, makes mistakes. Someone misses a note, someone else misses a cue, and the singer sometimes messes up the lyrics. It's part of the pressure and reality of live performance, of having to live up to the Real Thing of Morrissey and The Smiths when a bunch of fans are watching you, expecting perfection. As they should. Still, tribute bands make mistakes sometimes. We sometimes get too self-involved and forget about connecting with the audience. And other times, we could sound spectacular. On the best of nights, we are at one with the audience; we sound like Morrissey and his band if you close your eyes. Because at the end of the day, a tribute band is ruled by the music, the music that keeps bringing fans back for more, the thing that's bigger than all of us: Morrissey and the Smiths. Otherwise, why do it?

When undertaken with respect, commitment, and sincerity, tribute bands are a labor of love for everyone involved. Tribute band members are everyday amateur, semipro and in some cases, professional musicians, many with day jobs, families, partners, children, and other responsibilities to the community. Those of us who play in these bands are driven by many things, but always by our collective love of the music, by our deep and personal love for and connection to the Moz Smiths songs we play for others. For the sake of fandom, community, history, desire, love, and pure joy that comes with playing beloved songs for an audience of kindred spirits: this is why so many of us here form and join tribute bands. This is why we spend time, money, resources and energy to locate and assemble band members who, once committed, must then be willing to spend their own time, money, resources and energy to buy gear, drive to rehearsals, book and promote shows, design and sell merchandise, run social media sites. This is why we pay tribute at all.

The idea of tribute bands at all puzzles a lot of people. Such inquiring minds wonder, if you're gonna go through all that trouble to be in a band, why not play your own, original music? Why spend all that time rehearsing and practicing just to play someone else's songs? Well, mariachis do it all the time, and people love mariachis. Every Morrissey Smiths tribute band I have seen and spoken to boasts at least one member who plays original music in another band. Every band profiled here has members who have formed original bands, who tour in other original bands, who write original music. I think of Maladjusted's talented lead guitarist, Chuy Michel, an acclaimed Latin Alternative guitarist who plays original music with bands like Pastilla and Vampiro of Jaguares fame—the same Jaguares band that Morrissey supported in 2002. I think of everyone in Mariachi Manchester: Alexandro's 'day job' is playing guitar for ¡Aparato! when he's not teaching classes as a music professor at UCLA, while Gloria plays guitar and accordion with touring bands like Viento Callajero and Las Cafeteras. I think of my own sister, Monica, who rocked the keys for the alt-Latino band, Beatmo, and played bass for the lesser-know Latino garage punk/rock band, Tamales Fatales. And I think of our own Sheilas drummer and lead guitarist, Toni and Liz, who play in their original band, Exit Module. The list goes on and on. So who's to say that tribute band musicians do not play their own original music when they're not giving the ultimate gift of the tribute to the artists we love?

In Los Angeles, tribute bands (along with DJs and club promoters) are the tent poles that hold up the vast landscape of Morrissey Smiths fan scenes.[82] Moz Smiths tribute acts headline a variety of events, whether eighties new wave or Moz dance parties, rockabilly or rock en español nights, Cinco de Mayo or el Día de los Muertos. More generally, tribute bands invigorate local live music scenes, and in doing so they practice the preservation of musical histories and eras. Likening tribute bands to 'musicians who specialize in the historically-informed performance of Western classical music,' ethnomusicologist John Paul Meyers writes, 'Performing in a tribute band is an act based on having a sense of historical consciousness, on an idea that the music of the past is historically important enough to play again.'[83] Historical consciousness relates to memory and nostalgia, especially when considering that many of the first tribute bands formed after the original bands broke up or when a popular performer passed on. Take tribute performers who bring back to life dead music legends like Elvis Presley, Freddie Mercury, and Selena—my heart now drops at having to add David Bowie, Prince, and Juan Gabriel to this list. Like historical reenactments, these tribute bands mark a specific moment in time through recreating significant pop and rock music acts of the past. In these ways, tribute acts can be especially exciting for those fans who never had a chance to see the real thing perform.

And at the end of the day, that is the big point of the tribute band: to remind audiences of the original music, to recreate the memories for those who were old enough to 'be there,' to introduce this music to new generations of audiences. As long as there is audience demand for the music of the past—whether out of nostalgia, memory, fandom, desire for collective belonging—there will be tribute bands who will be there to play it. Life the gift-giver to the recipient, one can't exist without the other.

CHAPTER FOUR

Our Weekly Appointment
Breakfast with the Smiths, The World of Morrissey on Indie 103.1

CALLER: *"What up José, this is Angel calling from El Paso Texas and I wanna hear There Is A Light That Never Goes Out by the Smiths. Thank you, homes. Good show, I listen all the time."*

CALLER: *"Hullo, José, this is Colin calling from Bristol, in England, and I'd love to hear any song that Morrissey covers. Thank you."*

CALLER: *"Hi José, this is Jessica from El Monte, I met you this weekend at Moz Disco, it was so much fun! Anyways I'm calling to request Kiss Me A Lot and I wanna send it out to my husband Carlos, 'cuz it's our anniversary this week. We love your show, thank you!"*[84]

IT IS A TYPICAL WEDNESDAY MORNING, BREAKFAST time on the West Coast. I'm in my kitchen making coffee, scrambling eggs, putting away last night's dishes. No alarm clock, no campus commitments, no morning drive in traffic, just an easy Wednesday morning in Whittier before my writing day begins. The eastern sun rises and floods my kitchen with bright light, forcing my eyes open. I tap the Indie 103.1 app on my iDevice and wait for the sluggish wifi connection to wake up. It buffers just in time to hear José's[85] voice through the

123

tinny speakers: 'If you have stumbled across our little corner of the interwebs, you have found the only radio show that plays two full hours of nothing but music from Morrissey and the Smiths. Hello everyone, all you Breakfast Champions out there, welcome to *Breakfast with the Smiths, the World of Morrissey*. I am your host, José Maldonado, coming to you on Indie 1-0-3-1 in the heart of the Miracle Mile district of Los Angeles, California, as we do each and every week at this time for our weekly appointment, playing your requests of the songs that make you smile, the songs that make you cry, and the songs that make you dance your legs down to the knees.'

As the opening set of songs play, I imagine my fellow Breakfast Champions and think about who is listening and from where. It's noon in Boston, so the Battis sisters are likely lunching with the Smiths. Maybe Andrea, the English teacher in Tustin, is listening to the show with her second period sophomores. Donna Bishop in Manchester is probably stuck in evening rush hour traffic, while Mason from the Bay is on a plane to somewhere else. Later, during Roll Call, I see the requests rolling in for next week's show. Familiar names and handles and songs appear on the Twitter feed. From Germany, Serbia, Spain, Scotland, Ireland, and the Netherlands; in Indonesia, Japan, and the Philippines; throughout Latin America, like Mexico, El Salvador, Costa Rica, Chile, Argentina, Panama; and from coast to coast in the US, especially throughout California and Texas and cities like Chicago, Boston, and New York, Morrissey and Smiths fans from all over the place tweet at José Maldonado in hopes of hearing their songs played, their names said on the air this time next week.

As the epigraphs indicate, *Breakfast with the Smiths, the World of Morrissey* listeners literally map the world of international Morrissey fandom. The program effectively routes its worldwide audience of Moz fans—particularly those in the UK and Europe—through Los Angeles, thereby shifting the audience's listening experiences and referential contexts. In other words, *Breakfast with the Smiths* gives us Morrissey with a Mexican American accent: 'We look to Los Angeles for the language we use.' In doing so, the show and its listeners helps us to reimagine geographic, spatial, and historical relations between the local and global North and South, whether it be the North and South of England or North America and South America. *Breakfast with the Smiths* and its worldwide listenership thereby challenge preexisting cultural and national hierarchies that perpetuate notions of cultural authority and legitimacy.

'I Want to Start from Before the Beginning'[86]
Setting the Table for Breakfast with the Smiths

"'Is that Arthur Kane thumbing a lift?' 'Yes,' I say, turning up Indie 103.'
Morrissey, *Autobiography* (2013)

Before the beginning of *Breakfast with the Smiths*, there was Los Angeles, Morrissey, and his global-local fan following. There was a radio station on the air at 103.1 FM that was pushed onto the Internet. There was a famous international playboy-superfan-lead singer-occasional impersonator called the Mexican Morrissey, and there was his band mate Joe Escalante, the bass player of the Sweet and Tender Hooligans, who already hosted his own show on Indie, thus setting the table for *Breakfast*. There are plenty of places to 'start from before the beginning' of *Breakfast with the Smiths, the World of Morrissey* on Indie 103.1, before the rise of its regular fan base and international listenership dubbed the Breakfast Champions, and before its ascent as one of Indie1031.com's most popular programs.

Let's start with the Los Angeles station that Morrissey name-drops in *Autobiography*. Indie 103.1 FM debuted on Christmas 2003; the first songs aired were the Ramones' We Want The Airwaves and This Is Radio Clash by the Clash.[87] A year later, *Rolling Stone* dubbed it 'America's Coolest Commercial Station' for its programming and lineup. 'At a time when corporate-owned radio stations play the same proven hits in the same niche formats over and over,' writes Eric Pederson for *Rolling Stone*, 'a new Los Angeles station, Indie 103.1, is finding success the opposite way: by spinning an unpredictable mix of new groups and old favorites in the spirit of freeform FM stations of the seventies.'[88] Shows like 'Jonesy's Jukebox,' hosted by former Sex Pistol Steve Jones, and other original programs hosted by punk/rock veterans like Henry Rollins, Dave Navarro, and Joe Escalante—Maldonado's bass playing Hooligans band mate—kept Indie fresh and relevant for nearly six years by playing an eclectic mix of new music (Yeah Yeah Yeahs, White Stripes, Mars Volta), classic punk, UK pop and rock, even Johnny Cash.

In January 2009, corporate powers ended Indie's run on the terrestrial airwaves at 103.1 FM, and the station had to find new life on the world wide web. El Gato 103.1, a mixed-format Spanish language station that broadcasts music, news, and talk radio programming, replaced Indie on the air at 103.1 FM. News of Indie's unceremoniously abrupt exit from the airwaves received national media coverage in outlets such as *Mother Jones*, *Rolling Stone*, and the *Los Angeles Times*. Turns out that Indie's transition to an Internet radio station and on-air replacement by El Gato came as a result of the station's acquisition by Entravision, a Santa Monica, California based media corporation 'serving Latino audiences and communities with an integrated platform of solutions and services that includes television, radio, digital media and data analytics to reach Latino audiences across the United States and Latin America.'[89]

Entravision owns fifty-three television stations and forty-nine radio stations, most of which are exclusively Spanish language stations in the top Latino/a markets across the US, with heavy representation in the US-Mexican border states of California, Nevada, Arizona, New Mexico, Colorado, and Texas. The media company is headquartered in Los Angeles, a major city in the US-Mexico borderlands that 'represents the number one (and at times number two) radio market in the United States and boasts a forty-five percent Latino population.'[90] For this reason, Los Angeles's airwaves are coveted commodities for any commercial radio station, particularly for a company like Entravision that caters to Spanish-English bilingual Latino/a audiences.

Significantly, Indie1031.com is one of Entravision's few exclusively English language radio properties. Indie's format resembles that of the 'World Famous KROQ 106.7 FM' in its 1980s and 1990s heyday, which is to say that Indie draws many of its listeners from a large and diverse population of thirty- and forty-year-olds who grew up listening to the pioneering radio station's format and playlists that were replete with US indie/alternative and UK new wave bands. Groups like Joy Division, New Order, Siouxsie and the Banshees, the Cure, Depeche Mode, Pet Shop Boys, Erasure, and the like enjoyed wide rotation alongside acclaimed local bands such as the Red Hot Chili Peppers, Oingo Boingo and Jane's Addiction.[91]

So we have a nationally renowned radio station in Indie 103.1, its new incarnation online thanks to a corporate deal by a Latino media company, and a generation of listeners in Los Angeles still hankering for the good ol' days of Rodney Bingenheimer and Richard Blade on KROQ. Add to that the relative freedom of Internet radio programming versus the commercially mandated and federally regulated on-air programming, as well as the global, worldwide reach and accessibility of the online format, and we begin to understand Indie's unique sonic and cultural impact on the millennial radio landscape. All of these things are important pretexts for the conception and rise of *Breakfast with the Smiths*, a program that also owes some debt to another Fab Four from across the pond.

When Indie 103.1 went exclusively online, its directors were looking for programming ideas that would give the station a boost while working to secure some regular listeners. Indie bosses envisioned an 'indie/alternative rock' version of a show that would be modeled after the long-running weekend morning radio program, *Breakfast with the Beatles*. A three-hour radio show dedicated to the music and stories of the Liverpudlian quartet, including the respective solo careers of John Lennon, Paul McCartney, George Harrison, and Ringo Starr, *Breakfast with the Beatles* aired for many years during the late 1980s and early 1990s on LA's classic rock stations KMET and KLSX. The show was made famous by the late, great Deirdre O'Donoghue, who brought her signature program from the east coast of the US to Los Angeles.[92] It aired on Sunday mornings, when O'Donoghue's smooth voice and the Beatles setlists she played provided a friendly and familiar breakfast-brunch-

Sunday car-ride soundtrack for listeners across greater Los Angeles.

Breakfast with the Beatles was Indie's blueprint for a show that would follow a single-artist/band format. Program managers asked, if Indie 103.1 were to do a show like *Breakfast with the Beatles*, which band would fill in that blank: 'Breakfast with the _____?' What independent/ alternative band or artist has worldwide, timeless, nostalgic appeal? What band or artist has fans everywhere and loads of output and material to sustain a new show every week? Which indie/alternative band has an acclaimed global status like the Beatles? And who would host this show? Who would be the soothing, familiar signature voice of this two-hour one-band show?

Thanks to a little help from a friend, it didn't take long for Indie to figure it out.

Mexican Morrissey on the Radio
Hosting *Breakfast with the Smiths*
in the World of Morrissey

Indie execs initially approached morning show host Joe Escalante about helming *Breakfast with the Smiths*. From the station's perspective, Escalante made sense. He already had history with Indie since its days on the terrestrial airwaves when he took over the station's morning slot with his Morrissey song inspired program, *The Last of the Famous International Morning Shows*. The Vandal Escalante[93] also doubled as the bass player for the premiere Smiths and Morrissey tribute band, Sweet and Tender Hooligans, fronted by Maldonado, so he knew the music inside and out. To boot, Escalante studied law and worked as an entertainment lawyer; he hosted his legal advice show called *Barely Legal Radio* on Indie. In Indie's eyes, Escalante was just the guy for hosting *Breakfast with the Smiths*.

'But then Joe told them, "You don't want me, you want José. If there's any guy who would be perfect for this, *he's* the guy you want, not me,"' Maldonado tells me.[94]

We sit at the restaurant bar across from the Indie studios in the Miracle Mile district of LA. José drinks a Corona, I drink a glass of happy hour red wine while I listen, pausing only to scribble notes in my book. He shares the story of the time Indie came calling after Joe Escalante made the recommendation that the station call him. When the station asked Maldonado to host *Breakfast with the Smiths*, he said he jumped at the chance despite having no prior radio or media experience.

What he did have was an audience and international reputation as 'the Mexican Morrissey.' Born in the late 1960s in Burbank to immigrant parents from Chihuahua, Mexico, Maldonado grew up in LA and currently lives in Pasadena, an LA town that has plenty of Morrissey connections (and where Maldonado first met Morrissey). As the lead singer of the Sweet and Tender Hooligans since 1992, Maldonado has attracted a loyal following of fans who go to his Hooligans shows and show up at his popular DJ gigs at Mal's Bar (Moz Disco) and the Echo (Part Time Punks). Shirtless, perfectly pompadoured, and lifeguard-lean—Morrissey's song, Lifeguard On Duty, is a popular *Breakfast* show request, happily obliged by the host—Maldonado has amassed his own fan base, people who tweet him, want to meet him, go see him perform. His embellished embodiments of Morrissey oscillating wildly on stage, his lovely singing voice, and his spot-on Moz affect inspired Maldonado's friend and fellow performer, El Vez (known at the 'Mexican Elvis'), to christen him the Mexican Morrissey.[95]

Beyond performing as a singer and DJ, Maldonado has also appeared in several documentaries, television specials, newspaper features, and social media segments as a featured expert and commentator about the cultural phenomenon of Mexican/Latino Morrissey fandom. Accordingly, journalists, filmmakers, documentaries, and even academics look to Maldonado as the expert go-to for all things Mexican and Morrissey. So although he lacked previous radio or media experience, Maldonado had plenty of radio-friendly qualities as a performer, DJ, and recognizable public figure with built-in audiences throughout the world of Morrissey.

When I ask him what his early days on the radio were like, José smiles and shakes his head, takes another sip of Corona. He says he 'cringes' when he listens to recordings of his first few shows. While the show's rough blueprint was O'Donoghue's *Breakfast with the Beatles*, the station still experimented with the program's format. They tried co-hosts and guest reporters; early *Breakfast with the Smiths* collaborators included comedian and Morrissey fan, April Richardson, as well as guest reporter, Romeo Girl.[96] Maldonado eventually found his groove, and the show developed into its signature format that listeners enjoy: two hours of Morrissey and Smiths music chosen by listeners who tweeted or called in their song requests.

When the show first aired in February 2009, no one expected it to last more than a few weeks. '*Maybe* six months,' José says. Seven years later, *Breakfast with the Smiths, the World of Morrissey* is Indie's longest running show, if not its most popular. While Maldonado is a large part of the show's staying power as its personality and host—the show is unimaginable with anyone else behind the mic—there wouldn't be weekly *Breakfast with the Smiths* served at three convenient times without its loyal listeners, regular requesters, and audience of Morrissey Smiths fans from around the world wide web.

Roll Call: Tweet at Me, Breakfast Champions Keeping Our Weekly Appointment and Staying True to You

There is a faith in the moment of address that there is a public out there, and there is a faith in the act of listening that there will be some resonance with the audience.

Kate Lacey, *Listening Publics*[97]

In my own strange way, I've always been true to you
In my own sick way, I'll always stay true to you

Morrissey, Speedway

Like George Michael once sang, you gotta have faith. The *Oxford English Dictionary* defines 'faith' as a noun that means: 'The fulfillment of a trust or promise, and related senses. The quality of fulfilling one's trust or promise; faithfulness, fidelity, loyalty; trustworthiness.' In the first epigraph above, media and communications scholar Kate Lacey provides a useful framework for understanding the necessity of faith for both the radio host and the listening audience who are addressed. It highlights the shared responsibility of the host and the audience to the show's success, as well as the agentive qualities of fan audiences.[98] 'Faith,' in its literal, figurative and symbolic meanings, is at the core of *Breakfast with the Smiths* as a Morrissey fan-driven, fan-centered, and fan-hosted radio show that relies on the active participation of fans and listeners to sustain itself week to week.

In taking faith and fan agency as starting points for thinking about *Breakfast with the Smiths*, we create room for a more nuanced understanding of fans and subcultures like the Breakfast Champions. While much has been written about Morrissey fans as a faithful and devout group, worshipping a 'Mozziah,' the majority of these accounts border on pathologizing fans as 'cultish' and 'obsessed.' Very few books are written by fans for other fans; notable exceptions include Julie Hamill's *15 Minutes with You* (2015) and Dickie Felton's *Morrissey International Airport* (2012). Like Hamill, Felton, and other Morrissey fans who are part of and love our various communities of devotees, I am not interesting in perpetuating this characterization of Morrissey fans, or any fans, as crazy or obsessed. Rather, I turn to Lacey's statements about faith and audience listenership to offer a more favorable view of fans, and in particular the Breakfast Champions, as productive agents, as subjects rather than objects, whose faith and devotion (thank you, Depeche Mode) are central to the survival and longevity of the show.

Two hours goes by fast.

Before you know it, it's the top of the second hour and time for Roll Call. In *Breakfast* parlance, 'Roll Call' is the point in the show when Maldonado takes attendance, so to speak, by asking for tweets and song requests for next time: 'Alright Breakfast Champions, point your Twitter machines and in three-two-one-now, tweet at me with your song requests, and I will put you and your song at the front of the line for next week.' Like clockwork, the familiar handles, names and song titles show up on the feed, the first set of content for next week's show. We hear from reliable Breakfast Champions like Tina in Chicago, Jillian in Peru, Genevieve in San Diego, Stefan in Germany, Roberto in London, and Daily Moz from Maudlin Street. I see tweets like these ones:

From @girrlracer: *Hi @JoseMaldonado could you please play Lost for me next week? (Heart emoji) See you Sunday!*

From @Caress_101: *@JoseMaldonado "I Started Something I Couldn't Finish" #request #RollCall #bwts*

From @keenroy: *@JoseMaldonado request: heaven knows im miserable now. #lookingforajob #foundajob #bwts #rollcall*

As the favored modus operandi, Twitter serves multiple purposes as the lifeline of *Breakfast with the Smiths*. While the show also has an Instagram page, Maldonado will only take song requests that are called in or tweeted. Therefore, Twitter functions primarily as the show's main request line and a direct line to the host. It is the preferred method of listener participation: phone-shy Breakfast Champions take kindly to tweets. Plus, as the tweets above indicate, there is plenty of room in 140 characters to request a song, post a favorite lyric or two, give a shout-out to another fan, or simply respond to Roll Call.

Twitter also works as a strategic audience barometer. For our host, Twitter—and Roll Call in particular—is an effective tool to track listenership. Unlike corporate mainstream radio, there is no Arbitron system to track Internet radio audiences or measure Indie's ratings online. As Maldonado explains, 'When I do Roll Call, it's my way of taking the pulse of the show. Who's still listening, who has a song they want to hear next week or who just wants to give a shout-out to someone. And the station sees it, they notice the spike in tweets when people send in their requests during the show and at other times.' For Maldonado and

Indie 103.1 execs, the number of tweets, re-tweets, and 'favorites' during a broadcast provide a reliable indicator of who is listening to *Breakfast with the Smiths* and at which one of three convenient times.

Listeners and Breakfast Champions who follow each other and the host will notice that the most Twitter traffic comes during Roll Call on Wednesday and Sunday broadcasts of the show, timed so that it reaches prime listening hours through several times zones: mornings on the US west coast, lunch time on the east coast, midday in Latin America, rush hour in the UK and Ireland, night time in Europe. A rebroadcast of the show also airs at midnight Los Angeles time on Fridays, making it 8am Friday morning—breakfast time—in the UK and Ireland. Such timing of the broadcasts offers the widest windows of opportunity for listener participation in the form of tweets, Instragram posts, or call-in requests, which function to provide a real-time mapping of the show's listenership.

For a radio show such as *Breakfast with the Smiths*, listener activity accounts for a significant portion of content. Furthermore, tweets from familiar Breakfast Champions, as well as their mention on the air by José, are a signature part of the show that become moments we as listeners anticipate weekly. Among the show's listeners, *Breakfast*-time Twitter communications with the DJ and each another is common, as in the 'Roll Call' tweets above. Many Breakfast Champions dedicate songs to each other, while other listeners will call to dedicate a song to someone for a special occasion. Birthdays, anniversaries, a new job, and impending nuptials are some of the reasons listeners make requests. And nothing gets the *Breakfast*-time Twitter exchanges going quite like the announcement of Morrissey tour dates: fans tweet screenshots of their confirmed ticket purchases or photos of their Morrissey tickets that just arrived in the mail; once at the show, they tweet selfies and Moz Army/ Breakfast Champion group photos. Such is the real-life, on-the-ground camaraderie built through virtual social media relations that are routed through *Breakfast with the Smiths*.

As a regular listener, I look forward to every week to the creative renderings of song requests submitted by other Breakfast Champions.

They arrive on the Twitter feed in the form of pictures, memes and other digitized images that play on a song's lyrics, title, or theme, references that only fellow fans can decipher. For example, Tina From Chicago might send a picture request that contains several unrelated images that depict a song title. Think of seeing a picture of a lime minus the 'L,' next to a picture of a knot, next to a picture of the board game 'Sorry' to request the track I'm Not Sorry. Another picture request might depict a creatively arranged can of Bengali Beer inside a platform shoe.[99] These picture requests have become so popular that our host opened an Instragram account for the express purpose of posting these creative visual puzzles for all to see.

The picture requests are fun visual aids that invite audiences to figure out for themselves which song is being referenced. For fans who lean toward the literary, there are always Roberto Ferdenzi's wordsmithy anagrams. The London Breakfast Champion delivers creatively dexterous and cleverly entertaining tweets in which he arranges his song request in anagram fashion. Here are some examples of Roberto's signature tweets:

> *@RFerdenzi: Hola @JoseMaldonado #TheSmiths song request, in anagram form, for next week's #BWTS is... MARR SUITED ME. #TheItalianScallion #rollcall*

> *@RFerdenzi: Which #TheSmiths song is this an anagram of? OUTPATIENTS HERO:*

> *'OH, I'VE SUFFERED ON MY BIKE, HOY' (Hoy as in GB cyclist, Sir Chris Hoy)*

Unscramble the clue—because incredibly, Roberto manages to build a clue to the song's title into his anagram—and decode the titles: Meat Is Murder, Stop Me If You Think You've Heard This One Before. Roberto says he has created 'about 250 anagrams of Smiths/Morrissey song titles.'[100] These feats of wordplay led the 2015 *Mozarmy Fanzine* to commission Ferdenzi to specially compile ten Smiths and ten Morrissey anagrams, which they distributed to attendees at the third annual Moz Army Meet in Manchester.

In their linguistic suppleness and tongue-and-cheek humor, much like Morrissey's own, Roberto's anagrams are a unique expression of his particular fandom. They are a highlight for the audience and host alike because they foster creative and knowledgeable fan participation in solving the scramble. One of my personal favorites is this anagram: 'IS U.N. POOR FOOL? YES! BE NICE U.S., END WARS.' Or, for us mortals, World Peace is None of Your Business. Even José has fun; he publicly acknowledges Roberto Ferdenzi's remarkable talent and has given him an affectionate play-on-words nickname, 'The Italian Rapscallion.' This and other examples of fan activity, specialized tweets, and listener-host interaction provide the moments in the show that have effectively become part of the fabric of *Breakfast with the Smiths:* made for fans, by fans.

In these ways, *Breakfast with the Smiths* feels like a radio fan club. Nicknames, inside jokes, Morrissey Smiths lyrics, music, photos, news, trivia, and memories are shared, retweeted, and favorited in the forging of subcultural fan spaces online and offline. Furthermore, the request format of the show works one way by tapping into the nostalgia for request-line dedication shows, particularly in Los Angeles where large radio audiences grew up listening to Art Laboe on Sunday nights.[101] We imagine our fellow listeners wherever they may be, bonded through the show and the music, sharing memories sparked by a certain song. These interactive listening and participatory fan practices take on special dynamics that are unique to radio. As communications scholar Susan J. Douglas reminds us, 'Unlike other major technologies—automobiles, airplanes, or trains—that move us from one place to another, radio has worked most powerfully inside our heads, helping us create internal maps of the world and our place in it, urging us to construct imagined communities to which we do, or do not, belong.'[102] This idea that listeners imagine communities among each other by 'creating internal maps of the world' applies fittingly to *Breakfast with the Smiths*, an Internet radio show that boasts a global listenership. Douglas helps us to recognize the show's powerful capacity to map worldwide Morrissey Smiths fandom across space, time, and earthly geography.

I have met Morrissey Smiths fans from Argentina, Spain, France, Ireland, and Czechoslovakia who know about or listen to *Breakfast with the Smiths*. Although Maldonado's listeners come from all over the world, no doubt his biggest radio audience outside of the US-Mexico borderlands resides in the UK, home of the Moz Army. Check out the tweet from UK listener, nicknamed 'Saucy,' below:

> From @redorbrownsauce: *'I got off the tube 1 stop early so I could listen to @JoseMaldonado on @indie1031 before work! I'm now starting the day splendidly! #mozarmy'*

For fans like 'Saucy,' a daily tube commute or drive most certainly includes *Breakfast with the Smiths*, broadcasted on Friday mornings and Wednesday evenings there. The hash tag indicates the connection to the Moz Army, a Morrissey and Smiths Twitter fan club founded by North London Breakfast Champion, Julie Hamill. Maldonado credits Hamill and the Moz Army for helping to grow his audience throughout Morrissey's homeland; listenership is particularly strong in London, Manchester, and cities throughout England, Scotland, Wales, and Ireland.

The Moz Army, usually preceded by the social media hash tag, started with a group of UK Morrissey Smiths fans who were creating and circulating quizzes on Twitter every Friday evening, UK time. Hamill suggested the use of the hash tag during the Moz Army Quiz to make it easier for fans to find each other and for new participants to join in the fun. Moz Army members found each other on Twitter by listening to *Breakfast with the Smiths*. Soon, tweets from listeners in Cork to Liverpool to Cardiff to Camden began to roll in weekly thanks to the #MozArmy Hamill hookup. As Hamill explained to me in an email, 'José's show is the (three-times-weekly) convenient time for everyone to be on Twitter at the same time. It brings us together and we listen, interact, make requests and enjoy each other's shout outs... We warm to other fans who are like-minded and who try to ensure that the community stays happy and true. One of these fans is José, and we consider him to be a pillar.'[103]

Hamill regards Maldonado as a true fan, a pillar of the Moz Army community and a key figure in the #MozArmy's efforts to connect fans on social media. She paid the highest compliment when she included him among other Smiths Moz luminaries in her book, *15 Minutes with You: Interviews with Smiths/Morrissey Collaborators and Famous Fans* (2015). This special relationship between José and the Moz Army of Breakfast Champions reached a milestone at the Third Annual Moz Army Meet in April 2015, hosted by Julie Hamill. (Fig. 1) The event marked the first time that the Mexican Morrissey was a featured guest of the event: he met fans and listeners from all over the UK as well as those who traveled from Europe and the US. He performed a live set with the Moz Army Band, which included Andrew Paresi, Morrissey's drummer on his first three solo albums, on drums. Maldonado was such a hit that he was invited back for the Fourth Moz Army Meet in April 2016; four months later, he appeared with Hamill at her Los Angeles book launch event at West Hollywood's Book Soup, known amongst Morrissey fans as the singer's favorite LA bookstore.

The 2015 Moz Army Meet was held at the Star and Garter as it has been since the first Meet in May 2013. The 200-year-old Manchester pub is a stately double decker brick building just two stops down the Metrolink tram line from the famous Midland Hotel, where Morrissey has been known to enjoy afternoon tea on the rooftop. The Star and Garter is synonymous with the Smiths in Manchester, and is best known by fans as the home of the longest running Morrissey Smiths Disco night in the world, twenty-two years and counting, that continues to be held on the first Friday of every month. As such, the historic Manchester pub acts as a sort of headquarters for the Moz Army in the UK.

Like MorrisseyOke patrons at Eastside Luv, the Moz Army members have made the Star and Garter into a home for fans from all over.

'We always meet there,' says Hamill. 'It's a non-intimidating friendly atmosphere even for the shyest person to feel at home. For some people it takes a lot of guts to go and meet people from Twitter in the first place. Not everyone is comfortable socially, but when they go to the S&G once, they always come back, because the friendliness and heritage of the venue and the warmth of the Morrissey fans makes a person feel part of a special family.'[104] Here we can invoke Jamie Jones (whose book *I Blame Morrissey* was a raffle prize at the last Moz Army Meet), who writes, 'I knew that he had an army of fans, were they all like me? Knowing that we were all joined by this supernatural force that was Morrissey was a real comfort.'[105]

As both Hamill and Jones express, an important aspect of Morrissey Smiths fandom, or any strong fandom, is comfort. Many fans make these affective investments in making 'home,' feeling like 'family,' and finding 'comfort' with and amongst each other. These terms evoke powerful emotions for many people. For as much as comfort may be an illusion, or home may be an unpleasant place to be, we nevertheless seek comfort, we seek a place called home, of our own making. I go back to what I experienced and witnessed at the 2015 Moz Army Meet. It felt like being at the Moz Convention, the Moz Disco, and MorrisseyOke at home in LA, all at once. Even though I was the 'virgin' amidst the 'veterans' of the Moz Army scene in green and gray England, I never felt like I was amongst total strangers. It felt, in a sense, like home.

Breakfast with the Smiths on Indie 103.1 contributes to this affective sense of belonging for members of the Moz Army and Breakfast Champions. We can regard them as 'families of fans' that are co-created by the host and the listeners in ways that are particular to a radio show. Indeed, as Douglas reminds us, 'through the device of the radio we [are] tied by the most gossamer connections to an imagined community of people we sense love the same music we do, and to a DJ who often speaks to us in the most intimate, confidential, and inclusive tones. (Cousin Brucie of WABC in New York addressed us as 'cousins'; we were all part of the same cool family.)'[106] While the ways we listen to the radio have changed—smartphone apps and laptop computers instead of portable

Figure 1. Flier for
MozArmy Meet, 2015.
Credit: @RosyMires.
Used with Permission.

transistor radios—the feeling that we are solo listeners connecting with intimate friends and family through the radio remains constant.

'Appointment radio is a dying concept,' José says. We're at the bar, another round. These are the days of on-demand everything, when programs can be watched or accessed any time, when music can be streamed and listened to without a radio or boombox, when our media consumption habits are ruled by convenience and the individual needs of consumers.

Breakfast with the Smiths is appointment radio. One has to commit to tune in at the same time every week. It cannot be downloaded or otherwise accessed online once it has been broadcast. You have to make it a point to listen. And listeners, especially the committed ones who return to the show and station every week, are valuable commodities in the fickle and sometimes unpredictable world of radio programming. On any radio station or media network, let alone one with a checkered past such as Indie, any program could be here today and gone tomorrow, and no host is safe. No show, television or radio, can survive without a loyal audience. When ratings go down and listeners go away, so does the show and its host. Luckily, Morrissey fans are steadfast, faithful and true. Luckily for Maldonado, enough of them tune in regularly, some even 'religiously.'[107]

Despite a seven-year run that shows no signs of slowing down, a loyal audience of Breakfast Champions, and a listenership that grows every time Morrissey releases new music or tours, Maldonado will sometimes reveal, understandably, a little anxiety about the tenuous nature of on-air existence. It comes through in his occasional quips about his key card to the building that houses Indie's studios. 'As long as my key card still works and they let me into the building, I know I'm good for another week,' shares José. 'But I never really know, from week to week, if my key card will still work.'

For Maldonado, the tenuous nature of on-air existence is allayed in some ways by a faith that the Breakfast Champions will show up weekly, tweet their requests, and gladly keep his key card working. At the end of every show, before he cues the final set of songs, Maldonado delivers his signature sign-off line: 'Until next time, this is José Maldonado saying in my own sick way, I'll always stay true to you. Goodbye.' He borrows the closing lyrics of Morrissey's 1994 classic, Speedway. The song is quintessential Morrissey and a fan favorite. A soaring number, complete with the jolting sound effects of a buzzing chainsaw grinding in your ear after Morrissey practically whispers the opening lines: 'and when you slam down the hammer, can you see it in your heart?', Speedway literally roars to a start. The song is a personal favorite of the host to play on the air and perform with his band. And it is safe to assume that Speedway is also one of Morrissey's personal favorites; he has performed it consistently on his last several tours. During recent performances, the

Figure 2: The Star & Garter, Manchester, UK. Photo by the author.

band switches instruments to play the last verse—Boz Boorer goes to drums, Matt Walker gets on bass, Morrissey moves to Gustavo Manzur's spot behind the keyboards to play the tambourine, and Gustavo takes the mic at the front of the stage to sing in Spanish: *yo nunca dije, yo nunca dije!*[108]

Speedway's themes of faith and fidelity deeply resonate for Morrissey and his fans. In *Mozipedia*, Simon Goddard observes that Morrissey's closing lines in Speedway 'act as a symbolic holy communion for his audience for whom the words "true to you" were a sacred vow of unswerving allegiance.'[109] In this way, the specific phrase 'true to you' operates on multiple levels: as Morrissey's signature line, as Maldonado's pledge to his listeners, as fan shorthand for Morrissey devotion and loyalty.

Tweeter @ixpm: 'A loyal group of #BreakfastChampions, we are @ JoseMaldonado Thanks Champs for making this the best two hours of my week, week after week'

Religious and specifically Catholic overtones notwithstanding, I linger on 'faith' as an operative word in thinking further about the various specific contexts and forms of Morrissey fandom, especially this particular example of the radio show. I return here to the first epigraph that opens this section, taken from Kate Lacey's study, *Listening Publics* (2013): 'There is a faith in the moment of address that there is a public out there, and there is a faith in the act of listening that there will be some resonance with the audience.' Lacey helps us see, from a radio host and audience standpoint, the ways in which faith is shared, mutual, and routed through what 'resonates' with listeners. In this case of *Breakfast with the Smiths*, what resonates most strongly is Morrissey and his music. In Lacey's formulation, 'faith' frames Morrissey Smiths, host Maldonado, and *Breakfast* fans as public subjects who make active choices to believe in and express 'fidelity [and] loyalty' together' to someone or something: 'I'll always stay true to you.' It's not too unlike going to church on Sundays—indeed, *Breakfast with the Smiths* is rebroadcast on Sundays, where the faithful assemble to sing, pray, and rejoice in Morrissey's chapel of love.

We'll always stay true to you.

We Look to Moz Angeles; Or, I'm on a Mexican Radio Morrissey Fandom in a New Millenium

I hear the talking of the DJ
Can't understand just what does he say?
I'm on a Mexican radio. I'm on a Mexican—whoa-oh—radio

Wall of Voodoo, Mexican Radio

We look to Los Angeles
for the language we use
London is dead, London is dead,
I'm too much in love.
Morrissey, Glamorous Glue

In 1983, the Los Angeles new wave band, Wall of Voodoo, scored their only chart hit with the song, Mexican Radio.[110] Eleven years later, Manchester-born singer and music icon Morrissey would look to Los Angeles for the language he uses in his 1992 song, Glamorous Glue. Together, both songs serve as fitting reference points for lasting insights about Los Angeles, *Breakfast with the Smiths, the World of Morrissey,* the Mexican Morrissey, and the (global) North/South, bilingual and international circuits of fandom that make it all possible.

I have been listening to *Breakfast with the Smiths* since its first year on the air, back when it was on the radio, and I don't ever get tired of it.[111] I generally listen on Wednesday mornings, and I often return for a second helping of *Breakfast* on Sunday mornings. The best shows are like listening to your own Moz Smiths song playlist on random mode: a mix of canonical songs, chart hits, and popular songs—the songs about double decker buses and being a human who needs to be loved, just like everybody else does—with deep cuts, rare versions, and album extras. Any given week provides listeners with a well-rounded representation of Morrissey and Smiths musical output; Breakfast Champions request the songs, and Maldonado thoughtfully arranges them with a deejay's ear and a fan's heart. The set lists of songs are punctuated by the host's announcements of the latest Morrissey news, fan-interest stories, plugs for Hooligans shows, and the occasional guest there to plug a new book, theater show, or other Moz-fan related item. The two hours fly by as another edition of *Breakfast with the Smiths* just made our week.

At its best, the show represents a peerless display of transnational Morrissey Smiths fandom, as imagined and practiced, that emerges in our current era of globalized, mobile social media ubiquity. Ever the critical fan and listener, I also recognize that as a radio program, *Breakfast with the Smiths* is not immune to larger historical forces: radio has always been, and remains, a male-dominated field. Few radio programs burst that bubble, even those that make other kinds of significant cultural interventions.

I like to think of *Breakfast with the Smiths* as part of a larger historical and cultural moment in the US. In 2016, this is a country with over fifty-five million Latinos/as, forty-one million native Spanish speakers and eleven million bilingual English-Spanish speakers. According to a 2015 headline in the UK news outlet, *The Guardian*, 'US now has more Spanish speakers than Spain—only Mexico has more.'[112] We hear of the so-called 'Latin explosion' or the 'browning of America' (as if 'America' was not already brown, indigenous, non-English speaking) in a current moment marked by a historic 'demographic shift,' which is just a scientific, diplomatic way of saying that the minority are now the majority, that Mexicans and other people of color outnumber the white descendants of European immigrants and colonial settlers within the US borders. In these contexts, *Breakfast with the Smiths* represents a significant cultural and linguistic shift by routing its listeners, especially in the UK and Europe, through Los Angeles and thus via Morrissey's Mexican syndicate, which then shifts the audience's listening experiences and referential contexts.

A solid case in point is the host's pronunciation of certain names on the air. 'People love to hear their name on the radio,' something José said to me during our conversation at the bar. I come back to that often as I listen to him say the names of people who request songs for the show. There is joy in hearing the names of fellow Morrissey Smiths fans on the radio, whether they're down the street from you or across an ocean. There is something exciting, a fleeting moment of public recognition upon hearing your own name on the radio. And if you grew up hearing your name mispronounced your whole life, misspelled and misspoken by your gringo teachers and school mates who butchered it for years and years, you're grateful to not only hear your name said on the radio, but have it said right by the Mexican Morrissey for all to hear. *Hidalgo.* I

Badge given out at 2015 Moz
Army Meet at the Star and
Garter in Manchester, England.
Photo by the author.

realized a couple years ago that my joy in requesting a song and hearing
it played on the radio is unmatched by the pride I feel when I hear José
say my name correctly. La Profesora Mel *Hidalgo*. To this day, unless I'm
being addressed by my students Chicano/a and Latino/a Studies, I still
hear my name pronounced wrong, I still see the perpetual misspellings.
So yes, there is a bit of Vanity Smurf pride in me when I hear my name
said properly on the air by the Mexican Morrissey. As a native Spanish
speaker and LA Mexican, the host of *Breakfast with the Smiths* knows
how to say my name, accent and all. He knows my name doesn't come
from that Viggo Mortensen movie about a horse.

And it's not just my Spanish surname. When the Maldonado says the
names of callers or tweeters with Spanish names on the air, he does not
Anglicize his pronunciation as so many Mexican Americans have been
taught or learned to do in the name of assimilation: Maldonado makes
choices to say these names on-air correctly—the 'Rodrigos' and 'Marías'
and 'Felipes,' the 'Hernándezes' and 'Pérezes'—with a Mexican Spanish
accent, accents in the right places, Rs properly rolled. His decisions are
significant in their affirmation of Spanish, not dominant English, as the
normative pronunciation. We also hear the Chicano English of 'Paco
from Highland Park' and 'Leti from Moreno Valley' when they call to

145

request There Is A Light That Never Goes Out or I Know It's Over. In other instances, Maldonado will often address listeners from Mexico and other Latin American countries in Spanish, and he won't always translate. Rather than alienating audiences, however, Maldonado's speaking voice seems to have the opposite effect. It is inviting, inclusive; it is a 'soothing Latino lilt,' as one Breakfast Champion from London describes it.[113] No wonder José 'the Mexican Morrissey' was such a hit in Manchester.

Maldonado's unique distinction as the 'Mexican Morrissey' positions him as a radio host who also serves as a cultural translator, one whose communicative and enunciative choices create what Chicana feminist media scholar Inés Casillas calls 'interstitial space[s] that inform cultural practices and identities.'[114] Our *Breakfast with the Smiths* listening practices are thus informed by these small spaces of linguistic and cultural intervention created by Maldonado's voice and enunciations, as well as those Latino/a callers who make on-air requests for songs. In these ways, the show effectively challenges the dominant monolingual, English-only construct of public discourse and insists on privileging the bilingual vocabulary and accent of the US English-Spanish Mexican borderlands. In doing so, *Breakfast with the Smiths* figures prominently as a living example of a Morrissey fan product that could only emerge in the Los Angeles borderlands of the US and Mexico.

This brings us back to Wall of Voodoo's 1983 song. Mexican Radio is about 'border blasters,' which were powerful Mexican radio stations that transmitted broadcasts over thousands of miles north of the US-Mexican border.[115] These radio stations were the result of commercial broadcasting and equipment regulation agreements between Mexican and the US that were in effect from the 1930s through the 1980s.[116] The song Mexican Radio is a pop music rendering of the hybrid, bilingual, and culture-clashing realities of borderland life. It serves as an MTV-era touchstone of US cultural, political, and economic anxieties about Mexico and Mexicans that are both specific to the Reagan early-1980s era and continue to resonate in a post-NAFTA era of globalization.[117]

We can think of *Breakfast with the Smiths, the World of Morrissey* on Los Angeles's Indie 1031.com as a new kind of Mexican radio, a border blaster of a millennial kind that reaches far beyond the US-Mexican border through the world wide web. In all of its ways, from listener participation to the DJ's faithful address to its international fan-driven culture of participation, *Breakfast with the Smiths* effectively re-routes English-origin global Moz fan culture through Los Angeles, renders it in a bilingual Mexican American accent and thereby de-centers the UK as the seat and cultural arbiter of all things Morrissey. South becomes North, flipping the script.

This is not to say that 'London is dead' entirely. Rather, it is to illuminate all the ways in which *Breakfast with the Smiths* facilitates the creation of imagined communities among its listeners elsewhere in the world of Morrissey. The show's audience creates alternate maps of the world across time zones and national boundaries by connecting to each other through the show. Listeners then acquire new vocabularies rooted in Mexican Spanish bilingual Los Angeles culture through the voice of the Mexican Morrissey, through the critical embrace of Mexican American, Spanish language and Los Angeles Chicana/o-Latina/o linguistic and cultural referents that make *Breakfast with the Smiths* a 'Mexican radio' show that celebrates the music of an Irish-English pop music icon. In this way, *Breakfast with the Smiths* re-maps the center of Morrissey fandom and culture, turning from Manchester, UK (the north) to Los Angeles, California (the south). *We look to Los Angeles for the language we use.*

CHAPTER FIVE

Written Words on Paper
Morrissey as Muse

Such a little thing, a gentle tone of kindness
Or written words on paper, can you write?
How I love all of the very simple things of life
             Morrissey, Such A Little Thing Makes Such A Big Difference

BY NOW, WE HAVE A GOOD SENSE ABOUT WHY MANY cultural producers in the know, from Brooklyn to San Antonio to San Francisco to Los Angeles, quite naturally invoke Morrissey as a cultural symbol, a touchstone, a central part of our pop cultural landscape from the eighties onward. Morrissey moves us. He moves unabashed fans to go out and sing, dance, go veggie. In Moz Angeles, he moves virgins and veterans to get in their cars, drive to Boyle Heights, and try out their lovely singing voices at MorrisseyOke. He moves aspiring musicians and hams like me to form tribute bands and play our earnest versions of his songs to other loving fans in crowded bars across the Southland. He moves Breakfast Champions across the world wide web to call in or tweet song requests in a weekly radio appointment with the Mexican Morrissey for two hours of nothing but Smiths and Morrissey music. Morrissey moves inventive, enterprising fans to make arts and crafts like greeting cards and pencils and knitted dolls to sell online to other fans who will snap them up as fast as tickets to one of his concerts. He moves visual artists and graphic designers to imagine him on posters and T-shirts, whether as a cholo gangster, a mariachi, Vicente Fernández, or the Virgen de Guadalupe.

Morrissey moves many of us to write. He compels us to put pen to paper, to fill empty pages in diaries and write love letters disguised as poems, to tap out tweets to our followers who are often the only people in the social mediasphere who would get the references to punctured bicycles, backscrubbers, and balcony fools. There is evidence everywhere of the breadth and depth of Morrissey's influence on artists, musicians, and other creative fans in communities throughout Mozlandia.

For the writers throughout Mozlandia, Morrissey is the perfect muse. His looks, his lyrics, his style, and even his own literary output provide endless fodder for fans to write their own inspired works that pay tribute to Morrissey's wide-ranging influence. Since at least the turn of the new millennium, there has emerged a sizable body of writing on Morrissey. These writings range from the journalistic and interview-based book, like those by Simon Goddard, Len Brown and Julie Hamill, to the fan memoir by writers like Dickie Felton, Mark Simpson and Jamie Jones, to academic and scholarly inquiries by popular music scholars such as Eoin Devereux, Martin J Power and Aileen Dillane. Add these to the mountains of newspaper and magazine articles and blog posts that take Morrissey and his fans as their objects of inquiry.

Among Los Angeles Chicana/o and Latina/o writers alone, several high profile works since 2010 have referred to the Manchester singer in ways that reaffirm his cultural status for generations of fans. I can count a song by acclaimed band Ozomatli (Gay Vatos in Love, 2010), a debut novel by Brando Skyhorse (*The Madonnas of Echo Park*, 2010), a stage performance by Chicana performance troupe, Las Ramonas (*Las Ramonas Gone Wild*, 2011), a screenplay/film by Richard Montoya (*Water and Power,* 2013), a poem by East LA poet Verónica Reyes ('Torcidaness: Tortillas and Me,' 2013), a short play by Michael Patrick Spillers (*Whittier Boulevard*, 2013), and a film by Adelina Anthony (*Bruising for Besos*, 2016) among the cultural artifacts that center or invoke Morrissey as a Chicano-Latino cultural icon. Some of these writers are Morrissey fans, and even if they are not, they are at least privy to the undeniable ubiquity of Morrissey Smiths in the Mexican-Latino urban experience in the US and specifically in Los Angeles.

Clearly, there's wealth of writing inspired by Morrissey, enough to teach a few courses (I would love to teach one called 'The Literary Landscape of Morrissey') and write a few more books. But for now, as part of our literary tour of Mozlandia, I want to focus on a handful of works that were written by fans, for fans, and featured at fan-produced literary events that took place in the LA area in 2013 and 2014. We look first to a poem written by Bell Gardens, California native Vickie Vértiz, presented at a poetry event in El Monte, California. We then turn to *Teatro Moz*, a Morrissey short play festival and playwriting contest. These works by fan-writers take Morrissey's lyrics, musical influences, style, look, and life story as their inspiration for their own stories of self-discovery and desire. In doing so, they showcase how fandom can be actively mobilized as a platform for exploring the lived experiences of outsiders in order to imagine spaces of identity and belonging through Morrissey, 'a raconteur of the marginalized,'[118] and his music.

A Poem for Morrissey Lovers
Vickie Vértiz's Fan Tribute

Oh, what a night. Late September back in 2013. What a very special time for me, 'cause I remember what a night. My South El Monte-born Smithsfan loverfriend and I drove a few miles up the 605 to check out a Morrissey Smiths poetry night at a place in El Monte. We arrived at the venue, the now-defunct Florentino's Restaurant, for a one-night-only event called 'Heaven Knows I'm Miserable Now: Poems and Stories Inspired by the Smiths and Morrissey.' Amidst the warm spicy aromas from the Italian *and* Mexican food being cooked and served up, we listened to homegrown poets read their original writing, poetic tributes to Moz, delivered in an array of styles, forms and influences. The poetry reading was followed by an intimate acoustic set by a certain

Mexican Morrissey. While writers read and Mexican Morrissey sang, local artist and Morrissey fan Alicia Villegas sat in the back painting a portrait of the Mancunian muse, and vendors sold Moz-inspired art, jewelry, and prints. Attendees mingled with the poets and organizers, and others admired fine Morrissey-inspired art pieces by San Francisco visual artist, Shizu Saldamando, that adorned the walls. The audience was loving it all. Morrissey fandom was alive and well that night in El Monte, California.

The event was organized by the South El Monte Arts Posse (SEMAP). The group describes itself as a 'collective of artists, writers, urban planners, educators, scholars, farmers, ecologists, swap meet vendors, and youth dedicated to engaging with the South El Monte and El Monte community through the arts by rethinking our use of space and transforming how we inhabit it.' For the sake of orientation, it helps to know that El Monte and South El Monte, founded in 1910 and 1958, respectively, are cities located just a few miles east of Los Angeles: 'we are East of East,' explains SEMAP co-founder Romeo Guzman. The Southern California public television network, KCET, describes the history behind the founding of these two distinct cities: 'While El Monte was heavily regulated by racialized ordinances that segregated Mexican and Asian residents into barrios or camps, separate from white, home-owning residents, South El Monte was founded as a city where Mexican residents could own property.'[119] This fact speaks volumes of the well-known histories of segregation, displacement, and racial discrimination facing Mexicans that even Morrissey's Irish ancestors once faced on these US shores: no dogs no Negroes no Mexicans allowed, just like no Irish need apply.

Hemmed in by the 60 freeway, the Whittier Narrows Recreational Area, tracts of modest homes built in the sixties, and sprawling industrial zones, South El Monte remains a working class, predominantly Latino-Mexican urban community. El Monte in particular looms large in the East LA historical imaginary as a popular music destination for the area's youth back in the late 1950s and 1960s. Immortalized by the Penguins' 1963 hit (co-written by Frank Zappa), Memories Of El Monte, the city was home to the popular dances at Legion Stadium organized by local radio personality Art Laboe.[120] Artists such as Chuck Berry, Ritchie Valens, Jerry Lee Lewis and Ike and Tina Turner graced the stage of Legion Stadium, their fifties and sixties rock'n'roll and soul music moving masses of working class brown and black youth, who came from all over the San Gabriel Valley, to dance the night away at the venue that was hailed as 'the West Coast version of the Grand Ol' Opry,' according to the *Pasadena Star-News*.[121]

What made El Monte a cultural center of music and dancing was its location outside of the Los Angeles city limits. It therefore lacked the strict ordinances that prevented 'underage' teens from gathering at night. Popular music and race scholars like Gaye Theresa Johnson and George Lipsitz point out that during these postwar decades, live music and dance venues in towns like El Monte in the San Gabriel Valley to the east and Pacoima in the San Fernando Valley to the west—Pacoima is best known as Ritchie Valens's birthplace—routinely 'attracted interracial audiences outside city limits, where [brown and black youth] were relatively free of police harassment.'[122]

The children of the Art Laboe generation made El Monte and its environs a hotbed of the emerging East LA punk scene in the 1970s that gave us groups like the Bags, the Brat and Los Illegals. Members of the Gun Club, including singer Jeffrey Lee Pierce and guitarist Brian Tristan—stage name Kid Congo Powers—grew up in the El Monte-South El Monte-La Puente area 'east of east' LA.[123] This is the same Gun Club, by the way, that Johnny Marr was listening to all the way back in Manchester in 1982. Marr loves Kid Congo—at a Kid Congo and the Pink Monkey Birds show at the Echoplex in Los Angeles, Kid Congo himself showed me a picture on his phone of Johnny Marr holding a hand-lettered sign that read, 'Hey Kid!! Love you long time brother! Johnny x.'[124] Let it be known that one of the early influences of the legendary guitarist of the Smiths were 'the scratchy guitars of LA's The Gun Club'[125] played by none other than Kid Congo Powers, a gay Chicano punk rocker from La Puente, California. ('Another piece to this cool puzzle,' says my compadre, Nathan, bass player of Elvis Disciples and veteran of the

Whittier/SGV punk scene of the 1990s.)

This is the rich Eastside musical history that SEMAP organizers of the Morrissey poetry night evoke on the event's Facebook invite: 'From Legion Stadium to Punk in the 1990s, El Monte's been an important space for LA's music scene. The Art Movement reading series continues that tradition with this event full of poems and stories in honor of a shared love/hate relationship with the Smiths and Morrissey.' In doing so, the organizers place Morrissey squarely within this local legacy of multiracial musical gatherings and cultural practices created by and for outsider populations.

As the event organizers promised, we were treated to a lineup of poets who culled their inspiration from a variety of Morrissey and Smiths songs. One participant, Mike the Poet Sonkesen, delivered his tribute called 'Cento Knows I'm Miserable Now,' a freeform spoken word type of poem cobbled together from the lyrics of fourteen Smiths songs to address a dear friend named Cento. Graphic designer and poet Kenji C. Liu, an LA transplant via New Jersey, read 'May These Words Be Worth Speech,' his poem inspired by Morrissey's invitation to a nuclear bomb ('Come, come') in Every Day Is Like Sunday. South El Monte writer, artist, and SEMAP co-founder Caribbean Fragoza read her poem 'Central in Your Landscape,' inspired by Moz's song The More You Ignore Me, The Closer I Get. She writes, 'I have seen you waiting at crosswalks for the light to turn, I have seen you jaywalk with impatience, I have visited galleries and shopping centers and parking lots where you have been.' I imagine the poet addresses Morrissey, whose footsteps she traces all over this town where he once lived.

The highlight of the night for me was listening to Chicana poet Vickie Vértiz read her stirring epistolary tribute, 'A Xicano Love Letter.'[126] The poem as read by Vértiz at the event and as it appears in the event program is worth duplicating in full: [127]

Because we craved permission to be despondent in English
Desperate for words to hide erections for boys behind Trapper
Keepers/Needed to document in our journals those frequent Kotex leaks

Maudlin about how our parents didn't understand us, we yearned
To do this in private in the company of someone with rank

We hunted for you in crates,/Scraped pennies from the hands of
grandparents who collected cans to feed us/All to hear your 50s
guitar in the key of sorrow

We were born Juan Gabriel fans of twirl and flourish/Punching
farsantes[128] since the womb, we know posers when we see them/
You our savior for the disconsolation of being young/And Mexican/
Born here or not, and living south of the 60 freeway/No Movement
murals cushion our ninety-nine cent gray, our freeway interchange sky/
You taught me to hate the queen/Since the church thought I was dirty,
we were instant friends/You modeled desire for death by bus, side by side

We were your second chance American Manchester, empty tire factories and
soot-covered eyelids Bloody broken front teeth from gravel and steel-toes

Because we were strange/We fondled your open shirts and built a country
around you of sidelong glances and glum gladiolus

When you first saw our tight black jeans and creepers, you caught us like that
tiger/Recognized our crestfallen brown eyes, lined in black, our red lips/A
penchant for racing Chevys down Slauson with no headlights
We your wistful twins, that boy we won't share/You saw us make love in
cemeteries, mercurial daydreams/Shared our lust for trim sideburns, Elvis Vegas
beats to make us jump like beans

Forced fatalists by nations on all sides We're death-happy because it constantly
raps at our door/In the carcinogen heart of this Manchester Our black lungs
sing with you/Because every time we listen/It's our last day, too

The poem is striking on several levels. Rather than view it as a poem that reproduces stereotypes of depressed, 'death-happy' young Mexican fans of Morrissey, we can read Vértiz's poem as a powerful statement of affirmation, reclamation, and appropriation. After all, Mexicans are known to celebrate death in a way that honors the lives and memories of their loved ones during November el Día de los Muertos (Day of the Dead) celebrations that have now reached globalized commercial status (something to be really depressed about).

I immediately liked Vértiz's poem for what it does not do: unlike the other poems presented as part of the program, Vértiz's poem does not name Morrissey or the Smiths or quote any of his lyrics directly anywhere in the poem. Rather, Vértiz sketches an ontology of school-age Morrissey fandom by detailing the textured life experiences of young outsiders as seen through the prism of Morrissey's music and the social codes of fandom. She describes the very meaning of what it means (and what it looks like) to be a Morrissey fan for those whose lives depend on his music and lyrics for survival in a world that does not understand them. It is a tribute poem by a fan for other fans who know how to decode it through references to Morrissey's 'open shirts,' 'glum gladiolus,' and 'trim sideburns;' by recognizing words like 'maudlin' and 'rank;' by allusions to cemeteries, 'death by bus, side by side,' and the Queen.

The opening lines of the poem establish the intimacy and secretive, yet revelatory and confessional nature of a 'love letter,' and perhaps even a fan letter. Admissions of queer desire (boys harboring hard-ons for other boys) and embarrassing menstrual mishaps for the girls are the stuff of despondency for forlorn teens trudging through their lives 'south of the 60 freeway.' Proclamations of difference ('we were strange') are made by associating oneself with Morrissey as his 'wistful twin.' This metaphor brings to mind the part in Morrissey's *Autobigraphy* where the singer describes Chicanas and Chicanos as his 'syndicates.' In both ways, there exists a mutual recognition and shared savior sentiment as expressed in *Autobiography* and in songs like Ganglord with its choral refrain: 'And I'm turning to you to save me,' implores Morrissey. The poem also frames Morrissey as a savior to outsider youth, and his music a viable outlet of self-expression, particularly for those Mexicans 'born here or not' and whose lives are crisscrossed by freeway interchanges, carcinogenic pollution, and dangerous desires. In this sense, we can connect the poem to Ozomatli's song, Gay Vatos In Love ('The more I hear Morrissey/the more I feel alright') and Michael Patrick Spillers's short play, *Whittier Boulevard*. Both of these texts establish Morrissey as a figure of saving grace for the song's 'gay vatos' and the play's 'transbutch.'[129]

Furthermore, the poem is rich in cultural references that illuminate the specifically Mexican American affinities with Morrissey and the Smiths. Importantly, these are also cross-cultural, transnational references, such that Morrissey and the Smiths exist in a referential universe that also includes Elvis Presley and Juan Gabriel, an iconic Mexican singer—famous for his flamboyant stage performances and alternative masculinity—to whom Morrissey is often compared in borderland US-Mexican cultural contexts. Elvis resonates with Smiths fans familiar with the version of Rusholme Ruffians performed by the band on the live *Rank* album. The 'fifties guitar' sound of Rusholme Ruffians is a sonic reference to the Elvis song, His Latest Flame (1961), which the band plays in a perfectly blended medley of the two songs. The 'fifties guitar' sound also refers to the rockabilly hits of Morrissey's early 1990s heyday, when Moz was most popular with Mexican youth all over LA and the borderlands. In a fashion connection to The King, fellow tribute band artist Eddie Stephens (of These Handsome Devils and an Elvis aficionado first) reminds me that Morrissey's sideburns, his choice of fifties style pompadour (moreso part of his band's look), and a black suit he wore during the Oye Esteban tour serve as visual nods to Elvis's influence.[130] Indeed, Morrissey regularly performs cover versions of Elvis songs, as he has recently on tour in South America and elsewhere.

As for making sense of Vértiz's Juan Gabriel reference, let's turn briefly to the aforementioned song by acclaimed Los Angeles band, Ozomatli. In 2010, Ozomatli released a song called Gay Vatos In Love ('vato' means 'dude' or 'homie' in Chicano slang). Written at the height of California's Proposition 8 debates—Prop. 8 was a California ballot initiative that sought to deny same-sex marriage[131]—the song was the band's way to show their public support and advocacy for gay and lesbian 'equal rights,' while condemning anti-gay hate speech and discourse around the ballot measure. Gay Vatos In Love garnered some major media response in publications such as *Billboard*, *The Advocate*, *GLAAD* (the Gay and Lesbian Alliance Against Defamation), and the *Los Angeles Times*, which called it a potentially controversial song because it openly addressed and celebrated same-sex love and relationships in the predominantly Chicana/o-Latina/o communities in Los Angeles. More to the point, the band refers to Morrissey and Juan Gabriel in the song's lyrics. Juan Gabriel is a popular Mexican singer and balladeer known for his 'twirl and flourish' stage presence and being famously evasive of questions directed at his sexuality, like someone else we know.[132] 'Amor es amor,' sings Juan Gabriel: love is love, a rallying cry in the Proposition 8 era of same-sex marriage equality, akin to Morrissey's assertion that 'I am human and I need to be loved, just like everybody else does' in How Soon Is Now. In putting Morrissey and Juan Gabriel together, both Ozomatli and Vértiz, like many other borderland fans, acknowledge Morrissey as a significant cultural icon important to and recognized by gay, lesbian, and queer Chicanas/os-Latinas/os.[133]

Along with the Mexican Juan Gabriel reference, Vértiz's poem casts Morrissey as a linguistic authority figure, 'someone with rank,' whose English language gets appropriated by his young Mexican listeners who yearn to express themselves and put words to their 'strange' 'death-happy' desires while living their bicultural and sometimes bilingual realities of being Mexican in the US. Mexicans who grew up speaking English better than Spanish are often derided as 'pochos/as,' or ruined, whitewashed Mexicans, by older generations. In her opening lines and throughout her poem, Vértiz captures the specific in-betweenness experienced by borderland Mexican youth, 'born here or not,' who 'crave permission' to express themselves in English not understood by their parents. These are first, second, third generation Mexicans and Latinos/as who did not grow up speaking Spanish, mainly because the dominant US culture demands English as a primary language. We may have heard Spanish all around us all of our lives, but that doesn't mean we have the same access to Spanish as we do to English in schools and other public institutions. So we must look elsewhere for models, but not necessarily at the expense of our Mexican heritage.

As the poem suggests, 'our black lungs sing' with Morrissey because of the validation we feel through his music and lyrics. 'Morrissey made it okay to be a nerd, to be smart,' Vértiz said to me when we chatted about her poem at the event. This sentiment of 'feeling smarter' because one listened to Morrissey and the Smiths is a common theme shared among fans, particularly the Chicana/o-Latina/o fans who attended both public and parochial schools in the East LA area, home of the 1968 high school walkouts, and all over the US-Mexico borderland region.

Because of the historical inadequacies of Mexican American and Chicano/a education, particularly in the years leading up the 1968 high school marches for educational equality across California and Texas, brown students were often told they were not smart, or did not belong on the college track. The belief that Mexicans were only 'good' for manual labor as farm workers and domestics was reinforced and reproduced by a public school system that steered students into gendered vocational tracks: boys went into auto mechanic and wood shop courses, and girls went into home economics or secretary courses. In other words, counselors and teachers rarely encouraged an academic, college-bound academic program for Mexican students and instead, steered them away from bookish and intellectually challenging university preparatory classes.

On top of the institutional racism, there was also plenty of gender bias and traditional beliefs entrenched in the family and social structure, where parents often told boys to 'be real men' and work with their hands for a living, while telling girls their job was to find a man to marry and bear children. 'Why go to college when you're going to get married anyway?' was the message for girls, while for boys, it was 'worry about getting a good job to support your family.' Neither sex was to waste time reading books, and both would risk suspicious stares from family and friends for daring to be 'too smart for your own good.' This set of contradictory messages plays out in many works of Chicano/a literature: on the one hand, Mexican students were tracked into vocational training based on their gender, and when some of them challenged that discrimination, they were met on the other hand with the same heteronormative and gendered messages of 'know your place' from their traditionally rigid parents and peers. For queer students in particular, however, books and education were often the only way to find reprieve from both sets of repressive environments.[134]

So what's a bookish, outcast, 'strange' Mexican kid in 1980s and 1990s LA to do? Listen to the Smiths, of course, and take refuge in all kinds of books and music. This message resonates throughout Vértiz's poem. The sense that we feel 'smarter' from listening to Morrissey's music and poring over his lyrics is a point that resonates deeply with me. I'm pretty sure I became an English major in college because of Morrissey, who was aided and abetted by my 10th grade Honors English teacher, Mrs Walker. What Chicana or Chicano kid growing up east of east LA would ever know about Oscar Wilde (or Keats or Yeats) if it weren't for Cemetry Gates or record store posters of Morrissey laying in bed with a copy of an Oscar Wilde book on his pillow?

Plus, in the United States, ours is an Anglocentric formal education system that endows British culture—especially literature—with a high value. It is authoritative and correct. If we had to speak English, we might as well speak the English from the original 'motherland' of England. Morrissey was a good linguistic model for us school-age fans. The message in English classes all through school was, 'You have not been properly educated, you are not a real English major, unless you read the great British (and sometimes Irish) writers.' Therefore, commanding the English language, particularly the superior *English* English, was a powerful educational tool for Mexican kids born in the US who were also Smiths and Morrissey fans (and fans of British pop music more generally). Our grandparents or parents' Spanish is not our language in the same way English is. This is an historical fact which itself speaks to the double-colonized (first the Spaniards, then the Anglos) reality of generations of Mexicans born north of the border. We listen to Morrissey who sings in *English*: he speaks and sings proper dictionary words with an English accent. And his English is even better than the 'Standard American English' language that is taught to us in US schools, spoken to us in news broadcasts, and written in newspapers and textbooks.

And in another ironic twist, US Americans—proudly patriotic and hopelessly myopic in their exceptionalism—love them some British accents. Certainly an English, Irish, Scottish, Welsh, even Australian accent is much more welcome in the US cultural and political spheres than Spanish-Mexican accented English, its speakers too often targets of racism and bias. The British accent fetish remains a colonial condition of US society. There is much cultural capital in a British accent, especially to US Americans. We automatically think you're smarter, more handsome, more classy when we hear your British accent. It doesn't matter what part of England the accent is from, but the more Colin Firth or Hugh Grant or Royal Family or Downtown Abbey sounding, the better.

On reality television shows across the cable landscape, smart folks from England tell simple Americans how to do things right, whether it's how to run their hair salons (Tabatha Coffey) and restaurants (Gordon Ramsey, Robert Irvine, Jamie Oliver) or raise their kids ('Supernanny' Jo Frost). Brits are the arbiters of commercialized success in America, judging (if not creating and producing) reality talent shows like *American Idol* (Simon Cowell), *Dancing with the Stars* (Len Goodman), and *So You Think You Can Dance* (Nigel Lythgoe, Cat Deeley). Can we even imagine a Mexican or Asian or Arab judge in these authoritative positions as cultural gatekeepers in America? And of course, there is the incessant fawning over members of the Royal Family, lest we forget the oodles of British actors, the Kates and Benedicts and Emmas and Edwards, who win all kinds of American Golden Globe and Oscar awards and accolades. As Lawrence Buell writes, 'U.S. culture can be said to remain at least vestigially postcolonial so long as its citizens are impressed by the sound of an educated British accent.'[135]

And yet, Morrissey's accent is music to our colonized ears. In school, my Honors English and drama class group of friends and I knew there was something elite, lofty about knowing Englishisms because we heard them in a Smiths or Morrissey song. We listened to the songs and read books and used English words that even impressed our English teachers in school. There was work involved in finding out what those words in the songs meant—you had to look up 'vile' and 'maudlin' and 'plagiarise' in the dictionary (and realize that the −ise spelling was British, which we learned from all that Dickens and other BritLit we read in school); you had to look up 'Manchester' and 'England' and 'Queen Elizabeth' in the atlas or encyclopedia. These were not school lessons, but edifying life lessons learned from British pop music that had benefits in and out of school.

Mexican born, Los Angeles based writer Alex Espinoza describes these acts of linguistic and cultural appropriation as 'reverse exoticizing.' He says, 'I loved a lot of synthy pop like Depeche Mode, Echo and the Bunnymen, and Yaz. For me it was a culture and identity that was so different from anything that was around us... Instead of England as a colonial power taking over countries, I guess we were sort of colonizing them. There was this fascination with the look, the music, and the identity. Everyone wanted to go to gloomy England and write really depressing stories after listening to the Smiths... [I]t seemed so romantic. I think we fantasized a kind of sophistication to it. It felt very different from the reality we knew in places like La Puente, California,' a city also 'south of the 60 freeway' in the San Gabriel Valley populated mostly by Mexicans.[136]

Here, Espinoza speaks to the romantic fascination many of us had (and have) with Englishness, which we accessed primarily and most easily through UK popular music. 'We were sort of colonizing them' also points to a reframing of relations, a shift in power in some way: the colonized become the colonizer, at least to the extent of our romanticizing and cultural appropriation practices when it comes to Morrissey. Espinoza's comments also reflect the 'remote intimacies' expressed so vividly in Vértiz's poem. According to English and Gender Studies scholar Karen Tongson, 'remote intimacies describ[e] the communities for whom intimacies cohere across virtual networks of desire through radio, music, and television, on the Internet, and now through online social networking sites. Remote intimacies account both technically and affectively for the symbiosis that can happen between disparate subjects—like the storied connection between Latinos and Morrissey, for example, or between suburban queer kids of color and Anglophilic ear candy in general.'[137] Those of us in Southern California who grew up in the 1980s and 1990s listening to Richard Blade (an expatriate British DJ) on KROQ are familiar with these 'remote intimacies' that made us feel that the only bands worth our precious pennies were Depeche Mode, the Smiths, the Cure, and New Order.

Going back to Vértiz's poem, we can see the visual clues of these Latino Morrissey/'Anglophilic ear candy'-inspired 'remote intimacies.' They are found in the subversive fashion and style choices such as 'steel toe' shoes (preferably Doc Martens), 'tight black jeans,' 'creepers,' black eyeliner, red lips. 'Remote intimacies' are also expressed through critiques of monarchy and nations ('you taught me to hate the queen') and the embrace of the affective and emotional ('mercurial daydreams,' 'lust,' 'yearning') as modes of resistant self-formation. Some wore English punk and goth music influenced 'tight black jeans and creepers' and black eye liner, while others wore 'Morrissey-inspired cardigans and immaculate white T-shirts.'[138] Such were the unisex uniforms of the 'we,' the despondent youth, in Vértiz's poem. There is power in the 'we,' a sense of belonging and camaraderie among the 'strange' and 'death-happy' youth who reach for recognition among themselves when parents or others do not, cannot, understand them. In the 'we,' we find shared friendships, love, and affinities through our fan codes of communication.

In closing, I want to turn to the words of a former student after I showed him Vértiz's poem. He is a queer first-generation Mexican who went to an all-boys Catholic school in East LA. He loves the Smiths, and he shared some of his insights about why Latinos/as and Mexicans on both sides of the border have embraced Morrissey and his music so fervently. 'My older sister listened to all that stuff—not just the Smiths, but bands like the Sex Pistols and Bauhaus, Siouxsie and the Banshees, The Buzzcocks,' he said. He also discussed how his sister taught him that there are other ways to be Mexican in this country. 'We don't always have to listen to banda or speak Spanish well as long as we honor our roots and not totally assimilate to gringo culture. I think my sister saw some power in embracing the alternative and critical aspects of the English music she liked. And when I started listening to this music more, I realized I was getting something out of it that I never got in school or from my parents. The Smiths, Morrissey, all those bands, they gave us language and taught us to be conscious of the world around us.'[139]

Vértiz would surely agree.

CASA de Moz: Staging the World's First Theatrical Tribute to Morrissey

On 13 November 2014, *Teatro Moz* premiered at CASA 0101 theater company in Boyle Heights, East LA. Billed as the 'World's First Morrissey-Inspired Theater Festival,' *Teatro Moz* featured ten short plays by writers from the Los Angeles area and Brooklyn, New York. The event sold out quickly thanks to the buzz created by an *LA Weekly* article. Directed by Michael Patrick Spillers, a Missouri-born transplanted Los Angeles filmmaker and playwright, *Teatro Moz* was conceived as a way to pay homage to LA's culture of Moz fandom. Its production team, which included Spillers, Jaime Mayorquin, and CASA 0101 founder and playwright Josefina López, promoted the event as a Morrissey playwriting contest and celebration of his music, style, and artistic influence. The contest was judged by a guest panel of local 'Moz Experts'—including Alexis de la Rocha, co-founder and host of MorrisseyOke; Julian Ricardo, actor and lead singer of local Smiths and Morrissey tribute band, Strangeways; and your author, the 'PhD/academic' representative. The one-night-only performance of *Teatro Moz* was emceed by queer US Argentine writer, actor, and performer Karen Anzoategui.

The rich lyrics, song titles, themes and imagery from Smiths and Morrissey songs provided the raw material for the playwrights, fans themselves who delivered a body of work that covered Mozesque topics ranging from vegetarianism, homosexual awakenings, and stage-crashing fantasies. A talented ensemble cast of local actors brought to life each of the ten short plays as unique and memorable fan tributes. The event opened with Rocío Anica's 'The Golden Rule.' The play's main character, Betty Ramirez, is a 'feminist vegan college student' who still lives at home and must reckon with her immigrant, religious, suffering mother. She feels alone and fears her disapproving family will never understand her secrets. As the middle child and only daughter, Betty resents her mother's favoritism of her mijos, her sons: 'They always side with my brothers,' she complains to her aunt. Songs like Unloveable by the Smiths and Morrissey's I Have Forgiven Jesus—the inspiration for the play—give Betty the language she needs to make peace with herself and her home life.

Other dramatic plays included 'Spirit Board' by Josefina López, who cites Morrissey as the 'co-writer' of her play about three friends who attempt to reach the spirit of another friend with a Ouija board; Alyson Mead's 'Not to Bend or Break,' a comment on the impact of budget cuts on university campuses through a story about a college radio DJ's last night on the air; Jaime Mayorquin's 'Start with Now,' about two Chicano best friends in their mid-twenties who discover their romantic love for each other; and Oscar Argüello's 'Midsummer Nightmare,' a moving monologue about a brother's suicide.

In true Chicano teatro fashion, the rest of the plays were comedies meant to elicit a reaction from the audience, whose members no doubt saw themselves reflected in much of the content—more on that later. Ralph Ferráns gave us 'Rush into My Stage,' a funny take on fans' valiant stage-diving efforts at Morrissey concerts; Alison Lowenstein gives us a story about a married woman's secret fantasy to hook up with the lead singer of the local Smiths and Morrissey tribute band; and Oscar Agüello balances his sad monologue with 'Sister, I'm A...,' a humorous story about a brother and sister who scheme to meet Morrissey at the Sunset Marquis Hotel.

The winner of the *Teatro Moz* playwriting contest was 'Menudo is CENSORED' by East Los Angeles writer and novelist, Marco A. Vásquez. The play follows two characters, Vinnie Vásquez and Mundo González, on a sobering Sunday morning after a wild Saturday night at a club. According to the stage directions, '[b]oth look like your typical Morrissey fan. MUNDO has a shaved head. VINNIE has a pompadour.' No more descriptors are provided beyond the two characters' hairstyles, which serve as visual symbols of 'typical' Morrissey fandom in the context of Latino Los Angeles. As we get to know the characters and listen to them interact, we learn that their fandom extends well beyond their haircuts, for both Vinnie and Mundo speak in Morrissey lyrics and song references to make sense of Mundo's crazy night, to which Vinnie was a keen witness.

The play frames Vinnie as the gloating storyteller to Mundo's sorry hangover victim in such bad shape that he can't remember his exasperating drunken antics from the night before. Not even menudo—a spicy Mexican soup of tripe and hominy topped with onion, cilantro, oregano, and lemon typically eaten as an all-purpose hangover cure—can save poor Mundo, who concluded his night passed out in an alley next to a dog. The comedic exchanges between the two friends pivot around Vinnie's recap of Mundo's actions from the night before, which include his attempts to 'get his hands on some mammary glands' and making hotheaded threats to hang the DJ who did not play his favorite songs. In response, Mundo hangs his head and utters his disbelief, denying that he would ever threaten anyone and that he's all about 'love, peace, and harmony' before pitying himself for being 'hated for loving' the young ladies he tried to 'kiss a lot' at the club.

Mundo and Vinnie represent two types of 'typical' Morrissey fans that by now have become familiar figures in the popular imagination of Moz fandom. Mundo is the victim of unrequited love, prone to depression and drinking. He is someone we would see in the Smiths songs Stop Me If You Think You've Heard This One Before, the one who 'drank four and then fell on the floor and drank more,' and Heaven Knows I'm Miserable Now. Pompadoured Vinnie is the more astute fan with a wry and witty sense of humor. He makes important distinctions between Smiths and Morrissey songs in his assessment of Mundo's misfortunes. In one scene, a suddenly perky Mundo remembers hearing his 'favorite

Morrissey song,' Bigmouth Strikes Again, at the club. 'Actually, that song is by the Smiths,' corrects Vinnie, who proceeds to name Margaret On The Guillotine, a lesser-known deep cut from Morrissey's debut solo album, as his favorite song.

This line produced plenty of chuckles from the audience and us judges who recognized the existence of such distinctions. Whether at MorrisseyOke or tribute band shows or at the annual convention, we have found that fans often draw lines between being a Smiths fan or a Morrissey fan. Although often many are fans of both, there is usually a preference expressed for one or the other, and it becomes pretty clear in the fan scenes that many people invest in maintaining, sometimes pretty vehemently, the Smiths fan-Moz fan divide for all kinds of reasons. Smiths-dominant fans usually like Johnny Marr over Morrissey, or they like the younger, more androgynous Smiths-era Morrissey over the mature, manly figure of recent years; Moz loyalists appreciate his solo band mates and Morrissey's musical output post-Smiths, which is triple that of his Smiths albums. No matter the reason, it is pretty common for many fans to lean one side or other, as if supporting Team Moz Red United or Team Marr Blue City (like the stickers I saw floating around at the Moz Army Meet in Manchester). A case in point: the 2016 Smiths and Morrissey convention dedicated one day to the Smiths and one day to Morrissey. Vásquez plays with these Moz Smiths divides through his characters Mundo and Vinnie as a way to embrace the factions and fractures within fan communities.

My fellow judges and I chose 'Menudo is Murder' as the winning play for its sheer cleverness and comedic value. We liked Vásquez's deft arrangement of song lyrics and themes as the basis of his characters' dialogue and interactions. Vinnie and Mundo trade Moz lyrics like boxers trade punches, and we watch as eager spectators. Much like Vértiz's poem, Vásquez's short play gives us 'typical' fan characters who actively engage with the texts—words, music, themes—of Morrissey's solo and Smiths songs in order to make sense of their shared realities through a common language of committed fandom.

In my mind, there was another *Teatro Moz* contest winner. 'Let Me

Kiss You,' by Rosa María Rodríguez, focuses on Alondra, a sixteen-year-old student at St Mary's girls' Catholic high school who has never kissed anyone. She harbors secret feelings for her best friend, Cindy, a 'boy-crazy-goth-chick' who likes to pull pranks and get into mischief. Oblivious to Alondra's feelings, Cindy plays sneaky matchmaker between Alondra and Frankie, a handsome, popular and athletic 'rockabilly' type and 'big Moz fan' from St Michael's, the neighboring boys' school. The play's main action revolves around Cindy's scheme to get her friend to kiss Frankie, a senior who has had a crush on Alondra since his freshman year. Alondra, however, has no interest in making out with Frankie, the hot captain of the St Michael's football team.

Cindy's advice to Frankie, who has tried in vain to flirt with Alondra, is to appeal to her nerdy side: 'Dedicate a song to her, talk about books, or write her a poem. She's kind of a nerd like that.' The scene between Frankie and Alondra revolves around Frankie's Morrissey fandom and Alondra's subsequent dismissal of his music, and thus, Frankie's advances. We learn that Frankie likes Alondra because she's pretty, 'different,' and not 'silly' like the other girls who hang around St Michael's. Though she compliments Frankie's 'cool Moz shirt,' Alondra later admits that she doesn't 'know much about' Morrissey and only 'pretended to be into him' when she was younger. Frankie, unhindered, plays the Smiths song Ask to encourage Alondra to not be so shy with him. When he moves in to kiss her, Alondra rebuffs him. We find out that this is not the first time Alondra has rejected Frankie, who does not understand Alondra's refusal of his affections. She realizes that she would rather kiss her best friend, Cindy, and the play ends when Alondra does just that. As the lights fade, Morrissey's song Let Me Kiss You plays in the background.

Like Vértiz's poem, 'A Xicano Love Letter,' Rodríguez's play resonates with the queer sensibilities of Morrissey fandom, particularly as we have seen it expressed in certain Chicana/o and Latina/o works. Here, I think about queer Latino performance scholar José E. Muñoz, who writes, 'Queerness is essentially about the rejection of a here and now and an insistence on potentiality or concrete possibility for another world.'[140]

I think about Alondra rejecting her 'here and now' with Frankie and the heteronormative expectations of everyone around her. Queerness disrupts and rejects 'normal'/normative gender roles and sexual desires inscribed by cultural imperatives, religious ideology, institutional training or through discipline. Queerness denotes and describes the destabilization—if not destruction—of categorical norms of lived gender and sexual expressions. And destruction suggests danger for all parties involved, albeit in distinct ways.

In Rodríguez's play, the 'danger' is played out as a spectacle for Frankie, who spies on the girls' forbidden act, and as a sinful act in the eyes of the girls' teacher nun, Sister Anunciata, who chastises the girls when she sees them kissing, effectively ending the play. Queerness also expresses itself in the moment we see Alondra kiss Cindy while Let Me Kiss You plays while the lights go down. The scene has a gender-bending effect that punctuates the coming-out message of the play. In a reversal of gender roles, Alondra thus 'dedicates' the song to Cindy in the way that Frankie once dedicated a song to Alondra as a prelude to a kiss. In this way, Alondra appropriates the language of the song and assumes the masculine voice to express and act on her queer desire to kiss her best girlfriend.

As Devereux reminds us, 'Morrissey manages to sing from a range of viewpoints that address both male and female subjects. In songs such as Sheila Take A Bow he manages to shift gender positions mid-song,' thereby creating 'open polysemic texts.'[141] Those of us familiar with Morrissey's music know well the sexual ambiguity and the homoerotic desires as themes in so many of his songs, from Smiths-era tracks like Hand In Glove and The Headmaster Ritual to Morrissey's solo tracks like Piccadilly Palare and Dear God Please Help Me. Like Ozomatli's song Gay Vatos In Love as discussed earlier, Vértiz's poem, and a handful of other plays that were part of *Teatro Moz,* Rodríguez's play serves as another salient example of the particular ways in which queer fans in the borderlands appropriate Morrissey's image, music, and words in the service of their own homoerotic desires and expressions.

The words 'outcast,' 'outsider,' and 'alienation' are often used (some might say ad nauseum) when describing Morrissey's lyrics and sensibility. It makes sense then that fans of all stripes—queer, brown, disabled, working class, immigrant—are drawn to his music. Those of us who have been relegated to the margins fully embrace songs like the Smiths' Half A Person because too often, we have made to feel as such by dominant society. Mexican, Mexican American, Chicana/o, Latina/o fans in particular recognize and identify with Morrissey's existential struggle as a child born to Irish Catholic immigrants in the north of England. Josefina López, a Mexican born, Boyle Heights-raised feminist playwright, is one such fan.

López is best known for her work, *Real Women Have Curves*, her 1996 play that was made into a major motion picture starring America Ferrera in 2002. In 2000, López founded CASA 0101 (casa means 'home' or 'house' in Spanish), a community theater venue and arts space in the heart of Boyle Heights. In addition to being a major East LA performance venue that showcases original theatrical productions, CASA 0101 fulfills López's educational mission, providing low-cost or free acting and writing workshops for youth and adults.

CASA 0101 is also the home of *Teatro Moz*, which will enjoy a second, more full-scale production in September and October, 2016.[142] For López, the concept behind *Teatro Moz* makes sense: to celebrate the music of Morrissey Smiths and the unique multigenerational Mexican/Latino community of fans through Mexican and Chicano art forms. A fan herself, López sees the natural connections between her community and the Mancunian musician that her theater company celebrates. I have spoken to López about Morrissey Smiths and her take on these songs that continue to inspire artists and playwrights like herself. 'Morrissey sings corridos,' she says, referring to the Mexican narrative ballads that typically focus on the underdog and make social commentary: Mexican protest songs, if you will. López continues:

He tells stories in songs and understands the pain of living in a country that's a superpower which has little regard for other countries it considers inferior. Morrissey is powerful because he is willing to talk about the wounds and hurt of living in two worlds and feeling like you don't belong anywhere. He suffers the same oppression as Chicanos under Catholic indoctrination that dictates false expectations of what life should be and dares to challenge all the Catholic guilt and B.S. that sucks the life out of authentic self expression. He is a Chicano hero because he doesn't fight with his fists, but with words and wit and isn't afraid to show you he is powerful because he is unapologetically human.[143]

López's characterization of Morrissey as a 'Chicano hero' is drawn from her recognition of his ability to tell stories through songs, to use words, music, and performance as political weapons against oppression and injustice. From this perspective, the likening of Morrissey's songs to corridos is not so uncanny. Indeed, Morrissey's ode to Los Angeles, First Of The Gang To Die, has been called a corrido, a celebratory and mournful song about a Chicano outlaw named Hector.[144] And Mexican supergroup, Mexrrissey, arranges popular Morrissey Smiths songs like Every Day Is Like Sunday and The Boy With The Thorn In His Side into corridos, boleros, and other Latin American musical forms in their live shows.

The much-cited Catholic, immigrant, and working class connection between Morrissey and his Chicana/o and Mexican fans cannot be totally dismissed, for it's clear these are key historical and thematic frameworks for understanding this seemingly unlikely affinity between the two. Furthermore, Mexican and Chicano/a art forms like corridos and teatro are all about 'challenging the Catholic guilt' and other 'B.S.' that feed the oppressive system. Like Mexican corridos, Chicano teatro is another such political art form that has roots in community-based efforts to expose, challenge, and transform systems of economic injustice, institutional racism, and other forms of discrimination.

This brings us to *Teatro Moz* and the significance of López's CASA 0101 as its home venue. Its very name, *Teatro Moz*, rightly places the fan-produced Morrissey theater festival in the tradition of Chicano and Chicana theatre and performance. Teatro is a particular form of Chicano theatre that begun in the farm worker and civil rights movements in the mid-1960s. Luis Valdéz, a Chicano playwright and director (most famous for his play, *Zoot Suit*), is credited as the founder of the first organized Chicano/a theatre group called El Teatro Campesino, or the Farmworkers' Theater, in 1965. El Teatro Campesino 'drew on traditions from European drama such as commedia dell'arte, Spanish religious dramas adapted for teaching Mission Indians, a Mexican tradition of performances in California which began in the mid-ninteenth century, and Aztec and Maya sacred ritual dramas.'[145]

The signature form of El Teatro Campesino was its actos, or short one-act improvisational scenes that depicted the farm workers' political struggles and acts of resistance. According to Valdéz, the actos 'inspire the audience to social action,' 'illuminate specific points about social problems,' 'satirize the opposition,' 'show or hint at a solution,' and 'express what people are feeling.' I view many of the *Teatro Moz* plays as updated and extended actos in the El Teatro Campesino tradition. The acto as a theatrical and performance practice relies on comedic improvisational acting towards the political purpose of mobilizing audiences to work in the collective building of alternative spaces and traditions of expression. Much like we saw with MorrisseyOke, an event that functions as a way to build 'alternative spaces and traditions of expressions' in the middle of a rapidly gentrifying Eastside, the *Teatro Moz* event and the plays that are part of it also function as a way to appropriate Chicano traditions to tell new stories and express new realities of lived experiences, with Morrissey and the Smiths as its transnational, border-crossing soundtrack.

And these plays, for the most part, are funny. Chicana theatre scholar Yolanda Broyles-González discusses the central role of humor and the comic figure in the Mexican carpa performance tradition, itself a predecessor of the Chicano teatro/El Teatro Campesino movement. She writes,

Prime among the performance conventions of the carpa and the Teatro Campesino was a strong reliance on comedic technique and forms (particularly the comic sketch), on musical performance and dancelike movement. Virtually all explorations into social phenomena were conveyed through the medium of humor, often accompanied by music. The overriding tone of social critique and reflection was raucous... Yet in essence this humor was dead serious.[146]

Many of the contributing playwrights of *Teatro Moz* use comedy to explore such 'dead serious' issues as animal rights, veganism and vegetarianism; campus police repression and the defunding of campus organizations; depression and suicide; cultural and political oppression; and lesbian, gay, and queer struggles. Such themes and concerns are at the very core of Morrissey's body of work that embraces both the comedy and drama, the happy-sad of life. In the end, it is perfectly fitting that these fan-playwrights pay tribute to Moz through the Chicano art of teatro at a community theater in Boyle Heights.

Morrissey and Wilde are Ours

If you must write prose and poems, the words you use should be your own
Don't plagiarise or take on loan
'Cos there's always someone, somewhere, with a big nose who knows...
The Smiths, Cemetry Gates (1986)

Cemetry Gates is famously known (and misspelled) as Morrissey's admission of 'lyrical appropriation' in composing his own literary songs. Morrissey lifted bits from Shakespeare and films like *The Man Who Came to Dinner* and *Billy Liar* in Cemetry Gates, his ode to Keats, Yeats, and Oscar Wilde. Says Goddard, 'It was extremely ironic, if not deliberately self-parodic, of Morrissey to address the issue of plagiarism in a song which itself brazenly incorporated words which weren't his own.'[147] Plagiarism, the ultimate sin of original writing that, in some places, is punishable by law—think of copyright infringement and academic dishonesty policies at institutions of higher education—is at once a form of flattery and intentional act of borderline-legal appropriation. What essentially amounted to charges of plagiarism, very ironically, almost stopped *Teatro Moz* from happening at all.

Just two days before the Saturday night performance, after John Ochoa's article, 'Teatro Moz, the World's First Morrissey Theater Festival' ran in the *LA Weekly*, the offices of CASA 0101 started to receive phone messages and emails from a big nose who knows at the big corporate record label that owns the publishing rights to most of the Morrissey and Smiths catalogue. It turns out that the big corporate record label wanted us to pretty much cease and desist all references to Morrissey, all uses of lyrics in the plays' content, including titles, and refrain from performing any live versions of Smiths and Morrissey music as planned. This was a small, community-based presentation of theatrical fan tributes being held at a non-profit theater house that serves an educational function for all of Los Angeles. There were no plans to record or otherwise distribute or disseminate music and images of the night. And the whole point of the program was to feature original works inspired by Morrissey and his music. Scary words like 'unlicensed,' 'unauthorized,' 'copyright violation,' and 'sued' floated around. Why were they coming after us? Needless to say, these firm warnings from the big corporate record label shook up the CASA 0101 producers of *Teatro Moz*.

From the pile of submissions to finalizing the ten plays to casting, auditions, table reads and rehearsals, *Teatro Moz* was a community production, a labor of love in the spirit of the teatro tradition. Tickets sold out and the buzz grew. There was talk of a sequel of sorts at a later time due to more demand. No way were we canceling. In the end, out of respect for our artist and muse Morrissey, the *Teatro Moz* producers, cast, playwrights, consultants (myself included), and the CASA 0101 venue complied with the requests of the big record label.

What followed in the two days until show time was a feat of editing, rewriting, and improvising in order to get *Teatro Moz* off the ground while playing by the corporate record label's rules. Deep down, we knew, we wanted to believe that Morrissey himself would have approved of our efforts. He would have appreciated the playwrights' creative incorporation of his music in their works. But getting the event staged meant the arduous process of going through every single script and excising every line of lyric, every mention of Morrissey, and every reference to any song by the Smiths and Morrissey in all ten plays. The playwrights scrambled to change their titles and rewrite lines of dialogue; the actors re-learned the lines like champs. The producers canceled the trio of Latino/a musicians who planned to perform their stylized interpretations of some of the songs featured in the play. And CASA 0101 hired an entertainment lawyer just in case, even though it was hard to see what *Teatro Moz* was doing that tribute bands, karaoke events, and other fan-entities do all the time, and somehow within the rules and without the threat of legal punishment.

Was *Teatro Moz* really plagiarising or just practicing 'lyrical appropriation' in the highest form, in Morrissey's own way? As Jaime Mayorquin, one of the producers, told the *LA Weekly*, 'Obviously his music was influenced by a playwright, and now playwrights are being influenced by his music. It's a full circle.'[148] And renowned fandom studies scholar Henry Jenkins reminds us that 'appropriation involves both accepting certain core premises in the original work and reworking others to accommodate our own interests.'[149]

The *Teatro Moz* producers, playwrights, and actors did all of this to a T. Like the original Chicano actos, the short plays of *Teatro Moz* are products of their time. They 'satirized the opposition' with comedy and improvisation; they 'showed and hinted at a solution' when the big corporation came sniffing around; and they 'expressed what people were feeling' all around.[150] And like the Chicana punk rockers in 1970s and 1980s East LA who 'appropriated, reshaped, and critiqued imagery from unexpected sources, such as the British youth musical subculture,' the playwrights of *Teatro Moz* and the El Monte poets transformed Morrissey's aesthetics (and eighties UK new wave more generally) by taking his music, lyrics, and style as material for their own creative expressions of fandom.[151] We can see how these plays and poems together might represent some of the most meaningful tributes to Morrissey, himself a lover of playwrights, actors, poets, and the written word.

CONCLUSION

I Left the North Again, I Travelled South Again

OUR TRAVELS THROUGH MOZLANDIA HAVE TAKEN US from South (Los Angeles, the US-Mexico borderland region) to North (Manchester, UK) and back again, in the vehicle of Morrissey fandom. We spent most of our time in Moz Angeles, and we met some incredible people and fans who make it tick. From MorrisseyOke in Boyle Heights and our very own Mexican Morrissey's radio show, *Breakfast with the Smiths*, to the many live tributes including bands, theater, and poetry shows, fans of Morrissey's music create grassroots spaces of belonging, community, and celebration in a city that too often can feel too big, too impersonal, too superficial. And we only got to the tip of the proverbial iceberg.

It seems that every day, I see a flier or social media promotion for a Morrissey Smiths event somewhere in Los Angeles; some are new, some are annual, and some come around just once in a while. So many great fan events just did not make it into this book. As the writer, I often had to make tough choices about what to include and what to leave out. I wish I could have written about everything out there: there are many dance and disco nights, from Part Time Punks Smiths Moz night at the Echo, deejayed by José Maldonado; Morrissey and Smiths night at Pitfire Pizza in West Hollywood, deejayed by Hector Florrissey; Sing Your Life Sundaze at Footsies Bar in Highland Park, hosted by DJ Rosie Bojangles; and countless others at bars like Spike's in Rosemead and

Original Mike's in Santa Ana. There are art shows, like the Selena and Morrissey event in Pasadena (only in Mozlandia would fans think to bring together the slain Tejana singer and icon, Selena, with Morrissey, in a celebration of our mutual admiration for the two artists!), the Sing Your Life Morrissey art and tribute show produced by Ninoska Arte, and the Moz Art tribute organized by Andee Gomez, not to mention the Morrissey Smiths burlesque tribute shows. All these events and shows happen to celebrate Morrissey Smiths in Los Angeles. And we didn't even get to all the beautiful visual art itself, created by artists from Seattle and San Francisco to San Antonio, so deserving of its own treatment and attention here.

All this means that Morrissey fandom is not just alive and well in Los Angeles and beyond; it flourishes and grows exponentially with every new fan and each new generation, and it does so in ways that are unique to this border region of culture clashes, contradictions, and new cultural creations. Our fandom extends well beyond Moz Angeles. It crosses continents, busts through borders, and encompasses the globe, just like Morrissey's music and cultural influence does. As I write this, in early September 2016, Morrissey and his band are doing just that, crisscrossing the world on yet another world tour that will go through the end of November. By then, Morrissey will have made stops in Norway, Sweden, Finland, Germany, Turkey, Manchester, Israel, the US, Japan, China, Indonesia, Singapore, Thailand, and Australia. Morrissey will return to the US for the final leg of this tour, finishing up in the southwest US borderland states of California, Nevada, Colorado, and Texas.

The world of Morrissey fans is expansive and circles the globe, East West, North and South. I often wonder what other fans in other lands do to express their love of Morrissey. Do they create images of him as their cultural icons? Do they reinterpret his music in tribute band fashion? Do they write plays and poems inspired by his songs and lyrics? Are there dance nights, discos, karaoke nights in Berlin, Hong Kong, Tokyo, or Louisville? What other forms of Moz fandom might be circulating out there? What does Morrissey fandom look like in Singapore, Japan, Australia, Scandinavia? Perhaps it's time to consider the phenomenon of Morrissey fandom in other parts of the world, move beyond the US-Mexico borderlands and the Mexican, Latino/a, and Chicano/a fan cultures here that have piqued so much interest.

And yet here I am, writing this Conclusion from Limerick, Ireland, where I will spend the next six months on a fellowship researching, amongst other things, Morrissey and his transnational fan communities, starting with Moz Angeles. I left the South and traveled North, chasing the roots of this cultural phenomenon of Chicana/o-Latina/o and Mexican fandom of an Irish singer born to Catholic parents in the north of England, attempting to understand more about these 'distant relations' between Chicanas/os in the US, Irish folks in the UK, and the cultural connections that emerge between our shared histories. Morrissey's role as a global pop music icon is central, but my work does not end with him. We can look at the venerable Irish traditional group, The Chieftains, and their musical collaborations with Mexican singer Lila Downs; the acclaimed Mexican norteño group, Los Tigres del Norte; Mexican singer and lesbian icon, Chavela Vargas; and the East LA Chicano band, Los Lobos. I even found a taco truck in Dublin run by Mexicans from Guadalajara. South meets North through music, culture, and world community-building.

For all the ways in which these larger affinities of Irish, UK, Mexican, and Chicana/o-Latina/o cultures and peoples converge, for all the other ways in which we can look at these connections, nothing quite captures the depth of these relations like US-Mexican borderland Morrissey fandom and fan practices. The cultural references to Morrissey and his Latino, Chicano, and Mexican fans keep popping up on the pop culture landscape, like clichés. The Netflix show, *Orange is the New Black*, comes to mind. Early in the series, we meet Flaca Gonzales, a Smiths fan who hates 'that reggaeton shit' and wonders why none of these local radio stations play the Smiths. On season four, the show throws in another Morrissey reference, this time when a Dominican group of inmates sit in the prison salon, chatting about hair and speculating about 'why all the Latinos love Morrissey.' It must be his hair, they decide, before moving on to another topic.

On the one hand, I find it amusing to see the Dominican characters on *Orange is the New Black* pondering the 'Morrissey and Latinos' question; maybe it's not just Chicanos in LA and Tejanos in San Antonio who like Morrissey. Then again, the show has been accused of misrepresenting the Latina characters and relying on stereotypes in its depiction of the Dominican inmates. While I do appreciate the Morrissey references with regards to the Latina characters on *Orange is the New Black,* I also have to wonder to what extent the Morrissey-Latina/o, Morrissey-Chicana/o connection has become a stereotype, a punch line for mainstream pop culture. I turn here to one of my favorite writers, John Rechy, whom I cite in chapter one. In the Introduction to his wonderful novel, *The Miraculous Day of Amalia Gomez* (2001), Rechy describes how the word stereotype 'makes [him] wince' because of the judgment it carries. Stereotypes are 'easily spotted, easily derided.' He continues, 'Yet, examined closely, those "stereotypes" reveal a powerful source of enduring, often ancestral courage, even as, today, they challenge the insistence that they no longer exist. But they do, and they survive.'[152]

Ancestral courage. Survival. Power. We see all of these in the shared histories of struggle and resistance of Irish people in the UK and Chicano/a people in the US. We see see them in the fan creations and activities spotlighted in this book and other places throughout the world of Morrissey. I will take this stereotype, if it exists, of Mexicans, Chicanas/os, Latinas/os as Morrissey fans any day, if only to recognize the power we may find in it to take and make our place in this world.

I'm a Girl and I'm a Boy
My Fan Letter to Morrissey

THE RAIN FALLS HARD ON A HUM-DRUM TOWN...

It is raining today in Los Angeles, a rare occurrence in our drought-stricken existence. The wind blows, water hits the pavement, and I hear it all from my seat here at my kitchen table where the only view out the window is the apartment building next door. Drab concrete, grey skies, and it could be Manchester outside. The perfect setting for writing to you for the very first time, dear Morrissey.

This letter has been a long time coming. It's the fan letter that my seventeen, eighteen, nineteen-year-old self should have written, but that only my forty-two-year old self could now write. My first fan letters were to Olivia Newton-John when I was eight-years-old. I'm remembering others I wrote to adolescent idols like Terence Trent D'Arby, Siouxsie Sioux, Natalie Merchant, Indigo Girls. My letters were always youthfully earnest, and I was always a number one fan. This time, I won't claim to be your number one fan, simply that I have been your fan for a very long time and I have no plans to stop. Like a good mezcal, you get better, sweeter, more complex with age, and so does my fanlove for you.

I pledged my allegiance to you in 1991, when the songs from Bona Drag, Your Arsenal, Kill Uncle, Louder Than Bombs, and Strangeways, Here We Come were the only ones I ever wanted to listen to. I was seventeen, eighteen-years-old, and I was in Mrs Walker's Honors English class. There were only a handful of other kindred souls in my English and journalism classes who also spoke the language of Morrissey and Marr. Listening to you made us feel smarter than the plain and clueless peers at our high school in La Habra, California. We imagined your seaside towns, cemetery playgrounds, and ruffian fairgrounds as a way to find another, better place for ourselves at the north Orange County public high school we attended.

I could not wait to see you live in concert for the very first time. It was at UCLA's Pauley Pavilion in November 1991. You know what happened at *that* show. When the papers blamed you for starting the stage riot that sent fans looting the merch stands outside, even my own deep disappointment at having my very first Morrissey show cut way short before it really began did not stop me from writing an impassioned defense of you for my school newspaper, *The Scotch Tape*. Leave him alone, he was only singing! Morrissey is not naturally evil! I wanted you and the La Habra High School newspaper readership to know that the 'melee' was not all your fault, like the *LA Times* said, and that your fans still loved you.

But what a tease, man. I waited in line starting at 4 a.m. the minute those tickets went on sale for that UCLA show, and after months and months of anticipation of getting to see you in concert, all I got was sent home after barely three songs. The *Morrissey at KROQ* CD filled some of the void. My favorite was, and remains, that KROQ version of There Is A Place In Hell For Me And My Friends. That song made me feel like a little rebel in my house. Back then, I was a surly pre-queer, pre-Chicana, over-everything high school senior, bound for UC Berkeley to be an English major and study Oscar Wilde (because of Cemetry Gates) and Virginia Woolf (because of the Indigo Girls). In my room, before school, after school, in my headphones, in my car, on my way to work at my part-time Sam Goody music store job, I played that track on repeat, singing every word to the swinging live KROQ version, much different from the slower, more mellow solo piano track on *Kill Uncle*.

Playing and singing There Is A Place In Hell For Me And My Friends out loud was my way of claiming space in a place where I often felt out of place, whether at home, amongst family, or at school. I loved its assertiveness and air of defiance, its brattyness, its transgressive message, its insistence upon finding and claiming one's place, even if it is hell, but what is hell, anyway. The jangly guitars and rockabilly bass and your sneering vocals pushed the song through the cracks of my closed bedroom door and filled the hallway of my family's home. My younger sisters kinda liked the song, too. My goodhearted mama sometimes bopped her head and snapped her fingers along to the beat that reminded her of songs she liked from the sixties. My dad hated it. As a devout Catholic and now a deacon in the Church, he chafed at the song title and its sinful chorus. I would sing with a hearty voice in my best Morrissey vocal drone: *there is a place, a place in HELL, reserved for me and my friends/And if ever I just wanted to CRY, then I will, so I can, then I WILL!* When he'd get irritated enough to complain to my mom (he would rarely tell me directly), she would cheerily remind him that when they first met, his favorite song was Sympathy For The Devil by the Rolling Stones. 'It's the same thing, so leave her alone, honey,' she'd say.

I think you'd get a kick out of my mother, East LA accent (as she would say) and all. She married young and had me first, then my two sisters. Though she never went to college, she made sure my sisters and I all did. It's a big deal for Chicanas to get an education, she'd say, and she's right. My mama worked in a library her whole life, and she read a lot. She passed on her love of books to me and my sisters. It's one of the best things you and I have in common that I secretly delight in: both our mamas worked in libraries and opened our worlds to books. *There's more to life than books, you know, but not much more.*

I hate to say that I dumped you for a while in the mid-1990s, during my coming-out lesbian Lilith Fair phase. (At least I got to see Sinéad O'Connor perform there, in Indianapolis, of all places.) But then in 2000, I came back home to Los Angeles, and I found you again, thanks to my sisters who were a little older now but still listening to your 'old' rockabilly stuff from the early nineties and *Kill Uncle*. They loved Sing Your Life and King Leer because you sing about a homeless Chihuahua. And after I saw you at the Hollywood Bowl in June 2007, sixteen years after the UCLA 'melee,' I vowed that I would never break up with you again, Morrissey. I have stayed so true to you that it felt wrong going to see Andy Rourke deejay and Johnny Marr play.

You are number one in my eyes. And Moz, my sisters and I love you. Your music has stayed with us through two decades, going on three, and we have passed it on to our nieces. We recently formed a tribute band, playing your music, solo and Smiths. One sister plays keys, the other plays bass. And I sing. It's a tall order and intimidating at times. It's one thing to sing your songs while I'm alone in my car or buzzed at MozOke. But to sing them live with a band, ay. It helps that your songs are in my bones and that I know them by heart, and I love them (some more than others). It does not help that I lack testosterone. It is hard to sing your songs without it. 'I'm off-key, but I do my best,' like you wrote in your autobiography. I do have an advantage over the guy bands with songs like Interesting Drug and The Boy With A Thorn In His Side. But my voice is a woman's voice, and while it mostly serves me, it also betrays me.

Like the time I tried to get my hair cut at Trumper's in Mayfair. I wanted to go there because you did. I saw it on that Channel 4 documentary. I fantasized about it. I thought of that James Dean in a barber chair scene you recreated and that I see on T-shirts. Getting my haircut at Trumper's would be like that homage, a great fan gesture to express my Morrissey-love. I imagined sitting in one of those private booths getting my hair cut like you did, maybe even by the same hands. Busy scissors, busy clippers, bring it on.

When I landed in the UK for my research trip, I called Trumper's to book an appointment. But then they heard my voice on the phone and promptly, politely, informed me that they do not cut ladies' hair. I explained that I do not have a ladies' haircut, I go to barbers all the time in Los Angeles. Sorry, miss (ugh), our services are for gentlemen, but may we recommend a salon? Well, I was hoping to experience a haircut there, I said, this would be part of my research. I'm writing a book about Morrissey and his fans in Los Angeles, and I saw he gets his haircut at the Trumper's there in Mayfair. Would it be possible to make an appointment for a haircut, please?

I hung up the phone, dejected. They cited some archaic gentlemen only policy. Still, I had to go there. Maybe if they saw me, they'd realize I'm not a lady looking for a lady's haircut. So a few days after the phone call, my lovely travelling companion and I show up at Trumper's. My heart starts pounding. I marveled at the window display. It sure looked like they *sold* ladies' stuff. Floral fragrances, skin creams, hair dressings. We saw two ladies working the counter, maybe a good sign. It's not like they totally banned those of us with two X chromosomes from Trumper's.

But again, rebuffed. We're sorry, they said, we don't cut ladies' hair. *She* has a lady's haircut, I said, gesturing to my fem, but not me. So sorry, they said, our services are for gentlemen only. Damn. Hairdresser, you're fired. I felt a sudden pang of homesickness for my Chicano barbershops in Uptown Whittier where the guys know how to fade my hair 'like Morrissey' so I can get up there and sing, no biggie, just another butcha in the barber chair. But not in Mayfair. Pinche Trumper's. All they let me buy was some cologne and a pomade that smells like roses and takes forever to wash out. It doesn't even work that good. Consolation prizes that only remind me of what I couldn't get at that old Victorian gentleman's barbershop.

I tried and I failed. The fan in me still wants to get a haircut where you do, Moz. You must have a place here in Los Angeles. I'd have much better luck here.

I am forty-two and these are the ways my fandom gets fiercer. I've learned to express it in ways I never thought I would, like singing in a tribute band and setting foot in Trumper's. If I can't sound like you singing on stage, then I can at least invoke you through the only way my hearty Chicana butch body can: through dress shirts, dark jeans, sharp jackets, shiny black shoes, proper barber cuts. You represent a model of masculinity that merges with my own. Your perfect sideburns, your signature hair, your lovely shirts, your affective masculinity that does not reproduce gross hegemonic lockerroom beefaroni gender imperatives: 'I am not a man,' you sing, and I sing it with you.

I'm a girl and I'm a boy.

So thank you, Morrissey. Your music is the gift of a lifetime. Thank you for your songs, your style, your searing inspiration. Thank you especially for your written words, the ones you write for songs, the ones you sing to us, the ones you write in books (even *List of the Lost*). I connect to your words and language most deeply. Your lyrics have meant the most to me when I did not have my own words to express feelings of reluctant belonging, confounding ambiguity, tortured desires, profound love. In my mind, you write poetry and literature, and my reverence for your work is not unlike how I feel about James Joyce, Oscar Wilde, John Rechy, Ana Castillo, Sandra Cisneros, Helena María Viramontes. I want to write back, to engage you in conversation, treat your *Autobiography* (and, yes, *List of the Lost*) like I would treat *De Profundis*. You bring out the English major in me.

I am forty-two, and you mean just as much to me now as you did when I was seventeen going on eighteen. Even when I want to scold you for saying that shit about the Chinese, or liking Nigel Farage, or calling dykes lazy, or playing shows in Israel. Because even more so, I want to throw my arms around you, say thank you, *gracias*, for hanging a Mexican flag on your stage, and telling us that Bernie Sanders is the one, and putting three Latinos in your band, and consistently showing us what a living lyrical genius sounds like. Like the ocean, my fandom changes, shifts, deepens, morphs, but it is always there, anchored in your songs that save our lives. Finally, this could not be a proper fan letter without expressing my heartfelt gratitude for your artistic, political, and cultural contributions to the world. They are immeasurable. Writing this book and meeting so many of your fans has reaffirmed for me what I have known in my heart, soul, and bones for so many years: your music matters to us, and it changes lives.

Thank you for being here, thank you for being you.

With love, your number one balcony fool,

Melissa.
11 March 2016
Whittier, Moz Angeles, California

'Do I look like a lady to you?' Rejected at Trumper's and still needing a haircut in Mayfair, London, May 2014. Photo by Stacy I. Macías. Used with permission.

ABOUT THE AUTHOR

Dr Melissa Mora Hidalgo was born in Montebello, east of East Los Angeles, and lives in Whittier, Calfornia. She holds a PhD in Literature from the University of California, San Diego. She has taught courses in literature, ethnic studies, and Chicana/o cultural studies at UC San Diego and California State University, Fullerton. She is a Visiting Fulbright US Scholar affiliated with the Popular Culture and Popular Music research cluster at the University of Limerick in Ireland. Her other publications include short fiction, scholarly essays, and beer blogs. Dr. Hidalgo has been a Morrissey fan since 1991. She has never met him.

NOTES

1   Morrissey, *Autobiography* (Penguin Classics, 2013), p. 414.

2   Mexrrissey's roster rotates; for a full list of band members, see the group's website at mexrrissey.com.

3   Bastida penned an article for *Sabotage Times* called 'What It's Like Growing Up a Morrissey Fan in Tijuana,' 26 February 2016. In future academic projects about transnational fandom and the specific musical and cultural connections shared among Mexicans (both in Mexico and in the US), Chicanos/as, and US Latinos/ as and the Irish (in Ireland and in diaspora), I plan to look at Mexrrissey more in-depth as a transnational UK-Mexican cultural project.

4   Trish Ziff, 'Identity/Hybridity: Ideas Behind This Project,' in *Distant Relations: Chicano, Irish, and Mexican Art and Critical Writing*, 1995. p. 24.

5   A few notable visual-art exceptions to this pathologizing tendency come to mind. In 2012, Spanish photographer Aitor Saraiba put together a photodocumentary of 'Latin Morrissey Fans in Los Angeles.' In 2016, Anthony Amor and Julian Chavez published *To Me You Are A Work of Art*, a photographic homage to those tattooed Morrissey Smiths fans; this book features a foreword penned by Morrissey.

6   This subsection heading is a riff on the radio show 'Travel Tips for Aztlán,' a music show hosted by Mark Torres that airs on KPFK 90.7 FM, Los Angeles.

7   Gloria Anzaldúa, *Borderlands/La Frontera*, p. 25 (2nd edition, Aunt Lute Books, 1999; first published 1987).

8   See Simon Goddard, *Mozipedia* (Plume Books, 2010). I cite the entry for the Smiths' song Is It Really So Strange?

9   Anzaldúa, 'Border Arte: Nepantla, el Lugar de la Frontera.' Printed in *The Gloria Anzaldúa Reader*, ed. AnaLouise Keating (Duke University Press, 2009).

10   Oscar Reyes designed the Mexrrissey backdrops, including Moz as Frida Kahlo;

186

see also graphic T-shirt designs at cristocat.com and Etsy.com for Mexican and Latino-themed renderings of Morrissey. In a forthcoming essay, I explore several visual representations of Morrissey as various Mexican cultural icons, including the Yañez and Garry images on the covers of this book.

11 Marita Sturken and Lisa Cartwright quoted in Catherine S. Raméirez, *The Woman in the Zoot Suit: Gender, Nationalism, and the Cultural Politics of Memory* (Duke University Press, 2009), p. 22.

12 Cindy García, *Salsa Crossings: Dancing Latinidad in Los Angeles* (Duke University Press, 2013).

13 The traditional -a and -o endings of Chicana/o and Latina/o are gendered terms denoting the feminine or masculine form of a word. The -x ending, relatively new, represents inclusivity of all genders. As one article, 'The Case FOR "Latinx": Why Intersectionality Is Not a Choice,' by María R. Scharrón-del Río and Alan A. Aja, explains: 'Over the last few years, the use of the identifier "Latinx" (pronounced "Latin-ex"), born out of a collective aim to move beyond the masculine-centric "Latino" and the gender inclusive but binary embedded "Latin@," has received increasing attention and usage in popular to scholarly spheres.' See *Latino Rebels* (www.latinorebels.com), 5 December 2015.

14 These days, 'Chicana/o' may seem like a dated term; in my experience as a Chicana/o studies professor, I have noticed that few people born after the Chicano Movements use it to identify themselves, preferring more mainstream terms such as 'Hispanic' (a government term invented during the Nixon presidency) or 'Latino/a.'

15 Thanks to JoAnna Mixpe Ley, a Chicana feminist writer, teacher, and community activist from Boyle Heights, who shared this photo and the story behind it with me.

16 Deborah Paredez, *Selenidad: Selena, Latinos, and the Performance of Memory* (Duke University Press, 2009), p. 23.

17 Bertha Chin and Lori Hitchcock Morimoto, 'Towards a theory of transcultural fandom,' in *Participations: A Journal of Audience and Reception Studies* Vol. 10, No. 1 (May 2013). See also Chin and Morimoto, 'Introduction: Fan and fan studies in transcultural context,' *Participations* Vol. 12, No. 2 (November 2015).

18 Melissa Gregg and Gregory J. Seigworth, 'An Inventory of Shimmers,' in *The Affect Theory Reader*, eds. Gregg and Seigworth (Duke University Press, 2010), p. 1.

19 For further discussion of Morrissey's displays of allegiance to his Chicana/o,

Latina/o and Mexican fans, see Devereux and Hidalgo, 'You're Gonna Need Someone on Your Side: Morrissey's Latino/a and Chicano/a Fans.' *Participations: A Journal of Audience and Reception Studies* Vol. 12, Issue 2 (November 2015). participations.org

20　UK press outlets such as the *Guardian* and *Independent* have reported on an August 2016 interview Morrissey gave in Australia in which the singer expressed his approval of Nigel Farage. As early as 2013, Morrissey declared his near-vote for UKIP because he 'likes Nigel Farage a great deal.' After the Brexit referendum passed, Farage would go on to campaign with US counterpart Donald Trump in Mississippi. See 'Morrissey: I nearly voted for Ukip. I like Nigel Farage a great deal,' 10 January 2013 and 'Brexit leader Nigel Farage urges Donald Trump voters to "stand up to the establishment,"' 25 August 2016, both in the *Independent* online. In spite of this endorsement of Farage, clearly a Trump ally, Morrissey has been vocal about his anti-Trump ('Thump,' as the singer calls the Republican presidential candidate) and pro-Bernie stances on his website, true-to-you.net.

21　See Carolina A. Miranda's article, 'Morrissey with trumpets and taco t-shirts: Mexrrissey rocks the L.A. Regent,' in the *Los Angeles Times* 12 May 2015.

22　Wong went by the name 'Romeo Girl' when she was part of *Breakfast with the Smith*'s early days (see chapter four of this book), when she would give on-air dispatches from Morrissey shows and other fan events. I chatted with Wong at the Cat and Fiddle in November 2011.

23　Notes from a panel discussion with writer Nikki Darling and Chicana punk legend, Alice Bag, October 2012 at ONE Gay and Lesbian Archives, Los Angeles, California.

24　Henry Jenkins, 'Aca-Fandom and Beyond: Christine Bacareza Balance, Jack Halberstam, and Sarah Benet-Weiser.' 26 July 2011. *Confessions of an Aca-Fan: The Official Weblog of Henry Jenkins*, henryjenkins.org.

25　See Liz Ohanesian, 'LA Flashback: June 1991, When Mozmania Swept the Southland' in *LA Weekly*, 8 June 2009.

26　For more on 'Moz Angeles,' see the scholarly essay I co-authored with Dr Eoin Devereux at the University of Limerick: 'You're gonna need someone on your side: Morrissey's Latino/a and Chicano/a Fans,' by Eoin Devereux and Melissa Hidalgo. *Participations: A Journal of Audience and Reception Studies* (12:2) November 2015. www.participations.org.

27   From 'Who's the Daddy?' by Keith Cameron, in *Morrissey in Conversation: The Essential Interviews*, ed. Paul A. Woods (Plexus Publishing, 2007 and 2011).

28   'Do You F*@kin' Want Some?' by Stuart Maconie (1995), *Morrissey in Conversation.*

29   Morrissey's interview with Larry King was called his first 'in-depth, in-person interview' in over ten years with Larry King in Los Angeles in August 2015. However, in 2009, Morrissey did sit down for an in-person, but not in-depth, interview with Beto Cuevas of the popular Latin American rock band La Ley exclusively for the bilingual Los Angeles station LATV.

30   Goddard, *Mozipedia*, p. 230.

31   Morrissey's words from *Autobiography.*

32   *Los Angeles Times,* 'Inside L.A.'s Highland Park music scene, a hub of young artists, labels and vinyl stores.' 9 October 2015. www.latimes.com

33   This and other quotes in this section are from Jesse Tobias's liner notes to the *25Live* concert DVD.

34   I refer to John Rechy's essay, 'The City of Lost Angels,' published in 1958. Rechy—a Chicano writer born in El Paso to a Mexican mother and Scottish father—would rise to national prominence for his first novel, *City of Night* (1963), which depicted gay hustler life in late 1950s Los Angeles. Morrissey would love him.

35   Morrissey, *Autobiography.*

36   Goddard, *Mozipedia*, 'grave' entry (p. 149).

37   See 'Did You See This? Super Morrissey Bros.' at *Slate.com.*

38   Another burlesque troupe on the west side, Peepshow Menagerie, performs an annual burlesque tribute to Morrissey and the Smiths.

39   Goddard, *Mozipedia*, p. 392.

40   Morrissey quoted in Goddard, *Mozipedia*, p. 392.

41   *OC Weekly*, blogs.ocweekly.com (7 May 2014). Arellano refers to both Mexican-heritage/Mexican-descent people in the US and in Mexico; 'Mexican' here is also understood to describe specific cultural practices.

42   Sarah Kessler and Karen Tongson, 'Karaoke and Ventriloquism: Echoes and Divergences,' in *Sounding Out!* www.soundstudiesblog.com (May 2014).

43   Kessler and Tongson, 'Karaoke and Ventriloquism,' *Sounding Out!*

44   Stephen Royce Giddens, 'Singing Otherwise: Karaoke, Representation, and Practice' in *Studies in Popular Culture* Vol. 28, No. 3 (April 2006), pp. 93–109.

45 Giddens, 'Singing Otherwise,' p. 95.

46 *The Madeleine Brand Show* was a two-hour Southern California news, arts, and culture show that aired on Los Angeles public radio station KPCC 89.3 until 2012. Brand now hosts *Press Play*, a midday radio show that airs on another Los Angeles public radio station, KCRW 89.9. See 'Fans flock to Morrissey Karaoke in Boyle Heights,' 22 December 2011, at http://www.scpr.org.

47 10 September 2014 on laweekly.com. Text by Andy Hermann, video by Shannon Cottrell. The online feature, 'This Morrissey Karaoke Nights is Amazing,' highlights interviews with de la Rocha, the host and creator; Levi Petree, a regular attendee; and Julian Ricardo, lead singer of a local Morrissey and Smiths tribute band, Strangeways; and myself, discussing everything from Morrissey's appeal to Latinos/as, especially those of Mexican heritage, to the attraction of a monthly Morrissey and Smiths singalong event to Los Angeles area fans.

48 George J. Sánchez, *Becoming Mexican: Ethnicity, Culture, Identity in Chicano Los Angeles, 1900–1945* (Oxford University Press, 1993).

49 See 'Boyle Heights gets a makeover,' by Agustin Gurza in the *Los Angeles Times*, 17 May 2008.

50 See 'Boyle Heights residents force a fresh start on Mariachi Plaza project,' *Los Angeles Times*, 23 January 2015.

51 Leslie Berenstein-Rojas, 'The Cultural Mashup Dictionary: Gentefication,' KPCC 89.3, scpr.org (28 December 2011).

52 Alexis' father, Castulo de la Rocha, was one of the original creators and signatories of the historic *El Plan de Santa Bárbara*, a foundational Chicano Movement document and manifesto that spelled out Chicano students' educational demands during an era of civil rights resistance movements. Originally published in 1969, the document can be found on any number of Chicana and Chicano Studies department websites and archives.

53 Beto Cuevas is the lead singer for the Chilean rock en español band, La Ley. Cuevas's exclusive interview with Morrissey was conducted in 2007 when Morrissey performed at the Santa Barbara Bowl and Hollywood Bowl; both concerts were televised exclusively by LATV. The full interview can be found on YouTube.com.

54 See 'MorrisseyOke Founder Alexis de la Rocha Goes Big with New Synth-Pop Quarte, LEX,' by Liz Ohanesian, *LA Weekly*, 30 June 2015, and 'This Morrissey

Karaoke Night is Amazing,' by Andy Hermann, *LA Weekly*, 10 September 2014. As of this writing, LEX is preparing to make their debut at South By Southwest (SXSW), the premiere international new music festival held annually in Austin, Texas.

55   Uribe quoted in *New York Times* article by Jennifer Medina, 'Los Angeles Neighborhood Tries to Change, but Avoid the Pitfalls' (17 Aug 2013). See also the embedded video, 'Gentrify? No! Gentefy? Sí!'

56   *Oxford English Dictionary*.

57   Conversation with Gloria Estrada at La Parilla Restaurant on César Chávez Boulevard in Boyle Heights. 21 July 2016.

58   Elsewhere I provide an etymology and history of the use of the term 'pocho' in Mexican and Chicana/o communities. See Hidalgo, 'He was a sissy, really: Queering *Pocho* by the Books' in *Aztlán: A Journal of Chicano Studies* (Spring 2015).

59   For coverage of Uribe, his term 'gentefication' and his bar, see: *New York Times*, 'Los Angeles Neighborhood Tries to Change, but Avoid the Pitfalls' (17 Aug 2013); *Los Angeles Magazine*, 'Guillermo Uribe on the "Gentefication" of East LA.' (9 September 2014); and *Los Angeles Times*, 'Two bars—one Mexicano, one "Chipster"—show how an LA neighborhood is changing,' (7 April 2015).

60   Comments noted in May 2014.

61   Comments noted in August 2012.

62   George Lipsitz, *Footsteps in the Dark: The Hidden Histories of Popular Music* (University of Minnesota Press, 2007), p. vii–xii. See also this book's Introduction.

63   Lipsitz, *Footsteps*, p. xii.

64   Matt Garcia, *A World of Its Own: Race, Labor, and Citrus in the Making of Greater Los Angeles, 1900–1970* (University of North Carolina Press, 2001), p. 195. For more histories of the Mexican American generation in the early twentieth century and the emerging music scenes, see George J. Sánchez, *Becoming Mexican American: Ethnicity, Culture, and Identity in Chicano Los Angeles, 1900–1945* (Oxford University Press, 1993) and Anthony Macías, *Mexican American Mojo: Popular Music, Dance, and Urban Culture in Los Angeles, 1935–1968* (Duke University Press, 2008). For a related history of the rock and roll movement in Mexico, see Eric Zolov, *Refried Elvis: The Rise of the Mexican Counterculture* (University of California Press, 1999).

65   Georgina Gregory, *Send in the Clones: A Cultural Study of the Tribute Band*

(Equinox, 2012), p. 35.

66   Cover bands typically play a variety of songs from other artists, as if to focus on 'the most important aspects or events' (in our case, songs, bands, artists) of a specific genre (hard rock, punk) or decade (the 1970s, the 1980s). In 2003, the *Oxford English Dictionary* added 'tribute band' under its entry for 'tribute' to mean 'a band which plays the music of another more famous group (or performer), often imitating them in appearance and performance style.' We can think of tribute bands as 'subordinates' offering the gift of their studied, imitative performance to the 'superior' original band or artist (Morrissey and the Smiths), and we can think of the tribute band performance as a gift to the fans of the original band who come out and support their local tribute bands because they love the original music so much. For more about the distinction between cover bands and tribute bands, see Georgina Gregory, *Send in the Clones: A Cultural Study of the Tribute Band*, Equinox 2012.

67   Gregory, *Send in the Clones*, p. 40.

68   See Liz Ohanesian, 'In L.A.'s Suburbs, a Mini-Empire of '80s Bars,' in *LA Weekly* 28 January 2015. The article profiles Danny Sanchez's three eighties-themed bars in Bellflower, Fullerton, and Montclair. Other bars and clubs in Downtown, Chinatown, Downey, Rosemead, Whittier, and Santa Ana regularly host eighties dance nights and tribute bands playing the music of the Smiths and Morrissey, Siouxsie and the Banshees, Depeche Mode, Oingo Boingo, and Tears for Fears. Club Underground (which borrows the iconic red London Underground tube system logo as its own), Club Fun City, and London Calling are some of the promoters who host such eighties-themed parties.

69   John Paul Meyers, 'Still Like That Old Time Rock and Roll: Tribute Bands and Historical Consciousness in Popular Music.' In *Ethnomusicology* Vol. 59, No. 1 (Winter 2015), pp. 61–81.

70   Several media outlets have reported on Morrissey's recent cancer treatments as 'slowing' him down. Morrissey discussed his cancer treatments with Larry King during his landmark interview in August 2015. See other articles from August 2015 in *NME*, *Consequence of Sound*, and *Evening Standard* online.

71   Julie Hamill, *15 Minutes with You: Interviews with Smiths/Morrissey Collaborators and Famous Fans* (FBS Publishing, 2015), p. 31.

72   See the review 'Morrissey: You Are the Quarry: His finest album for a decade…'

in *NME*, 12 September 2005; 'Morrissey: You Are the Quarry' review in the *Guardian* by Alexis Petridis, 13 May 2004; reviews in *Pitchfork.com*, 19 May 2004 and *Los Angeles Times*, 17 May 2005; and of course, Simon Goddard's entry 'You Are the Quarry' in *Mozipedia*.

73   I heard this comment, or a version of it, from several people I spoke with, one of whom describes himself as 'more of a Smiths fan because of Johnny Marr.' He said, 'the songs on *Quarry* remind me of the old Morrissey from his early solo days. I loved the stuff on *Bona Drag* and *Your Arsenal*. Then I kinda lost track of him, but *Quarry* made me a Morrissey fan again.' From a conversation with Ernie Ceja, DJ and vinyl collector, wine and beer expert, and Whittier local. I was a regular at Ernie and his wife Lisa's wine bar, Vinatero, which operated in Uptown Whittier from 2006–2013. Every Friday at Vinatero was Vinyl Night, when Ernie would spin his seventies and eighties UK glam rock, punk, new wave, and freestyle dance records. I often discussed eighties music with him and Lisa over glasses of wine and beer. Their favorite band is Echo and the Bunnymen.

74   Interview with Eddie Stephens, 19 November 2015. Also from casual and ongoing conversations at shows and via telephone between November 2014 to February 2015. See also These Handsome Devils website and Facebook page.

75   I spoke to members of Strangeways after their gig at Spike's Bar in Rosemead, California, on 14 April 2012. I conducted a more formal interview with Julian Ricardo on 7 October 2012 in Downtown Los Angeles, California. I have had many follow up conversations with each of the band members at various events around town, including while serving with Julian as a guest judge at *Teatro Moz* in November 2014. On 24 July 2016, I chatted with Julian, guitarists John Arrieta and Ralph Paredes, and drummer Jorge Arroy via conference call (bassist Rawl was absent). Quotes and comments from this section are culled from these conversations between October 2012 and July 2016.

76   Gregory, *Send in the Clones*, p. 88.

77   This all-Morrissey track listing on Mexrrissey's album could be by design, but could also be because of copyright and permission factors. I heard from unconfirmed sources that Johnny Marr and the other ex-Smiths did not give permission to Mexrrissey to record Smiths songs, but Morrissey gave his permission for his solo tracks. While I have no way of verifying this statement, it makes sense given Morrissey's endorsement of the band on his official website, true-to-you.net.

78 I interviewed Alexandro D. Hernández-Gutiérrez at his East LA home on 20 November 2015; Moises Baqueiro joined us via phone. I conducted a second interview with Alexandro and Gloria Estrada in Boyle Heights on 21 July 2016. The comments in this section are taken from these conversations.

79 Manifesta! show at CSU San Bernardino, 12 November 2015.

80 Quoted in 'This Morrissey Karaoke Night is Amazing,' by Andy Hermann for *LA Weekly*, 10 September 2014.

81 As a masculine woman and self-identified queer butch, I do not always align with conventional notions or spellings of gendered terms. We are often called and assumed to be 'ladies,' 'girls,' and 'women.' I challenge it all, while acknowledging their wide usage as shorthand terms for feminine people, or people with biologically female attributes, assigned or self-realized. In referring to Sheilas Take A Bow and my band mates, I will use 'women' and alternate spellings of 'girl' ('gurl' and 'grrrl') to reflect our feminist gender politics.

82 Club promoters such as London Calling and Club Underground; Fun City; Savage Bros.; Inland Empire 80s; Rev it Up; DJ Eser's Breakfast Klub; and DJ Von Badsville are key to booking many of the tribute bands and organizing Moz Smiths nights at venues around Greater Los Angeles, including large fan events, themed dance nights, and Morrissey concert after parties.

83 John Paul Meyers, 'Still Like That Old Time Rock and Roll: Tribute Bands and Historical Consciousness in Popular Music,' p. 73. In *Ethnomusicology* Vol. 59, No. 1 (Winter 2015), pp. 61–81. For other scholarly analyses and other accounts of tribute and cover bands, see Shane Homan, ed., *Access All Eras: Tribute Bands and Global Pop Culture*, Open University Press 2006; Steven Kurutz, *Like a Rolling Stone: The Strange Life of a Tribute Band*, 2011; and Ted Moore, *Tribute*, 2015.

84 These are composite samples of the kinds of request call-ins made by listeners of *Breakfast with the Smiths*.

85 I will use both his first and last name interchangeably in referring to José Maldonado in this chapter.

86 First line of Morrissey's song, Maladjusted (1997).

87 See Indie-related articles in *Rolling Stone*, *LA Weekly* and *Los Angeles Times*, as well as the KDLD and Indie 103.1 *Wikipedia* pages for further references.

88 Eric Pederson, 'Free-Form Radio Lives,' *Rolling Stone*, 10 June 2004.

89 From Entravision website.

90 Dolores Inés Casillas, *Sounds of Belonging: U.S. Spanish-language Radio and Public Advocacy* (New York University Press, 2014). Kindle book loc. 321.

91 Currently, Indie 103.1's roster of online radio programming is comprised of fifteen shows, both homegrown and imported/internationally syndicated, all dedicated to a range of independent and 'alternative' music from around the world. Programs like *Passport Approved with Sat Bisla, Chaos with Full Metal Jackie, Retrograde with Dredd Scott, Something Different with DJ Santo,* and Indie's newest show, *Cocktails in the Kiddie Pool* with host Gia DeSantis, showcase the best of classic and contemporary independent music spanning the decades from the 1970s through 2000s. Tellingly, as with radio more generally, only two of the fifteen regular DJ hosts are women. See Susan J. Douglas, *Listening In: Radio and the American Imagination* (University of Minnesota Press, 1999) and Casillas (2014), *Sounds of Belonging,* for discussions of the male-dominated history of talk radio and programming in the US, including radio as a 'redefining invention for men' (Douglas, p. 12–3).

92 See *LA Weekly,* 'Dierdre O'Donoghue, 1946–201' and the *Los Angeles Times* Obituary, 'Dierdre O'Donoghue; Host of Radio's "Breakfast with the Beatles."'

93 Escalante is the long time bass player and founding member of the Vandals, a Huntington Beach (Orange County) punk band established in 1980.

94 Meeting and conversation with José Maldonado, DJ and Host of "Breakfast with the Smiths/The World of Morrissey," 13 October 2015. Miracle Mile, Los Angeles, California.

95 Conversation with Maldonado, 13 October 2014. See also Maldonado's interview with Julie Hamill in her collection, *15 Minutes with You.* For more on how the Mexican Morrissey got his name, see *The Black Table,* 'November Spawned a Mexican.' Maldonado says, 'The title probably began when we played on the same night as El Vez [a Mexican Elvis impersonator]. The night was being billed as "The Mexican Elvis meets The Mexican Morrissey." I've also been called "The Brown Morrissey."' While useful for this information, I remain critical of *The Black Table*'s characterizations of Mexican Morrissey fans in Los Angeles.

96 Richardson remains a friend of the show, occasionally appearing as Maldonado's guest. She is also a dedicated Morrissey fan: she followed Morrissey on tour in July 2015 and performed her stand-up comedy act, 'Louder than Bombing,' in each city he played live in concert. See 'April Richardson is Louder than

Bombing' at https://www.louisville.com. *Breakfast with the Smiths* also used to feature dispatches from Romeo Girl (Juliet Wong), a fan who would often report from Morrissey concerts and related events.

97   Kate Lacey, *Listening Publics: The Politics and Experience of Listening in the Media Age* (Polity, 2013), Kindle loc. 214. Lacey is a senior lecturer in media and cultural studies at the University of Sussex.

98   I follow Henry Jenkins, *Textual Poachers: Television Fans and Participatory Culture* (Routledge, 2012).

99   Sent in by Mason Nguyen of San Jose, California. 'I can't really take credit for the image, though,' Mason tells me in an email. 'I found it on the internet.' Correspondence in January 2015.

100   Email communication with Roberto Ferdenzi, 15 May 2015.

101   Art Laboe is a well-known L.A. radio host whose dedication show is syndicated throughout the US Southwest and is synonymous with 1950s and 1960s 'oldies-but-goodies.'

102   Douglas evokes Cornell scholar Benedict Anderson's influential concept of 'imagined communities,' which are '*imagined* because the members of even the smallest nation will never know most of their fellow-members, meet them, or even hear of them, yet in the minds of each lives the image of their communion' (p. 49). See Douglass 1999, p. 5/loc. 176; also, Anderson, *Imagined Communities: Reflections on the Origin and Spread of Nationalism* (Verso, 1991).

103   Email communication with Julie Hamill, 19 June 2015. See also 'Mozarmy Meet-Up: Interview with Julie Hamill' at http://kerbmumble.blogspot.com.

104   From email conversation with Julie Hamill, 19 June 2015.

105   Jamie Jones, *I Blame Morrissey: My Adventures with Indie-Pop and Emotional Disaster* (Britain's Next Bestseller, 2015), p. 76.

106   Douglas, *Listening In*, p. 22/loc. 538.

107   Email communications with Breakfast Champions from London, UK; Orange County, CA; and Los Angeles, CA, May–June 2015.

108   The UK's *Guardian* ranked Speedway fourth in a list of Moz's ten best solo offerings: 'Speedway's a song that's forever toying with you, pulling you this way and that, see-sawing from the verse's queasy guitar to the chorus's shuddering euphoria. And then there are Morrissey's lyrics: none of the usual snideness or sniping, and admitting that all his enemies may just have a point after all.' See

'Morrissey: 10 of the best,' in *The Guardian* online, 16 July 2014.

109 Goddard, *Mozipedia*, p. 412.

110 Mexican Radio was released on the band's 1982 album, *Call of the West*, and in 1983, became Wall of Voodoo's only song to land on the Billboard Hot 100 chart. REM's song Radio Free Europe, about 'border blasters' used in Europe during World War II, also charted in 1983.

111 The timeline I have presented in this chapter suggests that *BWTS* debuted online in February 2009, one month after Indie 103.1 moved off the airwaves and onto the internet. This is the date given to me by José Maldonado, an authoritative and trustworthy source. However, I do have memories of listening to the show in its early days when it was on the actual FM radio dial, and my friend and fellow Moz fan, JoAnna Mixpe Le, also confirms this—she, too, and I'm sure many others, remember when the show was on the air. While these particular timelines are not so crucial to the story—when the show premiered, whether it was on the air or online is not so important here—it is worth mentioning that it was on the radio airwaves at one time, which is when I first started listening, before it went online a short time later.

112 *The Guardian*, 29 June 2015.

113 Comments from Roberto Ferdenzi submitted via email, June 2015.

114 Casillas (2014), *Sounds of Belonging*, loc. 642.

115 For the history of such 'border blaster' stations from the 1930s–1980s, see Mexican Border Blasters Break for the Border on the *Modesto Radio Museum* website.

116 As one article states, 'Whether you're in downtown Los Angeles, halfway to Minneapolis, or, in the case of one powerful border blaster, nearly anywhere in the world, your radio is a target for the Mexican X-stations.' See 'Border blasters' blitz US airwaves from Mexico in the *Christian Science Monitor*, 7 July 1983. Not surprisingly, the language of this article resonates with US cultural anxieties about Mexicans that are rooted in nationalistic, racist and anti-immigrant discourses that have constructed Mexicans as 'illegal' border crossers and foreign invaders.

117 Wall of Voodoo's song and the promotional video picks up on these very political, economic and cultural anxieties by portraying a white US English-speaking male protagonist who experiences the bemusing encroachment of Spanish-language radio signals on his dial from the powerful transmissions coming from the Mexican side of the border. The border-blasting signals are saturated with

sounds and visions of bull fights, señoras cooking beans, and blaring norteño music that competes with a loud, fast-talking Mexican radio DJ. As such, Mexican Radio is what Lipsitz would describe as a pop song that 'resonate[s] with the hidden histories of nationalist division and multicultural reconciliation, of commodification and exploitation, of colonialism and transnational migration, of urban renewal, deindustrialization, and corporate greed.' See George Lipsitz, *Footsteps in the Dark: The Hidden Histories of Popular Music* (University of Minnesota Press, 2007), p. 273. NAFTA (North American Free Trade Agreement), passed by President Clinton in 1994, created a free trade zone between Canada, the US, and Mexico.

118 Power, Martin J. '"The Teenage Dad" and "Slum Mums" are "Just Certain People I know": Counter hegemonic representations of the working / under class in the works of Morrissey' in Devereux, Eoin; Dillane, Aileen, & Power, Martin J. (eds.), *Morrissey: Fandom, Representations and Identities* (Intellect Books, 2011), p. 95–118.

119 'East of East: Using Vacant Space to Create Place in South El Monte,' by Ryan Reft, 31 January 2013. kcet.org. See also 'El Monte/South El Monte' and 'East of East: Departures' at kcet.org.

120 See chapter six, 'Memories of El Monte: Dance Halls and Youth Culture in Greater Los Angeles, 1950–1974,' in García, *A World of Its Own*. I discuss this also in the previous chapter on tribute bands.

121 'Remembering El Monte Legion Stadium's Place in History,' by Frank C. Girardot, *Pasadena Star-News,* 3 February 2015.

122 Gaye Theresa Johnson, *Spaces of Conflict, Sounds of Solidarity: Music, Race, and Spatial Entitlement in Los Angeles* (University of California Press, 2013) and George Lipstiz, *Footsteps in the Dark: The Hidden Histories of Popular Music* (University of Minnesota Press, 2007).

123 'The Sky is Black and the Asphalt Blue': Placing El Monte in the Early East LA Punk Scene,' by Troy Andreas Araiza Kokinis, *Tropics of Meta: Historiography for the Masses,* 22 April 2014.

124 Special thanks to Kid Congo for showing me that picture on his phone, which he originally posted on his Instagram account. Personal conversation with Kid Congo on 4 May 2016 at the Echoplex, Echo Park, Los Angeles.

125 Simon Goddard, *Songs that Saved Your Life: The Art of the Smiths 1982–87* (Titan

Books, revised edition, 2013), p. 17.

126 Chicana feminist theorists such as Ana Castillo and Cherríe Moraga explain the significance of spelling Chicano/a with an X as a way to affirm and ground our politics in our native, indigenous American roots. See Castillo, *Massacre of the Dreamers: Essays on Xicanisma* (Plume, 1995 and 2014) and Moraga, *A Xicana Codex of Changing Consciousness: Writings, 2000–2010* (Duke University Press, 2011).

127 A revised version of the poem (complete with new its title, 'A Lover's Letter to Morrissey') was published in the neighborhood arts paper, *Brooklyn & Boyle*. It can also be found on Vértiz's website. See *Essays, Poems, and Stories by Vickie Vértiz* at vertiz.wordpress.com.

128 Spanish term for 'fraud' or 'phony.' The term here is also very likely a reference to a 1983 Juan Gabriel song called La Farsante.

129 Spillers's short play, 'Whittier Boulevard,' has been reworked into a short film of the same name and is, at the time of this writing, making the rounds on the film festival circuits. The play and film focus on Vic, a female-to-male trans teenager who seeks her/his father's permission to begin testrosterone treatments. The play focuses on Vic's interactions with her/his father, while the film picks up where the play leaves off. In the film, Vic (renamed André by the filmmaker) has fully transitioned to 'he.' We see his life shortly after he runs away from home: he wanders the streets of Boyle Heights in search of his love interest, a rockabilly singer named Sheila, and to find the support he needs from other queer and trans teens in the community. In both the play and film versions of 'Whittier Boulevard,' Morrissey's music and his idealized masculinity figure prominently in André's life. Songs like Everyday Is Like Sunday and First of The Gang To Die become the vehicles for André's expression of sexual desire, as well as his assertion of his emerging masculinity. I discuss both the play and the film at length in a forthcoming essay.

130 Interview with Eddie Stephens, 19 November 2015, in Whittier, California.

131 Proposition 8 eliminated the rights of same-sex couples to marry. Proponents sought to write the law of heterosexual 'man-woman' marriage only into the California state constitution. While it was actually passed by voters in 2008, federal courts in San Francisco struck down Proposition 8 in 2013.

132 During the editing stage of this writing, I was saddened to hear the news of Juan

Gabriel's passing on 28 August 2016 at age sixty-six. He died in Santa Monica, California, just a couple of days after performing at the Forum in Inglewood, where Morrissey also played to frenzied audiences in 1991. In the wake of Juan Gabriel's death, several obituaries, news pieces, and fan-written recollections remembered his importance as a queer Mexican performer. Nicknamed 'El Divo de Juárez' (The Divo from Júarez, Mexico), Juan Gabriel was the quintessential queer Mexican border artist and one of Mexico's proudest cultural ambassadors, even when he was derided for his 'effeminate' manner in a so-called macho society. The connections between Morrissey and Juan Gabriel made by fans are justified by both artists' coyness around sexuality, gender nonnormativity, and as crooner/balladeer figures, to name just a few points of relation. Rest in peace, JuanGa.

133 For an extended analysis of Morrissey and Gay Vatos in Love, see '"You're Gonna Need Someone on Your Side": Morrissey's Latino/a and Chicano/a Fans,' by Eoin Devereux and Melissa Hidalgo in *Participations: Journal of Audience and Reception Studies*, November 2015.

134 Elsewhere, I have written about the association of queerness with books in Chicana/o and Latina/o literature, particular for masculine subjects. See my essay, 'He was a sissy really: Queering *Pocho* by the Books,' in *Aztlán: A Journal of Chicano Studies*, Vol. 40: No. 1, Spring 2015.

135 Quoted in Tongson, *Relocations: Queer Suburban Imaginaries* (New York University Press, 2011), p. 127.

136 Alex Espinoza, quoted in Tongson, *Relocations*, p. 129.

137 Tongson, *Relocations,* p. 129.

138 Ibid.

139 Conversation with my former student, Oscar Flores (a pseudonym), in Long Beach, CA, 27 January 2016.

140 Muñoz, *Cruising Utopia: The Then and There of Queer Futurity* (NYU Press, 2009).

141 Devereux and Hidalgo, 'You're Gonna Need Someone on Your Side,' p. 203.

142 As this book goes to press, the cast and crew of *Teatro Moz* are preparing to stage a second, fuller production of the show for a four-week run from mid-September to mid-October of 2016. Co-produced by Josefina López, Jaime Mayorquin, and Michael Patrick Spillers, and directed by Spillers, *Teatro Moz* 2.0 features a new cast and additional musical direction under members of Mariachi Manchester and

Sheilas Take A Bow. This latest incarnation includes a live band, new plays, new cast members, and a prologue. The production also includes endorsements from Los Angeles-based pomade company, Handsome Devil.

143 Email communication with Josefina López, 11 January 2016.

144 See 'Mexico Loves Morrissey! But Why?' by John Schaefer for *WNYC Soundcheck*, 6 May 2015. www.wnyc.org.

145 'El Teatro Campesino,' UC Santa Barbara Library Special Collections website. For more histories and analyses of El Teatro Campesino and the founding of a Chicano teatro performance tradition, see Luis Valdez, *Early Works* (Arte Publico Press, 1990); Jorge A. Huerta, *Chicano Theater* (Bilingual Press, 1982) and *Chicano Drama: Performance, Society and Myth* (Cambridge University Press, 2000); Yolanda Broyles-González, *El Teatro Campesino: Theater in the Chicano Movement* (University of Texas Press, 1994); and Yvonne Yarbro-Bejarano, "Chicanas' Experience in Collective Theatre: Ideology and Form" (*Women & Performance: A Journal of Feminist Theory* Vol. 2, No. 2, 1985).

146 Broyles-González, *El Teatro Campesino*, p. 27.

147 Goddard, *Mozipedia*, entry for Cemetry Gates. See also Goddard, *Songs that Save Your Life*, p. 161–3.

148 Jaime Mayorquin, *Teatro Moz* producer and contributing playwright, qtd. in *LA Weekly* (John Ochoa).

149 Jenkins, 'Afterword: The Future of Fandom,' in *Fandom: Identities and Communities in a Mediated World*, eds. Jonathan Gray, Cornel Sandvoss, and C. Lee Harrington. NYU Press, 2007, p. 362.

150 Valdéz, *Early Works*.

151 Michelle Habell-Pallán, 'Soy Punkera, y que?' Sexuality, Translocality, and Punk in Los Angeles and Beyond,' p. 153), in *Beyond the Frame: Women of Color and Visual Representation,* Neferti X. M. Tadiar and Angela Davis, eds. (Palgrave, 2005), p. 219–41.

152 John Rechy, 'Introduction to the Grove Press Edition of *The Miraculous Day of Amalia Gomez,'* 2001.

A HEADPRESS BOOK
First published by Headpress in 2016

[email] headoffice@headpress.com
[web] www.worldheadpress.com

MOZLANDIA
Morrissey Fans in the Borderlands

Text copyright © Melissa Mora Hidalgo
This volume copyright © Headpress 2016
Front cover image: © Rio Yañez
Back cover image: © Vic Garry
Maps on pages 6 & 34: Michael Robinson, based on
ideas and sketches by the author.
Book design & layout: Ganymede Foley

The moral rights of the author have been asserted.

A CIP catalogue record for this book is available from the British Library

978-1-909394-42-1   ISBN PAPERBACK
978-1-909394-43-8   ISBN EBOOK
HARDBACK   NO-ISBN

WWW.WORLDHEADPRESS.COM
the gospel according to unpopular culture
Special editions of this and other books are available exclusively from Headpress